Empathy and the Phantasmic in
Ethnic American Trauma Narratives

Reading Trauma and Memory

Series Editors: Aimee Pozorski, Central Connecticut State University,
and Nicholas Ealy, University of Hartford

Reading Trauma and Memory offers global perspectives on representations of trauma and memory while examining the tensions, limitations, and responsibilities that accompany the status of the witness. This series attempts to bridge the gap between trauma studies and new directions in the fields of memory studies, popular culture, and race theory and seeks submissions that closely read literature and culture for representations of traumatic wounding, the limits of memory, and the ethical duty to depict historical trauma and its effects.

Given its breadth, this series will appeal to scholars in a number of interdisciplinary fields; given the specific angle of trauma and memory, it will capture those who see ethics and responsibility as key factors in their scholarship. Such areas include Holocaust studies; war trauma and PTSD; illness and disability; the trauma of migration and immigration; memory studies; race studies; gender and sexuality studies (which have recently had a resurgence with the #MeToo movement); studies in popular culture that take up television and films about witness; and the study of social and historical movements.

We are seeking projects that question how to honor the past through close readings of literature focused on trauma and memory—which would necessarily take on international perspectives. Examples include a consideration of literature, justice, and Rwanda through a postcolonial and trauma lens; recent thinking on the phenomenon of *American Crime Story* and the resurgence of interest in the OJ Simpson trial that parallel the narrative of the Black Lives Matter movement; and readings of the attempts of popular culture to address issues of historical injustice as exemplified by *12 Years a Slave* and HBO's *Westworld*.

Recent titles in the series:

Empathy and the Phantasmic in Ethnic American Trauma Narratives, by Stella Setka
Trauma in 20th Century Multicultural American Poetry: Unmuted Verse, by Jamie D. Barker
Ethics of Witness in Global Testimonial Narratives: Responding to the Pain of Others, by Kimberly A. Nance
The Latinx Urban Condition: Trauma, Memory, and Desire in Latinx Urban Literature and Culture, by Crescencio Lopez-Gonzalez
Literary and Visual Representations of HIV/AIDS: Forty Years Later, by Jennifer J. Lavoie, and Christine J. Cynn
Occupying Memory: Rhetoric, Trauma, Mourning, by Trevor Hoag

Empathy and the Phantasmic in Ethnic American Trauma Narratives

Stella Setka

LEXINGTON BOOKS
Lanham • Boulder • New York • London

Published by Lexington Books
An imprint of The Rowman & Littlefield Publishing Group, Inc.
4501 Forbes Boulevard, Suite 200, Lanham, Maryland 20706
www.rowman.com

6 Tinworth Street, London SE11 5AL, United Kingdom

Copyright © 2020 by The Rowman & Littlefield Publishing Group, Inc.

All rights reserved. No part of this book may be reproduced in any form or by any electronic or mechanical means, including information storage and retrieval systems, without written permission from the publisher, except by a reviewer who may quote passages in a review.

British Library Cataloguing in Publication Information Available

Library of Congress Cataloging-in-Publication Data Available

ISBN: 9781498583831 (cloth)
ISBN: 9781498583855 (pbk)

LCCN: 2020932596

For my mother, Annette Eachor Setka,
who taught me how to read,
and for my daughter, Zelda Summer Alexander,
who taught me how to see.

Contents

Acknowledgments ix

Introduction: Phantasmic Trauma Narratives 1

1 Phantasmic Africanisms: Igbo Cosmology in Octavia Butler's *Kindred* 23

2 Phantasmic Midrashim: The Midrashic Roots of Jonathan Safran Foer's *Everything Is Illuminated* 51

3 A Phantasmic Tribalography: The Case of LeAnne Howe's *Miko Kings: An Indian Baseball Story* 81

4 Projecting the Phantasmic 107

Conclusion: The Call to Infinite Responsibility 137

Works Cited 145

Index 159

About the Author 163

Acknowledgments

Although this project involved many hours of solitary writing, I owe its germination, development, and completion to a number of special people who supported and encouraged me in so many ways. This book would not exist if I had not enrolled in Holli Levitsky's "Trauma, Narrative, History" seminar in fall 2008. Holli's course was a transformative experience that changed the trajectory of my research and teaching interests, and her mentorship led me to the English doctoral program at Purdue University. There, Sandor Goodhart introduced me to the work of Emmanuel Levinas and encouraged me to think about the ways in which trauma literature invites conversations about ethical responsibility. I am deeply indebted to the generosity and guidance of Venetria Patton, whose course "Ancestral Presences in 20th Century African American Novels" shaped the way that I thought about the role of ancestral belief systems and the supernatural in narratives of cultural trauma. As the director of my doctoral committee and my stalwart champion, she challenged me to become a stronger writer and a more confident scholar. John Duvall endured endless conversations about my project and has continued to be one of my key mentors, providing practical support at many important moments of my development and supplying vital musical references for every stage of my career and personal life.

So many friends and colleagues have played an important role in encouraging me to push this project in new, provocative directions. Aaron DeRosa provided thoughtful feedback and much-needed encouragement when the project was in its earliest stages, and Heather Stanger Wicks has unfailingly offered me the sound advice and emotional support that I needed to work through moments of frustration when my words failed to do justice to the ideas behind them. Without the logistical support of Danelle Dyckhoff-Stelzriede and Elizabeth Drummond, I quite literally would not have been able to continue my research, and I am everlastingly grateful for the fact that they always said "yes." Many others were significant to this process in myriad ways, whether by offering strategic guidance, patient readings, moral support, or much-needed levity. These include Anthony Saavedra, Monica Osborne, Anastasia Lin, Robert Paul Lamb, Sandra Ruiz, Phil Kronebusch, Amy Woodson-Boulton, Sharon Oster, Emily Rutter, Ana Figueroa, Sofya Levitsky-Weitz, and my wonderful colleagues at West Los Angeles College.

I am so grateful to Martha Cutter and Gary Totten, whose editorial feedback helped me think through my ideas and generate a published essay of which I am especially proud. Chapter 1 of this volume was originally published (in an earlier form) in the spring 2016 issue of *MELUS* (41.1). I thank the editors of *MELUS* for allowing me to reprint this article.

Because a significant part of the construction of this manuscript has occurred since the birth of my daughter, Zelda, I gratefully acknowledge those who lovingly cared for her so that I could write. Special thanks to my lovely mother-in-law, Hollis Alexander, who never once said "no" when I needed a hand and slipped Zelda cookies when she needed them, and our babysitter, Lani Lolong, whose own daughter Leia has since become Zelda's best friend. Thank you to the many friends and family members who gave me the confidence I needed as a mother to continue the work that I do as a scholar: Monique Setka Wicker, Tanja Setka Edenfield, Heather Matas Hedesa, Lisa Logan, Marissa Ciardella, Nancy Bailey, Nancy Nazarian-Carroll, and Toni Moyer.

To my grandmother, Elizabeth Eachor, and my father, Marijan Setka: your love and belief in me have helped me to achieve my goals. In different ways, you both taught me the importance of kindness and generosity and the value of perseverance and stubbornness. I carry you both in my heart always.

To my beloved Ethan: thank you for insistently prodding me forward and never losing faith in me. You believed in this book, and you have helped to make it possible in so many ways, not least by leaving your beloved Los Angeles for West Lafayette, Indiana, so that I could pursue my doctorate. You consistently remind me that without a sense of humor, none of this means anything. Thank you for being my rock, my refuge, and my love, and for letting me acquire the pets whose presences, whether gentle or obnoxious, contributed to the atmosphere that enabled me to write.

Introduction

Phantasmic Trauma Narratives

The performance of an ordinary ritual at the beginning of the 1999 Showtime film, *The Devil's Arithmetic,* produces an extraordinary result: Hannah Stern, in the midst of reluctantly inviting the prophet Elijah inside to join her family's Passover Seder, is magically transported back in time and across the ocean to Europe. Although Hannah is desperately bored with both her family and their penchant for dwelling on the painful past, she soon discovers that the alternative universe in which she finds herself is not a reprieve from history. Quite the contrary: she has been transported to her family's shtetl in 1942 Poland, on the day that they will all be deported to Auschwitz. Through the mechanism of time travel, Hannah is forced to live the traumatic experiences she has refused to hear, and in the process gains her own memories of the traumatic past, which ultimately inform the development of her identity when she returns to the film's present. *The Devil's Arithmetic* thus poses a number of questions about the complicated relationship between traumas that have occurred in the past and their effects on present-day subjects: To what extent can cultural productions, like fiction narratives, with their ability to transport individuals through time and space, function as sites of memory for witnesses to historical traumas? What does it mean that authors from different cultural groups are adopting similar narrative modes to describe separate and distinct historical traumas? How and why do these texts use narrative modes rooted in culturally informed irruptions of the supernatural to build a bridge to the traumatic past? And finally, what does it mean that the audience is invited and even encouraged to engage in an empathic relation to a historical experience on which they may not lay a cultural claim?

In the wake of the civil rights and ethnic empowerment movements of the 1960s and 1970s, American black, Jewish, and indigenous writers have become increasingly invested in reevaluating the generational impact of historical trauma, as well as examining the role that such traumas have played in the formation of cultural identity.[1] This growing interest among American ethnic writers has coincided with the relentless forces of commodified mass culture and globalization, which have altered the means by which cultural communities construct narratives about historical traumas and the concomitant parameters of cultural memory and collective identity that such events shape. Because the traditional means by which an individual can acquire ethnic, racial, and cultural memories—that is, intrafamilial memories passed from one generation to the next, or those absorbed through community interaction—are becoming inadequate or altogether unavailable, narrative forms of representation, like novels and films, have gained importance as potential sites of cultural witnessing and memory. However, as public forms of remembrance, cultural productions such as these participate (or are implicated) in the broader commodification of mass culture. In other words, because narratives of historical trauma seek to forge or reinforce cultural memories of the past in a public way, they "do not belong to a particular group; that is, memories of the Holocaust do not belong only to Jews, nor do memories of slavery belong solely to African Americans" (Landsberg 2004, 2). Thus, just as time travel makes it possible for Hannah to engage her Jewish cultural history in a new way, *The Devil's Arithmetic* makes it possible for non-Jewish viewers to establish a felt connection to a cultural history not necessarily their own.[2]

Empathy and the Phantasmic in Ethnic American Trauma Narratives examines what I call phantasmic trauma narratives, a growing body of ethnic literature that employs supernatural phenomena and fantastical irruptions, rooted in the authors' respective cultural belief systems, to facilitate a sense of empathy for, or felt connection to, the past. Whether through ghosts, reincarnation, time travel, or a bending of the time-space continuum, these texts find ways to build bridges to the past and, by the same token, to extend the pain of traumas from long ago into the present moment. Taking as its focus works by American black, Jewish, and indigenous authors, this manuscript argues that the phantasmic irruptions contained in these works create opportunities for readers to connect, in an ethical way, to the cultural traumas invoked in these texts. In so doing, these texts also affirm the preponderance of cultural traumas in American ethnic communities, show how such traumas continue to manifest through the processes of what Marianne Hirsch (2012) refers to as "affiliative postmemory," and establish their particular traumatic histories, in ways that are both explicit and implicit, as representative of a broader shared human legacy of oppression and violence. In this way, these narratives provide spaces within which ethnic American writers can connect their inherited experience of historical traumas such as genocide and enslavement to the broader cultural fabric of American history.

This book engages a broad scope of multiethnic American literature at a time when the majority of ethnic literary critique generally proceeds in distinct ethnic or racial subject areas, and when transnational literary studies might seem more timely given the increasingly globalized nature of our world. However, the fact that few studies examine the ways in which multiethnic texts create spaces for thinking about cross-cultural empathy in the context of cultural trauma narratives is what makes this book a timely contribution to ethnic studies discourse, particularly given the racially divisive political rhetoric of the present moment. Inspired in part by the comparative and coalition-oriented scholarship of Kathleen Brogan, Caroline Rody, Chanette Romero, and Maria Rice Bellamy, this study adheres closely to the discipline of US ethnic studies while also engaging with postcolonial critical paradigms, specifically with regard to the debates within postcolonial studies regarding the hegemonic implications of contemporary trauma theory and magical realism as a discursive practice. More broadly, though, it is at the intersection of the ethnically specific and intercultural exchange or alliance that this study locates itself, to consider a body of contemporary literature that is characterized both by cultural specificity as well as by shared cross-cultural struggles. The texts under examination in this manuscript attempt to shift the act of reading from a passive experience to one of active engagement that inspires empathy and encourages ethical thinking.

In seeking to recover the past through phantasmic means, these texts resist the notion that history is sealed or closed off, privileging instead "the messiness of multiplicity to the sterility of monolithic narratives" (Lacey 2014, 102). Thus, I connect these texts by way of a genealogical approach, one that is well suited to analysis of dominant and counterdiscourses. As Lauren J. Lacey (2014) notes, adopting a genealogical approach to subject matter that addresses the interstices of trauma and history is particularly appropriate given "the traumatic processes that theorists have developed in relation to history. Traumatic history—both personal and cultural—appears to be inescapable, but not because history and trauma are simply one and the same, but because any thorough investigation into the nature of historical knowledge cannot escape the kinds of knowledge that push the limits of representation" (102). Because power and its fluctuations are undeniable factors in traumatic historical events, genealogical inquiry and the application of trauma theory—particularly a postcolonial approach to trauma theory—are useful lenses through which to engage the films and novels that I examine in this study. The phantasmic trauma narratives explored here challenge those aspects of existence that traditional histories, informed by post-Enlightenment sensibilities, tend to ignore or seek to discredit, as well as provide metacritical examinations of their own approaches to history and traumatic inheritance. For example, Octavia Butler's (1979) protagonist constantly questions her terrifying transitions between past and present; Jonathan Safran Foer (2002) directly addresses the relationship between history, memory, and story; and LeAnne Howe (2007) champions Choctaw language and understandings of time as modes of historical knowledge.

The integration of history and the phantasmic enables these authors, and the filmmakers I address in chapter 4, to create pathways toward empathy and ethical thinking. The device of time travel in *Kindred* (Butler 2003), *Miko Kings* (Howe 2007), *The Devil's Arithmetic* (1999), and *Sankofa* (1993) and the metanarrative structure of *Everything Is Illuminated* (Foer 2002) empower the writers and filmmakers with the ability to show how the relationship between past and present is mutually constitutive. If we agree with Kirby Farrell's (1998) argument that "trauma is a 'mind-blowing' experience that destroys a conventional mindset and compels (or makes possible) a new world-view," we can see how these texts engage the "mind-blowing" capacity of trauma in their stories of historical trauma as a means for recalibrating our sense of what is possible in our contemporary moment (19). By using culturally specific phantasmic elements and occurrences—such as Dana's ability to travel through time, or Ezol's ability to exist simultaneously in the past and present—the writers I address in this study find ways to gesture toward the ineffability of trauma, and to respond to or revise history even as they point to the failure of historiography to communicate trauma. Repeatedly, the novels and films discussed here draw attention to the inadequacies of Western ontologies and constructs of time for communicating the traumatic experiences of nonwhite, non-Christian subjects. Characters in these works find themselves negotiating new constructs of time and working through the tangled web of history/memory/story. Through these negotiations, they find pathways toward self-discovery and empathy for the suffering of others.

A POSTCOLONIAL AND POSTMEMORIAL APPROACH TO TRAUMA

In recent decades, scholars and creatives alike have become increasingly sensitive to the ethical problems that arise out of attempts to represent the other or, more broadly speaking, the historical experiences of other groups. This concern with the representation of the other has manifested itself most particularly in postcolonial and ethnic studies, as well in the realm of trauma theory, where the question of how to respond ethically to the suffering of others has dominated the discourses of that field since the early 1990s. Inherently interdisciplinary, trauma theory draws on psychology, history, literary and cultural studies, politics, sociology, and philosophy to ask questions about the impact of trauma and memory not only on the individual, but also on cultural groups. With the publication of foundational works by Cathy Caruth, Shoshanna Felman, Dori Laub, Geoffrey Hartman, Dominick LaCapra, and others, "trauma theory confidently announced itself as an essential apparatus for understanding 'the real world' and even as a potential means for changing it for the better" (Craps 2016, 55). In the works of these scholars, particularly that of Caruth (1990), we see the conjoining of a textualist approach with the language of pyscholanalysis that permits "*history* to arise where *immediate understanding* may not" (11).[3] This hybrid critical framework makes it possible to access through cultural productions traces of traumatic histories and experiences that resist representation and comprehension. Further, trauma theorists from Caruth onward have seen this critical practice as being equally concerned with questions of ethics. Caruth (1990) argues that the "new mode of reading and of listening" (9) demanded by the study of trauma can facilitate the forging of cross-cultural connections: "History, like trauma, is never simply one's own, that history is precisely the way we are implicated in each other's traumas" (24). The notion that "trauma may provide the very link between cultures" imbues the act of bearing witness with ethical significance (Caruth 1995, 11). Indeed, if bearing witness to the traumatic histories of others can foster empathic responses, opportunities for cross-cultural engagement and solidarity may follow.

However, what trauma and memory studies scholars—often working from deconstructionism—deem an appropriate empathic response differs significantly from those rooted in the neo-humanist school of literary ethics. While trauma scholars believe that the acts of reading and writing have ethical implications, they assiduously maintain that there is always a distance between testimony and text, since, as Robert Eaglestone (2004), observes, "the passage from world to text is far from straightforward" (605). By contrast, neo-humanists such as Wayne Booth and Martha Nussbaum assert that literary texts are an effective form of moral reasoning that can be used to inspire ethical responses in readers. Such critics rely on a neo-Aristotelian mimeticism that views literary texts as analogous to reality and therefore envision empathy as a straightforward form of identification. As many trauma and memory studies scholars argue, such easy identification results in a kind of emotional colonization in which the reader presupposes a sameness between self and other and therefore presumes to *understand* the suffering of the other. Rather than committing what Emmanuel Levinas (1969) terms "ontological imperialism" by presuming to comprehend the other, thereby erasing or writing over the other's alterity (44), trauma theory underscores the importance of acknowledging and respecting the other's alterity. If, as Levinas insists, failure to respect the alterity of the other represents a kind of violence, then a superficially empathic response to the other's trauma ultimately serves as a reinscription of that trauma. As a result, trauma and memory theorists are careful to distinguish desirable forms of empathy—

variously referred to as empathy (Landsberg; LaCapra), empathic unsettlement (LaCapra), or ethical witnessing (Kaplan)—from superficial forms of identification: sympathy (Landsberg); facile empathy (Caruth); empty empathy (Kaplan); projective identification (LaCapra); and surrogate victimage (LaCapra).

However, despite their apparent concern with ethical engagement, many of trauma theory's foundational texts—including those of Caruth—have failed to deliver on their promise for wider cultural engagement. As Laura Brown (1995) notes, trauma theory tends to privilege definitions of trauma derived from the experiences of dominant groups in Western society, namely "white, young, able-bodied, educated, middle-class men" (101). By marginalizing the traumatic experiences of those who do not belong to these categories, trauma theory does not frequently account for the culturally specific experience of historical traumas endured by nonwhite, non-Christian groups, nor does it allow for culturally specific responses to those traumas. Accordingly, there are limits to the empathy advocated by traditional trauma theory. As Susannah Radstone (2007) explains,

> It is the sufferings of those, categorized in the West as "other," that tend *not* to be addressed via trauma theory—which becomes in this regard, a theory that supports politicized constructions of those with whom identifications via traumatic sufferings can be forged and those from whom such identifications are withheld. (25)

Consequently, hegemonic definitions of trauma must necessarily be "revised and modified if they are to adequately account for—rather than (re)colonize—the psychological pain inflicted on the downtrodden" (Craps 2013, 21). Those who approach trauma studies from a postcolonial perspective, such as Michael Rothberg, Stef Craps, Gert Beulens, and Irene Visser, have called for a decolonization of trauma theory to address this monocultural bias, one that allows for broader definitions of trauma and recovery (Craps 2012) and openness to non-Western belief systems and their rituals and ceremonies in the engagement with trauma (Visser 2015).

My theoretical paradigm for analyzing phantasmic trauma narratives is influenced by Craps's (2013) conception of postcolonial trauma theory as one that "should take account of the specific social and historical contexts in which trauma narratives are produced and received, and be open and attentive to the diverse strategies of representation and resistance that these contexts invite or necessitate" (5). My analysis of the phantasmic trauma narratives in this manuscript attends to the culturally specific character of the phantasmic and how it is deployed and changes shape depending on the ethnic culture and belief systems from which it springs. The multiethnic scope of this book examines American black, Jewish, and indigenous interpretations of the phantasmic comparatively not only as a means of forging connections among the traumatic histories that they convey, but also as a way of highlighting the important confluences in the strategies of representation that they employ.

Of equal importance to my theoretical framework is Marianne Hirsch's (2012) conception of postmemory, as it provides a foundation for examining the residual impact of traumatic experience in the lives of survivors and their descendants, and, by extension, the ramifications of cultural trauma with regard to contemporary identity formation. Hirsch (2012) uses the term to describe "the relationship that the 'generation after' bears to the personal, collective, and cultural trauma of those who came before—to experiences they 'remember' only by means of the stories, images, and behaviors among which they grew up" (5). These transmitted memories, she explains, are so foundational and bear such affective significance that they

> *seem* to constitute memories in their own right. Postmemory's connection to the past is thus actually mediated not by recall but by imaginative investment, projection, and creation. To grow up with overwhelming inherited memories, to be dominated by narratives that preceded one's birth or one's consciousness, is to risk having one's own life stories displaced, even evacuated, by our ancestors. It is to be shaped, however indirectly, by traumatic fragments of events that still defy narrative reconstruction and exceed comprehension. These events happened in the past, but their effects continue into the present. (Hirsch 2012, 5)

The experience of postmemory is not identical to that of memory in that it is "post," or secondhand. However, it mimics memory in the sense that it carries with it an affective force. Although Hirsch originally formulated postmemory to give language to her experience as the child of Holocaust survivors, she argues that the intergenerational transfer of traumatic memory is not restricted to "the remembrance of the Holocaust" (Hirsch 2001, 11), nor is it strictly familial (Hirsch 2012, 7).[4] She explains that "postmemory is not an *identity* position but a *generational* structure of transmission" (Hirsch 2012, 35). As such, Hirsch (2012) argues, we can read broader applications of this form of traumatic memory as "*affiliative* postmemory," an "intragenerational horizontal identification" that makes the suffering of an inheritor of trauma "more broadly available to other contemporaries" (36). Thus, postmemory can be used to describe a broad range of cultural and historical experiences, and it enables subjects who are not personally associated with the traumatic event to feel for the suffering of others through public and private forms of mediation, including narratives, images, and historical and cultural artifacts. Phantasmic trauma narratives are a form of postmemorial work that builds on familial frameworks of transmission within their narratives to help readers achieve a sense of affiliative postmemory. By modeling examples of cross-cultural exchange and empathy within the context of traumatic histories, phantasmic trauma narratives encourage readers to develop felt connections to those histories and entreat us to be mindful of the ways in which we are implicated in the violent legacies of enslavement and genocide. For this reason, phantasmic trauma narratives are inherently coalition oriented and may provide potential starting points for activist cultural and political engagement.

EMPATHY AND ETHICS

Central to the project of the phantasmic trauma narrative is the desire to inspire within the reader a sense of empathy for the other and the other's inherited legacy of cultural trauma. I employ the term "empathy" to signify an ethical response that recognizes "the alterity of identification" (Landsberg 2004, 135).[5] The empathy that a reader of phantasmic trauma narratives may experience, then, is not dependent on a preexisting identification, nor is it a form of appropriation or ontological imperialism. Rather, the possible empathy that may arise from the process of reading narratives of trauma is one that allows the reader to feel for the suffering of the other while at the same time respecting the other's alterity.

While the interplay between a text and the reader's perception of that text is private and difficult to predict, the inclusion of phantasmic elements heightens the experiential nature of the reading process by disrupting or disturbing reader expectations and assumptions. As writing that distances itself from realism, the phantasmic trauma narrative creates impediments to the reader's reception of the events portrayed and the historical trauma that, even if not directly represented in the world of the narrative, looms large nonetheless. The outcome of this counterintuitive process is that we as readers not only read the text, but also react to it. In other words, we "comprehend the fictional text through the experience it makes us undergo" (Iser 1980, 189). The comprehension of the fictional text is not an *understanding* of the other's experience; rather, it creates the conditions whereby ethical engagement with the suffering of the other becomes possible. If Iser's argument stands, we can regard the phantasmic trauma narrative as constructing a reactive audience that is summoned, in a Levinasian sense, into a face-to-face relation with the other and the other's suffering. Of course, an individual reader may choose to deny the ethical summons, but the summons exists nevertheless.

In order to bring Levinasian ethics into conversation with the ethical aims of the phantasmic trauma narrative, we must contend with Levinas's (1989) assertion that literature, as a product of the imagination, does not create conditions for the ethical.[6] However, I argue that literature possesses the indirect potential for conveying what Levinas terms "the saying," or what Caruthian scholars term the "ineffability of trauma." While we might insist on the failure of language (the said) to represent traumatic experience, the fact remains that we cannot do without language, especially in the context of literature. This leaves us, as Monica Osborne (2018) explains, with the fact that "what cannot be said must be articulated through an exercise of what can be said" (21–22). It is through the "already said that words, elements of a historically constituted vocabulary, will come to function as signs and acquire a usage, and bring about the proliferation of all the possibilities of vocabulary" (Levinas 2008, 37). Reading trauma narratives as a form of saying that "which cannot be said but must be said" in order for recognition, reparation, and healing to occur, we as readers are charged "to identify the emergence of the saying within the said" (Osborne 2018, 22). The phantasmic irruptions that we observe in the phantasmic trauma narrative are, I argue, a form of saying that interrupts the said. The summons to responsibility emerges in the disruption of the said, and the tension between the saying and the said opens up the possibility for ethical reading, or rather necessitates, as Eaglestone (1997) suggests, a recognition of the "responsibility inherent in reading" (7). That is, readers are summoned to read ethically in order to recognize the saying that emerges from the said.[7]

By attending to the emergence of the saying within the said, the reader is brought face-to-face with the text, or figure. "The relationship with the other," writes Levinas (1986), "puts me into question, empties me of myself.... The I loses it sovereign coincidence with itself, its identification, in which consciousness returned triumphally to itself and rested on itself.... The I is expelled from this rest" (350–53). For Levinas, ethics emerges from the interruption of the self—which he describes in turn as an imperative, an obligation, a responsibility—that arises in the encounter with the face of the other. What Aimee Pozorski (2013) writes of photographs holds true for a written text: it has a speaking "face," "a face paradoxically composed of language that demands a witness and represents the residue of personal and collective guilt" (351). Hartman (1994b) writes in similar terms, asserting that reading is an ethical exchange because "the readings are addressed ... to the other as a responsive, vulnerable, even unpredictable being" (293). Thus, while Levinas himself originally theorized the face-to-face relationship as occurring between two human beings, subsequent theorists, such as Aimee Pozorski and Jill Robbins, have extended the ethics of Levinas beyond human interaction to human-text encounters. In *Altered Reading: Levinas and Literature,* Robbins (1999) argues that it is necessary to "face the figure otherwise, as language's ownmost figurative potential, as that which is most distinctive to language, that is, to face language *as* ethical possibility (54). Furthermore, Robbins identifies Levinas's interpretation of Jacques Derrida's notion of "the trace" as a means of enabling one to see a real and infinite other manifested in language. In other words, just as we recognize the otherness of other humans, we recognize otherness in the "face" rendered by language in a text. Indeed, as Robbins explains, Levinas's work "describes the ethical relation to the other as a kind of language, as responsibility, that is, as language-response to the other who faces and who, 'in turn' speaks" (54). The phantasmic trauma narrative renders a face that summons the reader in such a way that reading becomes a responsibility analogous to Levinas's (2008) conception of the responsibility that exists in the proximity to a human face or "neighbor" (84–86). In "facing the figure," we face not only the traces of trauma (the sayings) that emerge from within the text (the said), but also those alive today who bear the historical weight of that trauma.

By extending the "face of the figure" that we encounter in the text to the faces of the real humans implied by the text, we can see the way in which the phantasmic trauma narrative summons us to ethical responsibility that extends beyond the reading experience. That is, readers "become implicated in the situation being observed and obligated to the subjects of study" (Fernandes 2003, 84). The phantasmic trauma narratives I examine here challenge us to shift from passive readers into active witnesses who bear an ethical responsibility to respond, even if just by being truly open, to the stories of violence and injustice that we encounter. Just as a trauma survivor bears witness to an interlocutor, so does a cultural trauma narrative bear witness to readers. In this way, readers are positioned to become interlocutors. Dori Laub (1992) explains in his study of testimony that the interlocutor is not merely a passive observer, but rather an active participant in the "creation" of witness: he "is a party to the creation of knowledge *de novo*," and it is on him that the event "comes to be inscribed" (57). Laub's argument that the trauma becomes "inscribed" upon the interlocutor is analogous to the development of a felt connection to the traumatic event on the part of the reader. Although the interlocutor "preserves his own separate place, position and perspective" (58), he nonetheless "comes to partially experience the trauma in himself" (57). This is not an act of appropriation, but rather a process of opening oneself up to the suffering of the other. Thus, it is within the act of discerning the face of the other in the face of the figure and transitioning from passive reader to active witness that we are confronted with our responsibility to that other.

Active witnessing to the trauma of others is often modeled within the narrative worlds of phantasmic texts, and in the case of those I analyze in this study, we see this active witnessing extend across ethnic and cultural boundaries in the interactions of characters who are not only of different races, but also implicated in the historical trauma from different subject positions. The way that these characters negotiate their relationships to the past and to one another's experiences of the past creates opportunities for readers to consider their own relationship to—and, perhaps, implication in—the historical suffering of others. By creating complicated narrative worlds and engaging challenging ethical questions, these texts inspire active reader engagement of a kind that eschews passive empathy. They stage a narrative experience for the reader that establishes the possibility of ethical thinking and prosocial action.

DISTINGUISHING THE PHANTASMIC FROM MAGICAL REALISM

The prevalence of supernatural elements in ethnic trauma narratives—particularly the motif of a traumatic past that continues to haunt—has been the subject of several scholarly studies of multiethnic trauma fiction. Kathleen Brogan (1998), for example, has examined the trope of haunting in a number of ethnic American novels; this trope, she argues, functions as an attempt "to re-create ethnic identity through an imaginative recuperation of the past and to press this new version of the past into the service of the present" (3). She goes further to note that the paranormal mode of representation emphasizes "the difficulty of gaining access to a lost or denied past, as well as the degree to which any such historical reconstruction is essentially an imaginative act" (6). Maria Rice Bellamy (2016), building on Brogan's work, examines works that engage "trauma's ghost," or the "haunting resonance left by trauma, particularly those unrecorded, discredited, or repressed histories" that we so often encounter in ethnic American narratives of historical trauma (2). The notion of hauntings and specters as theoretical paradigms for the discussion of traumatic histories has become increasingly popular in the field of ethnic studies. Such works include Renée Bergland's *The National Uncanny* (2000) and Ivy Wilson's *Specters of Democracy* (2011), which examine how writers across diverse cultural and literary backgrounds limn spectral presences to fill in the gaps of an incomplete historical record by reinstating narratives that have been misrepresented, or altogether silenced, because they challenge mainstream historiography. Likewise, in his introduction to *Spectral America,* Jeffrey Andrew Weinstock (2004) analyzes the "preoccupation with ghosts" in twentieth- and twenty-first-century popular American culture, as well as the "'spectral turn' of contemporary literary theory" (4). Weinstock maintains that the "ubiquity of ghost stories in our particular cultural moment is connected to the recognition that history is always fragmented and perspectival and to the contestations for control of the meaning of history as minority voices foreground the 'exclusions and invisibilities' of American history" (5–6).[8] I incorporate this understanding of the spectral in my use of the term "phantasmic." Whether manifested as supernatural phenomena, as in *Beloved*'s ghost, or through the notion of an absent presence, as in *Everything Is Illuminated*'s lost shtetl—the phantasmic renders visible and undeniable that which time would have us forget, and enjoins us, as readers, to recognize our ethical responsibility to remember the sins of the past and to consider the ways in which past injustices inform those we encounter in the present.

This book builds on formulations of cultural trauma as a haunting presence that reinscribes itself on multiple generations by examining the cultural contours of the spectral presences and fantastic occurrences that arise in phantasmic trauma narratives. Further, it shows how such irruptions in these narratives reveal not only the traumatic histories themselves, but also the lingering and far-reaching consequences of those traumas on successive generations. This study argues that phantasmic trauma narratives encourage empathy not only for the historical situations, but also—and more importantly—for the contemporary inheritors of these traumatic legacies by exposing the reader to both the historical traumas and their long-lasting ramifications. My use of the term "felt connection" is similar to what Alison Landsberg (2004) terms "sensuous memories" (20), or what John Foster (1995) calls "felt histories" (273), a phenomenon that causes a person to respond to history's immediate impact in an emotional, and, ideally, ethical way. The connections these texts forge for their protagonists, and the cross-cultural exchanges that result from these connections, in turn act as models for cross-cultural empathy and ethical thinking for readers.

Phantasmic trauma narratives exist on a spectrum of the supernatural, with irruptions of the latter more pronounced in some works than in others. I use the term "irruption" in the spirit of Édouard Glissant (1999), whose *Caribbean Discourse* addresses how multiple—and at times contradictory—literary effects exist in texts by Caribbean and, more broadly, minority writers. Glissant argues that the existence of multiple literary effects stems from the fact that these writers are engaging with different modes of representation, practicing a principle of "Diversity" that is "spread through the dynamism of communities" (98). This understanding of diversity, Glissant suggests, emerges in response to the "sublimated difference" of "Sameness, which is ultimately saturated by sheer historical complexity and like a liquid overflowing its vessel, has everywhere released the pent-up force of Diversity" (99). Inherent in this "Diversity" is "the human spirit's striving for cross-cultural relationship" (99). The process that Glissant illustrates here is evident in phantasmic trauma narratives, wherein the "Sameness" of Western realism is punctuated by irruptions of the supernatural, which because they are culturally specific present a challenge not only to dominant historical narratives, but also to a Western ontology that seeks to erase or write over difference. These phantasmic irruptions reveal historical violence through a cultural perspective, or lens of being, which enables readers to recognize discordances between official and communal memory, as well as between documented history and lived experience. It is within the space of these irruptions (sayings) that opportunities for empathy emerge. Indeed, as Lyn Di Iorio Sandín and Richard Perez (2003) note, such irruptions in American ethnic literatures "shift the emphasis of authority from the unitary speaker to those who are receptive, who listen to and feel what Leslie Marmon Silko has called 'howls for justice'" (8). Although phantasmic trauma narratives employ culturally specific forms of the supernatural, they frequently presuppose just such a receptive, multicultural audience in the way that they model cross-cultural engagement in the text, as I explained above.

Because phantasmic trauma narratives are filled with spectral presences and supernatural irruptions, they are often incorrectly labeled as exemplars of magical realism.[9] The term is inaccurate, both as a description of the genre's aims and as a theoretical paradigm through which to analyze phantasmic trauma narratives. First, however, it is useful to explain how the two are connected: both phantasmic trauma narratives and magical realist texts—like those of founding practitioners Alejo Carpentier and Gabriel García Márquez—are forms of postcolonial discourse. Like magical realism, the phantasmic trauma narrative troubles realism's distinction between fantasy and Western constructions of "reality" to challenge the notion that conventional modes of historical knowledge provide access to extreme experiences such as slavery while at the same time underscoring "the relevance of alternative modes of knowledge and representation in the attempt to articulate such experience" (Adams 2011, 57). However, because magical realism is "premised on spurious racialist notions" that contrast a "rational" European civilization with a "primitive" indigenous mentality (Tudor 2010, 4), its usefulness as a representational mode for ethnic authors is questionable. At best, Rachel Tudor (2010) argues, "magical realism may be the product of the synthesis of the dialectical relationship" between Europeans and indigenous groups (4). At its worst, she continues, "magical realism is a dichotomous juxtaposition of an alleged superior and inferior relationship between two peoples analogous, symbolically speaking, to the long-lived dichotomous hierarchical relationship between men and women in Western society wherein [white] men are the privileged, superior, and normative category by which women [and nonwhites] are measured" (4). Further, as both a mode of writing and a theoretical paradigm, magical realism presupposes a modern, post-Enlightenment epistemology, wherein fantastic or supernatural occurrences are simply dismissed as unexplainable. Channette Romero (2012) explains that this epistemological and theoretical position is particularly problematic when applied to texts by people of color because it leads to "inaccurate representations of folk beliefs," which are shown as either being "false superstitions or free-floating ideas unconnected to any specific communities or theologies" (36). Because magical realism does not connect these beliefs to specific religious and spiritual practices, they are often misrepresented as literary devices. Magical realism's emphasis on post-Enlightenment epistemology is precisely what phantasmic trauma narratives resist; indeed, these texts actively engage their respective cultural ontologies as pathways toward alternative ways of knowing and resist magical realism's tendency to demystify these traditions.

Phantasmic trauma narratives subvert the hegemonic tendencies of magical realism by presenting the specific spiritual or religious traditions of ethnic communities as legitimate worldviews. For example, Gloria Naylor views her use of the supernatural as reflective of the African American communal perspective, and her works align spirituality with a nurturing female tradition: "I believe in the power of love and the power of magic—sometimes I think they are one and the same. . . . [T]he real basic magic is the unfolding of the human potential and . . . if we reach inside ourselves we can create miracles" (qtd. in Carabí 2004, 121). Toni Morrison is rather more direct: she disavows the application of the term "magical realism" to African American literature, arguing, "If you could apply the word 'magical,' then that *dilutes* the realism" and "the very shrewd, down-to-earth, efficient way" in which the African American community persists using "this other knowledge or perception, always discredited but nevertheless there" (qtd. in C. Davis 1994, 226, italics in original). For her, magical realism is "just another evasive label," "another one of those words that covered up what was going on," a "convenient way [for literary critics] to skip again what was the truth in the art of certain writers" (qtd. in C. Davis 1994, 226).

Other American ethnic authors have similarly rejected the label of magical realism. Louise Erdrich dismisses the term by saying that "the events people pick out as magical don't seem unreal to me. Unusual, yes, but I was raised believing in miracles and hearing of true events that may seem unbelievable" (qtd. in Chavkin and Chavkin 1994, 221). Louis Owens agrees, writing that magical realism "serves as a metaphor to tell us about our own existence," while "what's magical in Native American writing is part of the real world. It requires that the reader cross a conceptual horizon and enter into the Indian world in a new way" (qtd. in Blades 1993).[10] To many ethnic writers, supernatural occurrences are not exotic or psychological fantasies divorced from reality; rather, they are a "truth," part and parcel of ontological systems that precede and counter Western notions of rationality. As Alfred J. López (2001) reminds us, "'magical realism' . . . emerges as a Eurocentric attempt to apprehend within a Western criticism—and to graft a Western ontology upon—a body of texts that continually exceeds and escapes it" (144).[11] Karen Castalucci Cox (1998) concurs, noting that "it has become convenient for critics to label" what they perceive to be "disruptive features" as magical realism, despite the fact that "the authors themselves may resist such swift cataloging" (159). Thus, we can read efforts to dismiss these divergent worldviews and disruptive features as forms of hegemonic resistance to whatever threatens the supremacy—and legitimacy—of post-Enlightenment epistemology.

The phantasmic trauma narrative also diverges from magical realism in the type of audience it envisions. Magical realist texts typically assume a white, Western readership and in so doing reproduce the hegemonic structures that magical realism is purportedly used to uncover. Amaryll Chanady (1995) argues that the magical realist narrative has minimal impact on its white reader because "the reader considers the represented world as alien" (163). Chanady also maintains that "while the [white] reader accepts the unconventional world view [of nonwhite populations], he does so only within the contexts of the fictitious world, and does not integrate it in his own perception of reality" (163). Because magical realist texts tend to emphasize the otherness of the worlds that they depict, they thereby situate the reader and the subaltern subject in a hegemonic dialectic, and, in so doing, they limit opportunities for empathic response and establish barriers to ethical thinking. By contrast, supernatural events that occur in phantasmic trauma narratives are informed by specific cultural and spiritual beliefs, which means that these texts privilege the subaltern subject position and therefore avoid situating the reader in a hegemonic position from which she can essentialize and fetishize the "irrational" subaltern as an exotic object. Thus, another factor separating the phantasmic trauma narrative from magical realism is the way that it seeks to establish a trauma claim that indicts the privileging of white American historiographies over those of ethnic minorities. Because it is rooted in specific historical and cultural contexts, and because it seeks to encourage ethical responses in its readers, the phantasmic trauma narrative is also distinct from the ahistorical postmodernism that scholars have typically ascribed to magical realist texts. Moreover, the phantasmic trauma narrative disengages from magical realism and narrative realism not simply to critique and dismantle these familiar forms of representation, but also to communicate the reality of traumatic events such as slavery and genocide in ways that transcend conventional epistemologies, enabling the reader to experience a felt connection to the painful legacies of history.

EMPATHY AND THE PHANTASMIC

The texts I have selected for analysis highlight the residual impact of cultural traumas on those living in the present. Although phantasmic trauma narratives can be written from both contemporary and historical perspectives, the works that I examine in this study feature contemporary settings, positioning their protagonists at a historical remove from the traumas of enslavement or genocide. In these texts, "the present is seen as a symptom, the detritus of the significant relation between lived and remembered pasts and occluded futures" (Berlant 2008, 4). The way that these narratives juxtapose past and present encourages readers to make deliberate connections between historical events and their resonances in our contemporary moment. Readers are aided in this process by the presence of protagonists who are in some way dissociated from their respective cultural histories, which underscores the sense of historical distance experienced by the contemporary reader. Thus, when the protagonists begin their journey of historical discovery, the reader is more likely to feel invested in that process. For example, when *Miko Kings'* Lena discovers her ancestor Ezol's journal hidden in the walls of her house, we become invested in learning more about Ezol's story, which not only fleshes out Lena's fragmented understanding of her family history, but also enables her to recognize correlations between her tribal and familial past and her life in the present that had hitherto been obscured (Howe 2007). Similarly, when reading *Everything Is Illuminated,* (Foer 2002) we are called upon to empathize with Alex Perchov's confusion and guilt when he discovers, through a complicated interweaving of stories, images, and witnesses, that his grandfather was responsible for the death of his Jewish friend during the Holocaust. This process of discovery presents Alex and, by extension, the reader, with distressing questions of guilt and responsibility. In both cases, readers are encouraged to feel invested in the journeys of discovery undertaken by these characters as they struggle with the task of understanding a past that for them, as for us, has become increasingly obscured by time.

Phantasmic works that feature a historical setting seek to inspire a similar type of felt connection, albeit through different means. Some, like Toni Morrison's *Song of Solomon* (1977), Michael Chabon's *The Amazing Adventures of Kavalier and Clay* (2000), and Louise Erdrich's *Tracks* (1989), to name but a few, are set in the past, either during or in relative historical proximity to the cultural traumas they explore. Toni Morrison's *Beloved* (1987) provides an excellent example of this type. Set in the 1870s, the novel explores the relationship of its central characters—Sethe, Paul D, Denver, and Beloved—to the recent trauma of slavery. Nonlinear and populated by a variety of narrative perspectives, *Beloved* is structured in such a way that the reader is "kidnapped, thrown ruthlessly into an alien environment as the first step into a shared experience with the book's population—just as the characters were snatched from one place to another, without preparation or defense" (Morrison 1987, xiii).[12] Readers are transported back to the moment of slavery through the traumatic memories of Sethe and Paul D, but they also experience the postmemorial perspective of Denver, who must contend with the lingering impact of a trauma that she did not experience but has been shaped by nevertheless. Thus, the process of being "thrown ruthlessly into an alien environment" enables readers to develop a felt connection to characters' relative experiences of slavery's trauma. As noted by Christopher Okonkwo (2008), Chikwenye Okonjo Ogunyemi (1996, 2002), and others, the return of Beloved—and the multiple ghostly consciousnesses that she embodies—can be explained by the *ogbanje/abiku* of the Igbo and Yoruba tribes of West Africa.[13] Thus, Beloved is not simply a metaphor; she represents the repurposing of an African cosmology designed to tell the story of slavery and the intergenerational impact of its trauma in a new way. The disorientation wrought by first her spectral presence, then her physical rebirth, and, later, her sudden disappearance works in service to the disorienting quality of the narrative itself, heightening reader engagement with the traumatic memory of slavery. Thus, although they are not the primary examples I explore in this study, phantasmic trauma narratives with historical settings, like those I have identified above, bear the hallmarks of this narrative mode; that is, they use culturally specific forms of the supernatural as a means of enabling readers to develop a felt connection with the past and with the subject groups these texts explore.

In the chapters that follow, I show how American black, Jewish, and indigenous phantasmic trauma narratives encourage a felt connection to history, thus serving simultaneously as what Pierre Nora (1989) has called *lieux de mémoire,* or sites of memory, and cultural trauma claims. Reading these works of ethnic trauma fiction side by side is valuable not only for its contribution to the field of cultural trauma studies and for the way that it elucidates common concerns among different ethnic groups in America, but also for the way it lays bare the different cultural crises and concerns that drive such work. The texts I analyze in this study illustrate these concerns and demonstrate the ways in which the phantasmic trauma narrative's subversive and transgressive qualities are tools well suited for the task of writing about historical traumas and interrogating how and by what means they have been remembered by both the cultural group and society as a whole. These texts also explore the value of cross-cultural engagement as a strategy for resisting oppression.

In comparing narratives of African American enslavement, the Holocaust, and the genocide and dispossession of Native Americans, I do not seek to elide the historical or cultural specificities of these events. Rather, the goal of this study is to demonstrate a common impulse of narrative expression among contemporary authors from these ethnic groups.[14] In this sense, this project is inspired by the comparative and coalition-oriented ethos of ethnic studies.[15] *Empathy and the Phantasmic in Ethnic American Trauma Narratives* avoids what Manning Marable (2000) has called the "twin problems" of ethnic studies—cultural amalgamation and racial essentialism—by recognizing "both the profound divergences and the parallels in the social construction of ethnicity" (179). By attending to American black, Jewish, and indigenous exemplars of the phantasmic trauma narrative in separate chapters, this project honors the way each of these groups "retain their own unique stories, insights and reflections, triumphs and tragedies from their sojourns through

American life" (179). However, by examining the narratives of these groups under the aegis of a single study, I also highlight the deep structural parallels that these narratives reflect, particularly with regard to shared legacies of oppression and struggles for survival and resistance. The value of such work, argues Dean J. Franco (2006), is that "comparisons across ethnicities . . . sharpen our understanding of the differences between ethnic cultures, all the while highlighting the points of relation between dominant and minority cultures" (179). Indeed, comparative studies are valuable not only for the way that they underscore the differences between American ethnic groups, but also for their shared legacies of violence. Through such comparisons, we are better positioned to imagine progressive, cross-cultural alliances that work to resist and dismantle the political and social institutions that continue to oppress these groups.

The first chapter, "Phantasmic Africanisms: Igbo Cosmology in Octavia Butler's *Kindred*," posits African American uses of the phantasmic trauma narrative as an evolution of the neo-slave narrative that arose in the postmodern canon of the 1960s and engages the rich critical discourses surrounding the way that these novels have engaged the issues of historical memory, trauma, and embodiment. Using Octavia Butler's *Kindred* (2003, originally published in 1979) as a case study, this chapter shows how numerous neo-slave narratives composed in the post–civil rights era have engaged West African ideas of reincarnation as a way of connecting protagonists to their ancestral histories. *Kindred* adapts the Igbo notion of the *ogbanje*, also known by the English terms "born-to-die," or "spirit child," as a means of both spiritually and physically connecting Dana to the past. By drawing on West African cosmologies, neo-slave narratives like *Kindred* evoke the ideological and ontological capacities of African belief systems to connect readers to the slave past and to *lieux de mémoire* that are necessary for the construction of a collective African American identity in the aftermath of slavery. In their transgression of geographical and temporal boundaries, these novels highlight the inextricable ties between past and present and demonstrate how the painful consequences of slavery's legacy reverberate today. Further, by confronting their protagonists—and, by extension, their readers—with the past through phantasmic means, these novels bridge the epistemological and ontological gaps that the trauma of slavery presents.

The second chapter, "Phantasmic Midrashim: The Midrashic Roots of Jonathan Safran Foer's *Everything Is Illuminated*," argues that third-generation Holocaust novels address the Holocaust indirectly, through "traces" or fragments of history that function as clues to a deeper traumatic secret. Using Jonathan Safran Foer's *Everything Is Illuminated* (2002) as a representative example, I show how phantasmic irruptions in third-generation narratives function as invitations to read midrashically, deeply and critically, in a way that gives rise to ethical thinking about the Holocaust. Thus, rather than representing the Holocaust itself, each text deploys what Osborne (2018) calls "the midrashic mode," a reworking of an ancient rabbinic tradition as a means of restoring the protagonists' lost connections to Holocaust history and encouraging readers to think extensionally rather than representationally, creating new pathways for reader empathy. Through their literary invocation of trauma, these phantasmic midrashim—which incorporate elements of Jewish mysticism, folk beliefs, and supernatural occurrences—encourage an active discourse between writer, text, and reader that enables a felt connection to the Holocaust and a critical engagement with the way that it permeates our contemporary world.

The third chapter, "A Phantasmic Tribalography: The Case of LeAnne Howe's *Miko Kings: An Indian Baseball Story*," shows how contemporary Native American novels use tribally specific spiritual and storytelling traditions as a means of bending space and time to connect Native protagonists and non-Native audiences to indigenous histories. This chapter examines the way that LeAnne Howe's *Miko Kings* (2007) draws on Native spiritual traditions to create a type of "living thought" that connects readers to the past within the framework of a mode of writing that Howe (2002) calls "tribalography," which connects multiple facets of Native life to the surrounding world and "past, present, and future milieus," including, and perhaps specifically, "non-Indians" (42). In its efforts to reconstruct Choctaw history from a Choctawan perspective, this text also emphasizes more broadly the importance of indigenous languages and traditional stories as necessary elements of rebuilding and sustaining Native communities. Although the world into which Howe draws us is quite tribally specific, it offers important historical and linguistic contexts so that the novel is accessible to a diverse readership. By anticipating the non-Native reader, *Miko Kings* creates opportunities for felt connections to Choctaw history through the use of phantasmic strategies culled from Choctaw tribal traditions and beliefs. Drawing on the structure of Choctaw linguistics, *Miko Kings* manipulates the space-time continuum to connect the worlds of the past and the present, enabling the unearthing of painful historical secrets and revealing historic alliances that present models for contemporary cross-cultural engagement. Novels like Howe's demonstrate the powerful potential of phantasmic trauma narratives to act as both a site of memory and reclamation for Native Americans as well as a foundation for empathic understanding between Natives and non-Natives.

The book's fourth chapter, "Projecting the Phantasmic," shifts its focus to the phantasmic in film to explore how the power of seeing the images and hearing the sounds of historical trauma makes empathic responses more likely and encourages a greater degree of ethical thinking. In this chapter, I argue that films take the project of the written phantasmic trauma narrative further by constructing transferential spaces through which viewers might gain access to sensually processed memories of the past. Like the novels I discuss in the preceding chapters, the films I analyze in this chapter disrupt traditional narrative devices in order to communicate historical events and human experiences that are otherwise incommunicable. I examine three films: (1) *The Devil's Arithmetic* (1999), in which a Passover Seder precipitates a young girl's time travel back into wartime Poland; (2) *Sankofa* (1993), which invites audiences to travel back in time with an African American woman whose chronoportation abilities are connected to the mystical symbolism of the *sankofa* bird; and (3) *Older Than America* (2008), which transports viewers to the Native past through Rain, a young Ojibwe woman whose disturbing visions of the abuse suffered by Native American children in nineteenth-century boarding schools bear witness to attempted cultural extermination and help her testify against present-day encroachments on Native sovereignty. In its analysis of representative films by each of the ethnic groups discussed in this study, this chapter further elucidates the potential for cross-cultural connections described in the introduction. More specifically, this chapter encourages scholars to look at ethnic narratives and films that represent cultural trauma not simply as an attempt on the part of these artists to document their group's legacy of suffering, but also as an invitation for cross-cultural understanding and empathic engagement.

In the conclusion, I return to the Levinasian notion of infinite responsibility, which provides a useful theoretical prism through which to view the ethical project of the phantasmic trauma narrative. Further, I examine the way in which the phantasmic trauma narrative can be read as a vehicle for what Marianne Hirsch and Nancy K. Miller (2011) term "a contemporary politics of acknowledgment" (14), which recognizes historical traumas and which can be used to foster productive interethnic alliances in the future. The political potential of these works can perhaps be explored most effectively in the context of the classroom, where special attention to the best pedagogical practices for teaching phantasmic trauma narratives may increase their potential for galvanizing activist responses.

The novels and films that I address in this study illustrate the complicated relationships that exist among traumatic histories and familial and cultural legacies and demonstrate that the phantasmic opens important new possibilities for readers to establish felt connections to the suffering of others. By engaging these texts in conversation with trauma theory, memory studies, and Levinasian ethics, I show that the inheritance of cultural trauma can be a destructive force because of the way that its consequences resound, obstructing its inclusion in public memory. The phantasmic enables writers and filmmakers to bridge the distance between past and present in ways that reaffirm the belief and value systems of oppressed peoples. By implicating readers in those histories, phantasmic trauma narratives have the potential to effect empathic responses and motivate ethical thinking.

NOTES

1. Following Jeffrey Alexander (2004), I understand cultural traumas as events that cause members of a collectivity to feel that they "have been subjected to a horrendous event that leaves indelible marks upon their group consciousness, marking their memories forever and changing their future identity in fundamental and irrevocable ways" (1). Alexander's sociological approach to cultural trauma as something that is performative in nature is not intended to deny the reality of historical events or the violent legacies that they engender, but rather seeks to describe the means by which a shared understanding and narrative of trauma is "imagined" by cultural agents and then reproduced in cultural productions such as literature, music, art, and film (9). Further, he argues that cultural agents who represent trauma in these ways project a "trauma claim" to society to seek recognition and reparation (12). Similarly, Ron Eyerman (2001) also regards collective trauma as a "cultural process," and similarly asserts that "trauma is mediated through various forms of representation and linked to the reformation of collective identity and the reworking of collective memory" (1). My study draws on Alexander's and Eyerman's formulations of collective trauma by reading each text as a product of cultural processes geared toward establishing a trauma claim to be addressed and acknowledged by mainstream society.
2. The 1999 Showtime film, *The Devil's Arithmetic,* is based on a 1988 novel by Jane Yolen of the same name.
3. Irene Visser (2015) rather forcefully argues that "it is necessary to discard Caruth's emphasis on a new perspective on history when this is predicated on the dissolution of historical factuality" (254). I agree with Visser's argument that nonwhite, non-Christian trauma narratives do eschew "the anti-historical, phylogenetic, and mythic trauma of Freudian theory" in favor of narratives that tell the story of concrete historical experiences. However, many literary scholars, including Kathleen Brogan, Chanette Romero, and Maria Rice Bellamy, as well as postcolonial trauma theorists such as Stef Craps and Gert Beulens, have convincingly argued for the validity of Caruth's statements about how the study of trauma can provide a bridge between cultures.
4. Hirsch (2012) writes, "*Familial* structures of mediation and representation facilitate the *affiliative* acts of postgeneration. The idiom of family can become an accessible lingua franca easing identification and projection, recognition and misrecognition, across distance and difference" (39).
5. While sympathy is defined as "a (real or supposed) affinity between certain things, by virtue of which they are similarly or correspondingly affected by the same influence" and thus presupposes a position of sameness, empathy is "the power of entering into the experience of or understanding objects or emotions outside ourselves" (*OED*).
6. As R. Clifton Spargo (2004) explains, "The Levinasian suspicion is that imagination, as a cognitive act ordered by the rules governing all our knowledge, always reduces alterity to a play of the *same,* that which is already signified by language and thought" (276).
7. The text that perhaps most clearly illustrates this summons can be located in the epistolary exchanges between Alex and Jonathan Foer's *Everything Is Illuminated,* which I examine at length in chapter 2.
8. Weinstock (2004) also traces the "'spectral turn' of contemporary literary theory" (4), noting that "the figure of the specter in literary and cultural criticism has become so common that one may refer to contemporary academic discourse as, in some respects, 'haunted'" (5). Such works include Jacques Derrida's *Specters of Marx* (1994), Jean-Michel Rabaté's *The Ghosts of Modernity* (1996), Avery Gordon's *Ghostly Matters: Haunting and the Sociological Imagination* (1997), Peter Buse and Andrew Stott's *Ghosts: Deconstruction, Psychoanalysis, History* (1999), Peter Schwenger's *Fantasm and Fiction* (1999), and Danelle Dyckhoff-Stelzriede's "Representing Spectral Subjects in Historical Crime Fiction" (2017).
9. The term was first used in a literary context by Arturo Uslar Pietri, a Venezuelan critic who, in 1947, became the first to use it as a means of describing an emerging trend in Latin American fiction. As Alfred J. Lopéz (2001) explains, "when Uslar Pietri first invoked the term *realismo mágico,* it had already been in circulation for over 20 years; the German art critic Frank Roh was the first to give *Magischer Realismus* critical currency within the context of

post-Expressionist painting of the 1920s" (244). The term was then taken up by Alejo Carpentier in the preface to his 1949 novel, *El reino de este mundo* (*The Kingdom of this World*), who used the term *lo real maravilloso* to express the idea that the geography and history of Latin America are both so extreme as to appear magical.

10. Owens (1990) offers his own term, "mythic verism," to describe supernatural occurrences in contemporary works that arise from indigenous storytelling traditions.

11. In *Posts and Pasts: A Theory of Postcolonialism*, López (2001) further explains the hegemonic implications of the term magical realism:

> A European term applied to a "non-European" literature which . . . retains its irreducible difference, its mark of a radical alterity, which only begs the question: What of this act of *naming* . . . imposed on it from without, in a futile European attempt to categorize and thus "understand" it by this process of naming—which is already itself an act of appropriation, a bid to harness the wild, "exotic" text within a reasonable European critical framework—to "master" the other's difficult text? Here the act of naming emerges as the allegory of a colonial fantasy: the mastery of reading as a reading of mastery. (143)

12. Phantasmic trauma narratives tend to be nonlinear and often include different narrative perspectives. These features have often caused them to be categorized as postmodern. However, phantasmic trauma narratives, like the novels by contemporary women of color addressed in Romero's *Activism and the American Novel* (2012), "use religious and spiritual traditions in ways that are culturally and historically specific and explicitly political, making them distinct from the ahistoric postmodernism with which literary critics have tended to collapse them" (38).

13. See Christopher Okonkwo's *A Spirit of Dialogue: Incarnations of Ogbanje, the Born-to-Die, in African American Literature* (2008), Chikwenye Okonjo Ogunyemi's "An Abiku-Ogbanje Atlas: A Pre-Text for Rereading Soyinka's *Aké* and Morrion's *Beloved*" (2002), and Fethia El Hafi's "Punished Bodies in Soyinka's *The Bacchae of Euripides* and Morrison's *Beloved*" (2010).

14. Like Dean J. Franco (2006), I assert that ethnic literary criticism "ought to be comparative," and that this is an ethical imperative (6). Franco's ethic of comparison "is dialectically derived from the literature and culture itself, and from the two fundamental thematic concerns of ethnic literature, history and geography. . . . [C]ultural difference in the United States is produced by history, including the histories of slavery, colonialism, and genocide, as well as physical displacements of people through immigration and exile. . . . Moreover, for contemporary ethnic Americans, the very fact of their social difference and often marginalization is traceable to these historical events" (6–7).

15. See Daniel Y. Kim (2013, xvi–xviii); Caroline Rody (2009, xii–xiii); and Manning Marable (2000).

Chapter One

Phantasmic Africanisms

Igbo Cosmology in Octavia Butler's Kindred

The neo-slave narrative that arose in the postmodern canon of the 1960s critiqued and redefined white patriarchal understandings of history and identity. It did so, Timothy A. Spaulding (2005) writes, by "revitalizing the historiography of slavery" and rejecting the parameters of narrative realism in order to blur the boundaries between the past and the present (4). Since then, what has emerged out of this blurred temporal boundary is a unique form of African American cultural history that seeks to record traumatic history. This literary movement manifests in what I call the phantasmic trauma narrative, which uses culturally specific modes of the fantastic or the supernatural to engage the traumatic past and give voice to those marginalized by white historiographic accounts. The phantasmic trauma narrative provides a space within which African American writers can connect the event of slavery to the broader cultural fabric of African American history. Octavia Butler's *Kindred* (2003) invokes the phantasmic by incorporating elements of Igbo cosmology as a means of explicitly connecting its contemporary protagonist with the trauma of her slave forebears as well as implicitly connecting her with the spiritual worldview of her more distant African ancestors. However, what makes *Kindred* such a compelling example of the phantasmic is not only the way that the text engages Igbo ontology as the mechanism of Dana's travel, thereby denying Western delineations of time and being, but also the way that it encourages readers to link Dana's experiences to issues of trauma, repression, and cultural memory.

 Reading *Kindred* as a phantasmic trauma narrative grants us a greater critical purchase on the way the novel engages issues of trauma, historical memory, and embodiment. Admittedly, a great deal of the scholarly discourse about *Kindred* has already attended to the novel's engagement with these issues to varying degrees. Critics such as Kelley Wagers, Marc Steinberg, Linh Hua, and Lisa Long have added to our understanding of the text's experimentation with temporal and physical boundaries as engaging with the broader historical reclamation work of the neo-slave narrative.[1] However, no scholarship to date has explored the connection between the novel's temporal experiment and Butler's documented interest in West African ontological traditions, nor have scholars noted the way that Butler mobilizes those African traditions in service to her broader strategic appeal to reader empathy.[2] As recent work in the interdisciplinary field of empathy studies indicates, reader identification is critical and "often invites empathy, even when the fictional character and reader differ from one another in all sorts of practical and obvious ways" (Keen 2006, 214).[3] This chapter shows how *Kindred* opens up possibilities for empathy by permitting readers access to the experiences of a contemporary character whose reactions to the past anticipate their own. Butler's adaptation of the West African *ogbanje* figure—a spirit being capable of traveling between worlds—is what permits this access, connecting Dana to the past and offering readers a felt connection to slavery that encourages them to ask what it would mean to respond to history in an ethical way.

The chapter begins by defining the phantasmic trauma narrative and showing how it can be used as a tool for articulating cultural traumas and encouraging empathic responses from multiethnic readers. It then proceeds by tracing the West African roots of the *ogbanje*—known as the "born-to-die" or "spirit child"—and its recent incarnations in American literature; I argue that the figure is adapted by *Kindred* to suit a specifically African American context. Specifically, I demonstrate how the text galvanizes the border-crossing potential of the *ogbanje* figure as a means of facilitating reader identification with Dana. This identification permits readers access not only to her lived experience of slavery, but also to her experience as a contemporary black woman negotiating issues of race and gender in the twentieth century. The felt connection that arises as a result of this identification encourages readers to consider the ways in which history continues to inform discussions of race in the present day. The novel guides readers in this line of ethical questioning by modeling cross-cultural empathy as performed by Dana when her failure to bear witness to her own traumatic experience causes her to recognize the historical suffering of other groups. Finally, I chart how the novel's enactment of repetition compulsion in Dana's final, voluntary return to Maryland stands as a reminder to readers of the need to confront the historical traces of slavery that remain in our social, cultural, and political institutions.

THE PHANTASMIC NEO-SLAVE NARRATIVE

Broadly conceived, the phantasmic trauma narrative is characterized by unsought and often unwelcome intrusions of the traumatic past in the world of the present. In the case of African American texts that engage the phantasmic, these intrusions are connected to the slave period, usually in the form of contact with ancestral spirits who endured the slave experience; representative works include Phyllis Alesia Perry's *A Sunday in June* and *Stigmata*, Paule Marshall's *Praisesong for the Widow*, Julie Dash's *Daughters of the Dust*, Gloria Naylor's *Mama Day*, and August Wilson's *The Piano Lesson*, which engage pan-African beliefs in the ancestor figure to reaffirm connections to African cultural values and traditions that have been forgotten or suppressed by postslavery generations.[4] Facilitating these historical connections are supernatural elements that "evoke Afro-diasporic ways of knowing that were suppressed by Enlightenment rationality" (Dubey and Goldberg 2011, 602). Henry Louis Gates, Jr. (2014), specifically roots these ways of knowing in traditional African cosmologies: "Violently and radically abstracted from their civilizations, these Africans nevertheless carried within them to the Western hemisphere aspects of their cultures that were meaningful, that could not be obliterated, and that they chose, by acts of will, not to forget: their music, . . . their myths, their institutional structures, their metaphysical systems of order" (3–4). The fact that Africanisms abound in contemporary African American novels that contend with the slave past is a testament to the persistence of the African diasporic heritage. Gates further explains how African belief systems and traditions evolved in the African diaspora:

> Slavery in the New World, a veritable seething cauldron of cross-cultural contact, however, did serve to create a dynamic of exchange and revision among previously isolated Black African cultures on a scale unprecedented in African history. Inadvertently, African slavery in the New World satisfied the preconditions for the emergence of a new African culture, a truly Pan-African culture fashioned as a colorful weave of linguistic, institutional, metaphysical, and formal threads. (4)

This pan-African culture that Gates describes accounts for the variety of Africanisms that can be traced in contemporary African American novels that look to the past. In addition to those texts mentioned above, one thinks of Perry's *Stigmata* (1998) and *A Sunday in June* (2005), which invite readers to experience historical trauma through the experiences of protagonists who share a consciousness with their slave ancestors in a manner suggestive of Yoruban reincarnation beliefs. Other texts, such as Dash's *Daughters of the Dust* (1999) and J. California Cooper's *Family* (1991), draw on Kongo cosmology to engage the slave experience in a way that transcends the distance of time and space. Collectively, these texts creatively repurpose African cosmologies in an American context to negotiate questions of race, gender, subjectivity, and historical memory.

In the context of the phantasmic trauma narrative, these Afro-diasporic epistemologies are important because they provide an added critical purchase on the historical recovery work that neo-slave narratives such as *Kindred* seek to achieve; that is, they recover the slave past, but they do so in Afrocentric terms. As Lisa Long (2009) argues, the goal of neo-slave narratives such as *Kindred* and *Stigmata* extends beyond the maxim "never to forget" (463); rather, they align with Cathy Caruth's (1996) assertion that the psychological impact of a traumatic event continues to haunt those who have survived because "it is not locatable in the simple violent or original event . . . but rather in the way that its very unassimilated nature—the way it was precisely *not known* in the first instance—returns to haunt the survivor later on" (4). This, Long explains, is what drives writers like Butler and Perry to "dramatize the reality of a past—and subsequently, a theory of history—*always* mediated by a particular modern consciousness" (463). Where Long's critique falls short, however, is in its dismissal of the "supernatural" engagement in these novels as "the sort of experience possible only on the pages of science fiction novels" (463).[5] As Butler herself has noted, *Kindred* is "obviously not science fiction" ("*Black Scholar* Interview" 14); indeed, what motivates Dana's time travel is not explained by science but rather by the repeated life cycle of the *ogbanje*, which is delineated in greater detail in the following section. Viewed through the lens of the phantasmic trauma narrative, the supernatural aspects of Butler's text become understood as a new ontology—an American *ogbanje*-ism—that connects West African spiritual traditions to an African American context and gives rise to a new way of conceptualizing the relationship between historical memory and cultural trauma.

The phantasmic trauma narrative solidifies this relationship through its contemporary protagonist, who, like the reader, initially identifies with the traumatic past from a position of alterity. Like Dana, the reader is experientially unfamiliar with the trauma of slavery and therefore shares the protagonist's lack of identification with the events being portrayed. As a result, the reader experiences a journey of discovery alongside the protagonist's own, which enables her to develop a felt connection to a trauma that she did not experience and one, moreover, to which she may not have a cultural connection. Thus, when *Kindred*'s Dana finds herself transported to the antebellum world of her ancestors, we are invited to share her fear, confusion, and ultimately refusal to accept the conditions of slavery. In this way, the novel opens up a space for readers to feel connected to the experiences of the protagonist.

The novel's deployment of *ogbanje*-ism is intricately connected to its related project of reader identification, which is central to the phantasmic trauma narrative as a mode of writing. Thus, it is not surprising that *Kindred*'s investment in reader identification has been noted by a number of scholars. Lisa Woolfork (2009) observes that "Dana's responses to the past are meant to serve as a mirror for contemporary readers" (33) and asserts that reader identification with her character is rooted in the fact that she is a "sympathetic twentieth-century woman who can bring the past into greater relief" (34).[6] While she derides it as "sentimental," Linh U. Hua (2011) accedes that *Kindred* encourages "readerly identification with Dana as a twentieth-century voyeur, reserving room for this identification to fluctuate as Dana situates herself ambivalently in Maryland" (397). Likewise, Long (2009) suggests that this sense of identification with Dana is what ignites reader empathy. In her study of *Kindred* and *Stigmata,* she observes that "as student responses to these novels indicate, contemporary Americans—both white and African American. . . all want to imagine that we would be the defiant and brave African American slave or white Underground Railroad worker. We would not be the ones maimed or killed—surely not the ones doing the maiming and killing" (463–64). Long's emphasis on bodies in pain correlates to my sense of the phantasmic trauma narrative as inspiring in the reader a felt connection to history. She notes, "The protagonists may suffer a slave's pain, but it is a pain . . . experienced by twentieth-century minds" (475).

The distance that Long emphasizes here is a critical one, for even as phantasmic trauma narratives seek to inspire empathy, they do so while underscoring the essential difference between the subject position of the reader and the other, therefore avoiding the pitfalls of what Emmanuel Levinas terms "the imperialism of the same" (1969, 39). In this sense, the goal of the phantasmic trauma narratives overlaps with what Laurie Vickroy (2002) sees as the objective of trauma fiction that attempts to rearticulate the lives and voices of marginalized people: "to try to make readers experience emotional intimacy and immediacy, individual voices and memories, and the sensory responses of the characters" (xvi); this is achieved, she argues, when texts succeed in "absorb[ing] readers into personal and historical trauma" (xvi). Phantasmic trauma narratives such as *Kindred* cannot endow readers with the sort of understanding that can only result from actual experience, nor can they deliver an equality of response; indeed, each reader's reaction to a given text is influenced by the specificities of her own subject position and life experiences. However, as Suzanne Keen (2006) asserts, "when texts invite readers to feel, they also stimulate readers' thinking" (213).[7] Susan Rubin Suleiman (1994) agrees, arguing that "we all project ourselves into what we read, especially into narrative" (48). Suleiman goes further to note that "just as it has been claimed that all writing . . . is in some way autobiographical, so it can be claimed that all reading is" (48). What phantasmic trauma narratives can do, then, is to help condition how a reader thinks about history and therefore potentially shape the way that she evaluates her ethical obligations with regard to that history in the world of the present.

One of the challenges that writers of African American phantasmic trauma narratives face is the fact that this sort of felt connection to history is not easy to achieve, especially because slavery is an experience that is difficult to represent "in the realistic or naturalistic traditions in which much of American literature has been cast" (De Weever 1991, 4). Christopher N. Okonkwo (2008) observes that many neo-slave narratives contain supernatural characters, who imbue the text with "telekinetic, affective, and ideological possibilities" that would otherwise be impossible in a wholly realist text (46). The influence of African belief systems on the construction of American neo-slave narratives is a useful paradigm for analyzing the way that *Kindred* uses West African cosmology as a way of linking past and present. These adaptations of culturally specific beliefs, or the phantasmic, center on Igbo ideas of reincarnation. Specifically, *Kindred* evokes the ideological and spiritual capacities of the Igbo *ogbanje*—also known by the English terms "born-to-die," or "spirit child"—as a means of connecting its protagonist to the moment of slavery. The novel restores Dana's connection to the slave past by adapting *ogbanje*-ism—the ability to travel between worlds—as a literary trope that permits her movement across time and space. Dana's ability to transgress these boundaries raises important questions about the way that the remembrance and reconstruction of the traumatic slave past informs how individuals relate to their cultural heritage and, more broadly, how readers relate to historical experiences on which they potentially may not lay a cultural claim.

THE *OGBANJE* AS PHANTASMIC AGENT

The novel establishes Dana as an *ogbanje* during her first time travel episode, beginning in 1976 Los Angeles and following her over the course of six time travel episodes to early nineteenth-century Maryland, where she is transformed by her traumatic encounter with slavery and her involvement in the lives of her ancestors, both black slaves and white masters. Her *ogbanje*-ism is rooted in her ancestral tie to Rufus Weylin, the white slave owner who fathers her maternal family tree with his slave, Alice Greenwood. Neither Rufus nor Dana can explain their supernatural connection, nor can either control the forces that propel Dana back and forth through time and space, although they gradually come to understand that Dana is summoned to the past when Rufus's life is threatened and is returned to the present when her own life is endangered.[8]

In keeping with other literary adaptations of the *ogbanje*, Dana is a "space- and time-traveling telepath" whose connection to her ancestor is enabled by her "capacity for intuitive and extra-sensory communication" (Okonkwo 2008, 15). While Dana is not telepathic in the traditional sense of the term, she does share something of a telepathic connection with Rufus that causes her to time travel when he is in danger, and her unpredictable returns to antebellum Maryland replicate the *ogbanje*'s refusal to be grounded by mortal rules of space and time. Her first unexpected sojourn to antebellum Maryland illustrates this point: struck by a sudden sensation of dizziness and nausea, she reacts with fear as her vision "blur[s] and darken[s]" (Butler 1979, 13). Without any knowledge of what is happening to her, Dana is transported to another world where she hears the desperate screams of a drowning child. Running to the rescue, she resuscitates the child and, just as he revives, looks up to discover a rifle pointed at her by an irate white man. Convinced that he will shoot her, Dana again experiences dizziness and nausea and, when the blurriness of her vision subsides, discovers herself once again kneeling in her living room, "several feet from where [she] had fallen minutes before," but now "wet and muddy" (14). From this very first encounter, we see that coalesced in Dana's "alien-ness and spatial-temporal travel are the sub-themes of permeability of (cosmic) borders, separation from home/ancestry, migration, and exile" (Okonkwo 2008, 15). Her ability to connect these two worlds in a material way—by bringing fragments of the past into the present and vice versa—underscores the critical role of *ogbanje*-ism as a tool for enabling readers to engage the past from a new perspective.

That Dana—who at the beginning of the narrative has "virtually no historical awareness" (Beaulieu 1999, 118)—finds herself phantasmically linked to the past demonstrates a concern that the traumatic lessons and ramifications of slavery have not been passed down to the present generation of African Americans. The sense of connectedness through time and across generations that arises from Dana's *ogbanje*-ism reflects the African cosmological view that all entities are rooted in a "cosmic totality" that links everyone and everything together as inextricable parts of a cosmic whole, which in turn enables a "cosmic consciousness" shared by the living, ancestors, and the unborn (Soyinka 1976, 3).[9] More specifically, it is through this sense of cosmic unity that the Igbo peoples of West Africa—one of the principal tribes from which African Americans are descended[10]—attempt to make sense of the world and of their lived experiences. The West African cosmological belief in the interconnectedness of all things and beings—living, ancestral, or in between—clearly drives Dana's time travel episodes, which transform her from a person lacking in historical awareness to one intimately acquainted with the stark physical and psychological conditions in which her slave ancestors suffered and persevered.

Traditionally understood, *ogbanje* is an Igbo term used to signify spirits who (1) manifest themselves in human flesh by taking over or causing a pregnancy, (2) are born into the human world, and (3) die young, only to begin the cycle all over again. Like its Yoruba counterpart, *abiku*, the *ogbanje* may be understood as a "constellar concept" because it "embraces various beliefs about . . . the relationship between the real world and that of spirits" (Quayson 1997, 122). As "part human and part spirit beings" (Achebe 1986, 27), the *ogbanje* is traditionally thought of in Igbo culture as "a spirit child, one fated to a cycle of early death and birth to the same mother" (Achebe 1980, 32). As Christie Achebe (1980) explains, "The literal meaning of ogbanje is thus one who *comes repeatedly* or one who dies and comes again" (33, emphasis added).[11] Moreover, Misty Bastian (2002) explains, the *ogbanje* "embodies, in the human world, a mischievous, spiritual person—one who is interested in human life, who could almost be said to experiment with the idea of being human, but who is not him/herself human and who has little interest in committing to a human lineage" (59).[12] Further, its cycle of death and rebirth is believed to be continuous and is often repeated within the same family, as the literal translation of *ogbanje* suggests: "one who is engaged in repeated reincarnation" (Nzewi 2001, 1404). However, the term differs from Western understandings of reincarnation because, as Achebe (1980) writes, it belongs in a "mysterious and supernatural etiology" (33). Whereas reincarnation, for the Igbo, "symbolizes a rebirth after a full life cycle" and is therefore considered "desirable," *ogbanje*-ism is considered a "perversion of that natural life pattern which gives hope of an auspicious life after death" (33). As a result, the *ogbanje* is considered to be an "elusive, mysterious, and incomprehensible" presence (33), one that essentially enslaves the parents to whom it is born.

Although the concept originated in Africa, scholars of African spirituality and its impact on American literature, such as Chikwenye Ogunyemi and Christopher Okonkwo, agree that the idea of *ogbanje* was introduced to the American colonies by enslaved West Africans, who gradually integrated their native beliefs with the Christianity of their masters. As a result, the *ogbanje* has quietly assumed a place within the African American literary tradition, functioning both as an avatar for the liminal space between the worlds of the living and the dead as well as a symbolic connection between the cultures of Africa and African America. Toni Morrison (1994) underscores this connection when she observes, "The gap between Africa and Afro-America and the gap between the living and the dead and the gap between the past and the present does not exist" (247). If, as Venetria Patton (2013) asserts, the "ogbanje figure is ideal for illustrating the continuity between these seemingly disconnected spaces" (130), we can understand why it has been repurposed as a literary trope with increasing frequency over the past thirty years, beginning with the publication of Butler's *Mind of My Mind* in 1977.[13]

However, the majority of African American novels that employ the *ogbanje* as a literary trope do not exactly duplicate the qualities and experiences associated with that special category of children in the Igbo culture of Nigeria.[14] In its adaptation by African American writers, the *ogbanje* figure has been reshaped to fit uniquely American contexts and hermeneutical purposes. That it is increasingly found in narratives touched by slavery reflects a desire on the part of African American writers to syncretize their African heritage with the distinctive experience of American slavery and to reconcile the historical silences that it wrought with the need to feel the past. *Kindred* embodies these twin drives by staging a return to the past through the *ogbanje* as a cultural vehicle. Assessing the complicated interplay of history and memory in *Kindred*, Guiliano Bettanin (2008) suggests that neo-slave narratives

> mean to be innovative as they seek to rediscover and rewrite a significant part of history that was deliberately forgotten and denied. ... Yet, we must remember that while the original slave narratives aimed to recover history, neo-slave narratives are based on a re-invention of history, a re-invention which is conscious of the principle that every narration of history, be it a chronicle or a piece of fiction, was born from a process of interpretation from which it cannot be separated. (96)

Butler's novel reinvents the American past by imbuing it with an African sensibility, thereby not only rejecting a Western view of history as a linear progression of events, but also insisting that a reappraisal of the slave past be framed within a non-Western cultural context.

In this spirit, *Kindred* creates a literary device that provides a conduit to the past, retaining the primary qualities of the spirit child—such as its ability to move between worlds and its intrinsic sense of otherness—while eschewing its secondary qualities, such as its malevolence, selfishness, and mischievousness, for the sake of encouraging reader empathy for Dana's plight. The novel's slight adjustments to the *ogbanje* form act as a syncretization that permits Butler to account for her specifically American context and offer her readers a new way of connecting to slave history. Most importantly, *Kindred* substitutes the dialectics of life and death of the traditional *ogbanje* narrative with the dialectics of present and past, freedom and enslavement. The novel mobilizes key aspects of the *ogbanje* as a way of providing access to the past, and in doing so creatively repurposes its ontological peculiarity to frame Dana and to negotiate questions of race, gender, subjectivity, and historical memory.

Further, Butler uses the *ogbanje* as a phantasmic tool for reinterpreting the complexities of being a black woman in post–civil rights America and for exploring the ways and means by which both black and nonblack individuals can remember and feel history. In this, *Kindred* anticipates projects like Butler's own *Wild Seed* (1980), Tananarive Due's *The Between* (1996), and John Edgar Wideman's *The Cattle Killing* (1997), in which the idea of the *ogbanje* is "consciously reconstructed and resounded as title, character, theme, plot device, and epistemology" (Okonkwo 2008, xv). These *ogbanje*-centered texts capitalize on literature's ability to appeal to readers in a way that emphasizes the "embodied—felt—and connective use of narrative" (Wagers 2009, 26). Further, these texts recognize that literature's impact on readers is connected to its ability to "*make* history" (Reilly 1986, 90). Indeed, as John M. Reilly (1986) observes, "fiction creates its own objects" (88). Further, it serves as a vehicle for cultural histories that function not only as a way of preserving cultural memory for a particular group, but also as a means of documenting and packaging those memories in a way that can be accessible to other groups. For Butler, the *ogbanje* figure offers a unique way of connecting readers to the moment of slavery.

When asked to classify her novel, Butler explains that, unlike her other works, *Kindred* does not fall within the boundaries of science fiction because there is "absolutely no science in it" (Butler, "*Black Scholar* Interview" 14), and indeed, the mechanics of Dana's time travel are never explained or even questioned. Instead, Butler describes *Kindred* as a story designed to "make people feel" the experience of the novel's protagonist. She continues by explaining that her goal in writing *Kindred* was not to make readers "understand what it felt like to be a slave," but rather to "confront a modern person with that reality of history. It's one thing to read about it and cringe that something horrible is happening. I sent somebody into it who is a person of now, of today, and that means I kind of take the reader along and expose them in a way that the average historic novel doesn't intend to, can't" (Butler 2003). Thus, the novel's objective is to offer readers a way into traumatic history that takes into account their present-day perspectives.

To some extent, *Kindred* resembles magical realist works' confidence that readers, like the characters, will accept fantastic events as part of the textual landscape. However, Butler establishes the realistic moments of her text—the physical and psychological violence of slavery—within the context of phantasmic occurrences. By casting the novel's fantastic events in realist yet ambiguous terms, Butler asks us to perceive those events not as science fiction, but rather as the products of a phantasmic phenomenon that links Dana's present-day existence with her ancestral past. Butler's resistance to *Kindred*'s categorization as science fiction makes perfect sense, given that Western science does not allow for the spiritual categories recognized by non-Western cultures. Instead, she draws on an entirely different ontological mode to transport her characters into the past, and, in so doing, rejects both science, which would require a "rational" explanation for Dana's time travel, as well as magical realism, which would require readers to simply indulge the text's flight from reality without allowing for the possibility that Dana may be operating within a culturally specific African ontological system.

Butler's privileging of Igbo ontology over Western views of time and space reflects Channette Romero's (2012) assertion that "contemporary novels by women of color explore the relationship of people of color's temporalities to mainstream Euro American notions of time in an effort to prompt their readers to consider how concepts of temporality relate to ideology" (59). As Vine Deloria Jr. (1973) argues, this exploration is crucial to the recovery of non-white histories and identities because "Western European identity involves the assumption that time proceeds in a linear fashion; further it assumes that at a particular point in the unraveling of this sequence, the peoples of Western Europe became the guardians of the world" (63). By juxtaposing Euro-American and Igbo notions of time and ontological possibilities, *Kindred* asks readers to become more aware of "the ideologies associated with divergent worldviews, ideologies that the linear concept of time works to elide" (Romero 2012, 59). Thus, by adapting the boundary-crossing capacities of the *ogbanje* as a vehicle for Dana's journey of historical discovery, the text not only underscores the inextricable, though often forgotten, connections between the slave past and the shape of present-day America, but also challenges the ideologies—both religious and scientific—that have historically justified the existence and perpetuation of slavery in America and that seek to negate ontologies that fail to square with Western belief systems.

READER IDENTIFICATION AND *OGBANJE*-ISM

It is easy to imagine why readers of *Kindred* have overlooked Dana as an *ogbanje* figure: neither the word *ogbanje* nor its English translations, "born-to-die" and "spirit child," are mentioned anywhere in the novel, and Dana is not a literal adaptation of the spirit child who seeks multiple rebirths with mischievous and perhaps even malicious intent.[15] By contrast, she is an adult who is compelled to time travel against her will. She has no control over her returns to the early nineteenth century and very quickly comes to fear them. And rather than displaying the selfishness of the traditional *ogbanje*, Dana is compassionate, self-sacrificing, and kind. Nonetheless, the position that Dana occupies in the nineteenth-century world of her ancestors mirrors the ontology of the traditional *ogbanje* figure in significant ways. Indeed, her multiple returns and (near-)deaths mimic the birth-death cycle of the born-to-die: her brushes with death in the world of the past return her to the present. Moreover, Dana's character map mimics that of the spirit child archetype in the way that it harnesses the *ogbanje*'s "stupendous capacity for telepathy and time travel" (Okonkwo 2008, xxiv). By rendering permeable the boundaries of time and space, the text highlights the inextricable links that exist between the contemporary world and the traumatic past that gives it its form. The novel's use of the *ogbanje* figure not only permits Dana to bear witness to the past, but also enables her to reclaim and critique it.

Significantly, in using the spiritual capacities of the *ogbanje* as a vehicle for Dana's time travel, the text challenges us to ask *why* Dana is physically propelled back into the past, rather than how or by what means her time travel is achieved. The fact that the novel leaves the question of why Dana has such an intense connection to the past ambiguous is important because it encourages crucial interpretive engagement on the part of the reader, who as she becomes more involved in the fabric of the story begins to anticipate and empathize with Dana's reactions to the antebellum world into which she is transported. Christine Levecq (2000) affirms the novel's uncanny hold on its readership when she argues, "In spite of the repeated emphasis on history's textuality, it is precisely the confrontation with the reality of slavery that constitutes the main appeal of the novel" (529). As a result of this connection, the empathic reader affectively identifies with Dana and her first-person subject position in the drama of the novel. By suspending the rules of narrative realism through its use of the *ogbanje* trope, the text bridges the distance between reader and protagonist, permitting the formation of a powerful emotional identification.

Ultimately, empathic reader responses to this novel are predicated on an understanding of the way that Dana's fluid subjectivity and her empathy for the suffering of others inspires us, in turn, to think about our own subjectivity in relation to historical trauma and its victims.[16] Recent research from social psychologists David Kidd and Emanuele Castano (2013) reinforces this idea by demonstrating that literary fiction improves a reader's capacity to understand what others are thinking and feeling and may, in turn, inspire prosocial behavior. Similarly, in *Empathy and the Novel*, Keen (2007) affirms "the robustness of narrative empathy as an affective transaction accomplished through the writing and reading of fiction," but she hesitates "to tether readers' empathy to certain outcomes of altruistic action" (xv). While I share Keen's sense of caution, I am more concerned with delineating the strategies by which phantasmic texts, in this case *Kindred,* seek to elicit empathic responses and, in so doing, create opportunities for ethical thinking.

Our ability to connect with Dana's experience is made easier because the novel is narrated through her perspective, and thus we view antebellum Maryland through her eyes. As a result, we are afforded a closer proximity as she is faced with the challenge of traversing racial, gendered, and geographical borders while at the same time negotiating dual consciousnesses and identities.[17] The *ogbanje*'s in-betweeness recalls the postmodern black subject's liminality, which locates its origins in the cradle of slavery, the collective memory of which has had a part in shaping contemporary African American identity.[18] *Kindred* capitalizes on the liminal status of the postmodern black subject as the basis of this connection and cleverly uses the *ogbanje* trope as a means of situating the reader in a liminal position similar to that of the Igbo spirit child. Dana literalizes this connection between the postmodern black subject and the *ogbanje* figure by continuously—if at first inadvertently—crossing and recrossing traditionally inviolable boundaries of time and space and, later, by actively challenging racial and gender distinctions.

The novel realizes the connections between the past and present on three different levels. The first level establishes Dana as an *ogbanje* figure, and it is through her liminal status that we gain access to the slave past. On the second level, we see how Dana's *ogbanje* status in her ancestral community—as a gendered, racial, and supernatural other—emphasizes her distance from history as well as her disconnection from the suffering of her slave forebears. Her awareness of this distance is manifested in repeated, failed attempts to write about her experience of and relation to the traumatic past without being consumed by it at the same time. Thus, on the third level, Dana's personal encounters with the violence of slavery prompts us to recognize the gaps between the lived reality of slavery and the official historical record, as well as the pervasiveness of systems of oppression in the contemporary moment. Dana's struggle to make sense of the imbrications of the traumatic past and her present-day life resonates as a call for us to remember and bear witness to slavery and its lasting impact on American culture.

From the moment of her first encounter with Rufus on the riverbank, Dana becomes a point of fusion between past and present, a wormhole through which the reader gains access to the trauma of slavery in a more immediate way. In this capacity, she evinces qualities of the *ogbanje* and its Yoruba counterpart, the *abiku*.[19] Ogunyemi (1996) notes an important confluence in these two versions of the born-to-die:

> *ogbanje/abiku* . . . itself as a status or condition epitomizes "rememorying," to borrow Toni Morrison's word in *Beloved* for the notion of returning to the past and reconstructing it for contemporary uses. With reiteration and revision, one establishes a tradition of newness as an agency for progress. This idea is in consonance with the fact that *Ogbanje* retains an original core, in spite of the repetitions. (67)[20]

Like *Beloved, Kindred* presents rememory as a form of memory that is both "emotional" and embodied, "what the nerves and the skin remember as well as how it appeared" (Morrison 1995, 99).[21] Because she is a phantasmic agent with whom readers can identify, Dana's time travel enables an important "rememorying" of the past for the reader. In this way, we understand Dana as an American adaptation of the *ogbanje*, for while she does not literally die, it is by virtue of her intimate relationship to death that she is permitted to reverse her journeys to the past.[22] More importantly, because she herself struggles with questions of ethics and responsibility in a way that encourages the reader to do the same—as I discuss below—she acts as an agent for progress.

Terrified and confused by her initial journey to the past, Dana can only explain to her horrified husband that the experience "almost killed" her and confess her suspicion that "it could happen again . . . it could happen anytime" (17). Her fears are confirmed when she is called to the past a second time and learns that Rufus is "the focus of [her] travels—perhaps the cause of them"; indeed, she is "drawn to him" (24). Piecing together clues from Rufus's dress and diction, Dana quickly discerns that she has traveled back in time to antebellum Maryland and, dimly recalling an ancestral connection to that time and place, realizes that the child sitting before her is her "several times great grandfather, but still vaguely alive in the memory of [her] family because his daughter had bought a large Bible . . . and had begun keeping family records in it" (28). Gradually, Dana realizes that like the woman who unwittingly recalls the *ogbanje* into her empty womb following the loss of a child, believing that the birth of a new child will replace the absence left by death, so Rufus unknowingly calls her to him when death menaces him, thereby yoking her into a seemingly endless cycle of appearances and disappearances, mimicking the traditional death and rebirth cycle of the Igbo *ogbanje*.

As she begins to make sense of the mysterious bond that links her to Rufus, Dana also comes to recognize "the paradox" that her connection to Rufus represents (29). She knows, for example, that Rufus's life depends "on the actions of his unconceived descendant. No matter what [she] did, he would have to survive to father Hagar, or [Dana] could not exist. . . . If [she] was to live, if others were to live, he must live" (29). To ensure her own existence in the future, Dana must ensure Rufus's survival in the past. However, Dana's preservation is predicated on her involvement in still more violence: the rape of her foremother Alice. And for Dana, there is no way out of this dilemma: "It was so hard to watch him hurting her—to know that he had to go on hurting her if my family was to exist at all" (180). Thus, while Dana does not outwardly resemble the *ogbanje* in temperament, she does model the *ogbanje*'s tendency to privilege its own self-interest at the expense of others.[23] Yet her willingness to preserve the life of an often sadistic slaveholder and her complicity in the rape of Alice serve a deeper symbolic purpose as well: they force Dana to acknowledge the idea that "in this country there is always a great deal more kindred than we have always chosen to recognize" (Butler 2004). For Butler, the trauma of slavery has made us all kindred, and just as Dana is complicit in Alice's rape, so too are we all complicit in the perpetuation of slavery's racist underpinnings in contemporary cultural and political institutions.

Most notably for the nineteenth-century people she encounters, Dana's appearance, demeanor, and sociopolitical sensibilities set her apart from the rest of the community. Her alterity can be explained by her *ogbanje* status: as Bastian (2002) explains, "to be an *ogbaanje* is to be categorized other—and to bring alterity home in a way that transcends the more ordinary, bifurcated 'otherness' of gender" (59). And Dana is indeed marked by an otherness—inscribed on her both in terms of appearance and character—that is expressed through her strong sense of individuality that situates her in opposition to authority figures, who generally perceive her as "insolent" (66) and "impudent" (219). She manifests the *ogbanje*'s persistent "disloyal quest" for another home (Ogunyemi 2002, 664)—1976 Los Angeles—and in so doing establishes important contrasts and links between the antebellum world and post–civil rights America.[24] Writing about the *ogbanje-abiku*, Ogunyemi (2002) explains that it "disorients" its "parents and the community" because of its "many incarnations and cultural pluralism" (664). And Dana does indeed disorient both branches of her ancestry, white and black alike. Repeatedly throughout the novel, she is told by Rufus and others that she "don't talk right or dress right or act right" (30). With her short haircut, penchant for wearing pants, educated manner of speaking, and post–civil rights social sensibilities, Dana defies nineteenth-century race and gender norms, for which she is branded at the outset as a "strange nigger" (24). Balking at being identified by a derogatory racial slur, Dana endeavors to define her identity in post–civil rights era terms, as is evident in the following exchange: "'Your mother always call black people niggers, Rufe?' 'Sure, except when she has company. Why not?'. . . 'I'm a black woman, Rufe. If you have to call me something other than my name, that's it. . . . [Y]ou do me the courtesy of calling me what I want to be called" (25). Her indignant response to this appellation immediately upsets the established master-slave dialectic by contesting Rufus's right to name her.

Interestingly, Dana's *ogbanje* qualities are refracted in the novel's inversion of the oppressor-oppressed dichotomy by which the Igbo traditionally understand the relationship between the *ogbanje* and its parents. While the "life-and-death drama enacted between an Ogbanje-abiku child and his/her parents is . . . an ongoing struggle for power, control, and self-autonomy" (Okonkwo 2008, 40), Butler recasts Dana as the subject of oppression who ultimately struggles to wrest her freedom from her forefather. It is important to note that we only recognize the inversion of traditional *ogbanje*-parent power dynamics when viewing the past from Dana's twentieth-century point of view. However, if we adjust our perspective to examine Dana as Rufus sees her—as a black woman who not only defies and resists conventional nineteenth-century perceptions of black people, but also refuses to allow her black captivity to reaffirm Rufus's white freedom—we discern more clearly the ways in which she manifests spirit child characteristics. Indeed, if Dana acts as an *ogbanje*, Rufus plays the role of *ogbanje* parent. Just as Igbo parents "resort to bribery" in a desperate attempt to convince their *ogbanje* children to remain in the world of the living, so too does Rufus entreat Dana to remain with him (Ogunyemi 2002, 664). His attempts to manipulate Dana range from offering her "gifts" ("Here, Dana, here's a new book I bought for you in town," or, "here's some cloth, Dana. Maybe you can make something from it" [258]) to appealing to her empathy for the other slaves (he allows her to teach the slave children to read and write) and to her sense of guilt and responsibility (arguing that "if [she] had any feelings" for his slave offspring [256], she would stay "to protect their freedom" [259]). Their fraught relationship reverses traditional hierarchy of the parent-child relationship, and therefore extends and rewrites the metaphysical idea of the *ogbanje* to illustrate the master-slave dialectic as it plays out in the novel and, by extension, in American history.

Considering this contradiction, Dana reflects, "I was the worst possible guardian for him—a black woman to watch over him in a society that considered blacks sub-human, and a woman to watch over him in a society that considered women perennial children. I would have all I could do to look after myself" (68). Although Dana finds her relation to Rufus problematic, Elizabeth Beaulieu (1999) argues that this is Butler's intention; indeed, she "prioritizes both womanhood and blackness by reversing the conventional equation and demonstrating her female protagonist's necessity in a world that actively campaigned to deny her every fundamental right" (122). Thus, Dana's status as an *ogbanje* not only reverses the parent-child dynamic by situating her as Rufus's "guardian," but also permits her to transgress the boundaries of race and gender prescribed by Rufus's cultural environment. Moreover, Dana's impulse to correct Rufus's racist terminology clearly reflects twentieth-century sensibilities that have been cultivated by the liberal environment of 1970s California. Angelyn Mitchell (2002) agrees, noting that as "a post-integrationist Black woman, Dana possesses a clear sense of her individuality. Strengthened by her racial pride, her personal responsibility, her free will, Dana embraces her ability to define herself in both her past and her present" (64). Dana's postintegrationist, postfeminist sensibilities disturb the slave community as well, whose members regard her comportment as distinguishing her from the rest of the slaves. Indeed, they deem her manner of speaking as an effort to "try to talk like white folks" and consider her "more like white folks than some white folks" (74). Some, like Alice's ill-fated husband Isaac, openly judge her for her perceived "white" qualities and consider her speech to be evidence of race betrayal: "She don't talk like no nigger I ever heard. Talks like she been mighty close with the white folks—for a long time" (119).

Despite the seeming freedom that Dana's mobility and liminal status grant her, she is nevertheless caught in between, both in between centuries and in between races. Because she is equipped with the "hindsight, insight, and foresight" characteristic of the Igbo *ogbanje* (Ogunyemi 2002, 665), Dana "confuse[s] everybody" and is perceived as a threat to the white people in power and "some kind of traitor" to the black people they enslave (Butler 1979, 255). At once "too white" and "too black," the "kind of black who watches and thinks and makes trouble," Dana unsettles the antebellum worldview of her ancestors and challenges the white patriarchal authority that seeks to categorize her by race and gender (255). Further, she moves fluidly across borders of difference with a seemingly limitless freedom that is nonetheless circumscribed by her in-betweeness: Dana exists in two different centuries, but gradually begins to feel out of place in both worlds. She is free in the present day, but is also enslaved there by hegemonic cultural practices, just as she is enslaved in the antebellum South, but free by comparison to her black ancestors. Her temporal mobility—the ability to travel between the past and present—belies the fact that as an *ogbanje* figure subject to the whims of her white master-forefather, she is enslaved by her ancestral history as well.

INSPIRING CROSS-CULTURAL EMPATHY

Because she is perceived as a transformative being—at once both white and black, a subject of slavery and yet a citizen of 1976 America—Dana is an object of mystery to the antebellum community she touches. However, as a creative writer, she is capable of harnessing and explaining this mystery for an audience of readers. As both Catherine Acholonu (1988) and Ogunyemi (1996, 2002) suggest, the creative writer is something of an *ogbanje* figure in her ability to imagine and negotiate the distance between real and imaginary worlds, and I suggest that it is with this in mind that Butler makes her heroine a writer, one for whom boundaries between the real and imaginary, past and present, are not circumscribed (Acholonu 1988, 104; Ogunyemi 2002, 667).[25] As an *ogbanje*, Dana does indeed possess an "innate power to effect transformations" visible to others, a creative power that parallels that which she exercises as a writer (Ogunyemi 2002, 666). And while Dana earns her living in the present day as a writer, Butler shows us that she finds the challenge of communicating her lived experience of the past to be a nearly impossible task. Her first attempt to articulate her traumatic encounters with Rufus and his world in writing is met with failure: "Once I sat down at my typewriter and tried to write about what had happened, made about six attempts before I gave up and threw them all away. Someday when this was over, if it was ever over, maybe I would be able to write about it" (116).

Although Dana finds writing somewhat therapeutic—"Sometimes I wrote things because I couldn't say them, couldn't sort out my feelings about them, couldn't keep them bottled up inside me"—she nonetheless feels compelled to destroy her writing, convinced that "it was for no one else" (252). Dana's impulse to testify to her firsthand experience of slavery is stymied by the fact that the worlds she must navigate are not divided by the traditional boundary between real and imaginary that she negotiates in her creative writing projects; indeed, both of the worlds in which she moves are equally real and are divided by the weight of time and space. Moreover, she is challenged by the "burden of narrating the extreme" and of giving shape to the "overwhelming, incomprehensible, and formless" trauma that has not been sufficiently communicated by the official historical record (Miller and Tougaw 2002, 7). No longer simply an observer of history, Dana is now a participant in it. Yet even as an active agent in the lives of her ancestors, Dana does not have the power to alter the course of history; the past is intransitive.

Because she cannot rewrite the (hi)story of her ancestral past, Dana carries the weight of imparting to the historical record an affective account of the incomprehensible acts of horror that she has witnessed. Wagers (2009) also recognizes the impact of trauma on Dana's writing, arguing that "*Kindred* carries out its reconfiguration of history . . . chiefly through a change in Dana's understanding of the meaning and practice of writing. Her sense of narrative shifts from the goal of producing a marketable commodity to an awareness of the more vital, shared use of narrative as a mode of explanation and understanding in a community" (27). Unlike the fiction writer, who as Morrison contends is charged with the task of imagining the past, Dana finds herself writing autobiography, her own lived sense of history, and is creatively paralyzed as a result. She struggles to witness against what Morrison has described as a "national amnesia" about the trauma of slavery as well as the traumatic effects of institutionalized racism that persist in her own century (Morrison 1994, 257). In an effort to make sense of her personal experience of slavery, Dana looks to the historical record and "read[s] books about slavery, fiction and nonfiction" (116). This desire to contextualize her experience requires Dana to move beyond her own subjectivity and draw on latent historical knowledge of concurrent and related cultural traumas to navigate the ideological and cultural landscape of the antebellum South; Dana's search for knowledge brings her closer to locating her individual identity within the broader scope of a shared ancestral and cultural identity.

The first circumstance that prompts Dana to draw on historical knowledge is during her second time travel episode, when with Rufus's help she leaves the Weylin plantation for Alice's cabin. Under the cover of night, she avoids the road, admitting that "the possibility of meeting a white adult here frightened [her], more than the possibility of street violence ever had at home . . . [because] if they saw [her], they might take [her] along with them as their prisoner. Blacks were assumed to be slaves unless they could prove they were free—unless they had their free papers. Paperless blacks were fair game for any white" (33–34). Here, Dana anticipates the potential dangers that confront her by drawing on a rather vague historical knowledge of the period. Beaulieu (1999) points out that at the beginning of the text, Dana "has virtually no historical awareness" (118), which is best demonstrated by her callous references to her unemployment agency as a "slave market" (Butler 1979, 52). Confronted with the reality of a traumatic past that she only recognizes through sedimented representations of history—"like something I saw on television or read about" (17)—Dana realizes the need to gain more knowledge about the foreign world to which she is repeatedly returned.

More than once, she thinks "back to [her] reading" and popular culture knowledge as a means of navigating the past, such as when she imitates the submissive body language of a slave when around white slave owners, or when she packs modern-day history texts and maps to aid her in escape attempts. However, these representations prove inadequate for Dana, who quickly becomes aware of her liminal position, at once outside and yet within the past. We observe Dana's awakening to her liminal status in her reaction to the brutal whipping of Alice's father by white patrollers: "I had seen people beaten on television and in the movies. I had seen the too red-hot substitute streaked across their backs and heard their well-rehearsed screams. But I hadn't laid nearby and smelled their sweat or heard them pleading and praying, shamed before their families and themselves" (36). Here, it seems clear that the novel privileges "experiential knowledge over text-based knowledge," though, as Susan David Bernstein (2003) notes, "this lesson is inevitably text-bound to its readers" (153). However, because *Kindred* goes to such lengths to make the distinction between these two types of knowledge explicit, and because its project is dedicated not only to commemorating the slave past but also to encouraging reader identification with that traumatic event, *Kindred* "produces something like a document whose origin belongs to the past . . . but whose effects belong to both the present and the future—to the living readers whose post-traumatic responsibilities are both retrospective and prospective" (Miller and Tougaw 2002, 7). Lauren J. Lacey (2014) furthers this argument to assert that it is during those moments when Dana draws comparisons between her experience as a witness and "the inadequate representations of history available to her in 1976 . . . that Butler draws the reader's attention to the production of historical knowledge in the contemporary world, and pushes the reader to ask what it would mean to react to history in a truly ethical manner" (74). In this way, Butler encourages the reader to move beyond emotional response into ethical thinking.

With Dana serving as our proxy, the text draws us into the painful world of the American South and asks us to become witnesses to the horrors of slavery and, in so doing, to open ourselves up to the possibility of achieving a felt connection to the past. By encouraging this kind of engagement, the text invites the reader to identify with Dana's complicated subject position, which is characterized by an uneasy occupation of the unsteady territory between participant and observer, a present-day subject immersed in history. Supporting this view is Gregory Jerome Hampton (2010), who observes, "The narrative of *Kindred* is elevated to more than a tale told to an audience by a narrator. It becomes an experience which is shared by Dana and the reader. The reader, like Dana, becomes a passenger gaining access to a passage through time, beyond the formation of Dana's family history" (3). Robert Crossley (2003) goes further to emphasize the visceral response that *Kindred* evokes from readers: "The route [Butler] pursues to her readers' heads is through their guts and nerves" (274). These observations resonate with Butler's (2003) comment that her intention in writing *Kindred* from the perspective of a contemporary protagonist was "to make people *feel* the book" (emphasis added). For Long (2009), Butler's stated goal gives rise to a need for a "pedagogy of the body" (477), one that accounts for the fact that "although readers cannot embody the slave experience, they, too, are invaded by the painful [narrative]" (478). She goes on to note that "it is a pain that many readers are unwilling to endure" and points out that some readers are indeed resistant to what they perceive as "the persistence of slave experience in African American writing as forcing racial violence on an 'innocent' citizenry" (478). However, in my experience of teaching in college literature classrooms, even those who resent being confronted with slavery through the experience of reading *Kindred* are often prompted, as the result of that experience, to begin asking questions about what constitutes an ethical response to cultural trauma. This act of questioning is important in itself for the way that it advances discourse about historical events and our responsibilities with regard to those events in the present. Just as Dana's *ogbanje* status renders her vulnerable, so too does it remind readers of their own violability. This exposed position is an uncomfortable one, and it is from this uncomfortable state that critical questions of ethics and responsibility arise.

The precariousness of Dana's position is further illustrated during her third trip to the past. Together with Kevin, Dana lives on the Weylin plantation for several months. Being stuck in the early 1800s for such a prolonged time means that they have to adopt suitable roles and routines; to this end, Kevin acts as Rufus's tutor and Dana assumes the role of Kevin's slave, and they keep the fact of their relationship hidden. However, Dana is troubled by the ease with which they seem to acclimate to this unfamiliar life: "It seemed as though we should have had a harder time adjusting to this particular segment of history—adjusting to our places in the household of the slaveholder" (97). She is concerned that their journey back to such a troubled, racist past does not elicit from them more resistant attitudes and is alarmed by their seemingly easy adjustment to the social mores that governed plantation life. Later, however, she realizes that they have not become complicit in this lifestyle, but are instead spectators: "We weren't really in. We were observers. . . . We were watching history happen around us. . . . We never forgot we were acting" (98). By recognizing her participation in the past as performance, Dana moves closer to achieving the historical consciousness that the text endorses as a mode of cultural memory. Although she does experience the trauma of slavery in a bodily, visceral way, she never forgets that her experience of the past is mediated by her own growing historical foreknowledge.

Dana's acceptance of her spectator status is challenged soon after, however, when she and Kevin observe the slave children playing a game intended to simulate a slave auction. Horrified by the reality that these children have formulated their identities and self-worth by white racist standards, she struggles with her role as a detached observer, and questions Kevin's insistence that they are unable to change history: "You might be able to go through this whole experience as an observer. . . . I can understand that because most of the time, I'm still an observer. It's protection. It's nineteen seventy-six shielding and cushioning eighteen nineteen, and I don't know what to do. I ought to be doing something though. I know that" (101). Woolfork (2009) reads this moment as the definitive point at which "Dana crosses the boundary between observer and participant," propelling her toward a very physically driven "experiential involvement" in the traumatic past (27). However, for Woolfork's claim to be fully substantiated, Dana would have to eventually abandon her present-day subjectivity, eschew her historical foreknowledge, and fully immerse herself in the slave consciousness. For Dana, as for the reader, it is not possible to fully shed who she is. The *ogbanje* never loses sight of its own liminal status; indeed, its awareness of its own in-betweeness is part of what enables it to cross and recross boundaries. Michael Kreyling (2010) insists that the text "keeps Dana a spectator" by imagining that "remembering the present [is] a way of realizing the past" (190). Further, he suggests that by reversing memory, *Kindred* "is able to enter the 'unrecoverable' territory of the mind and temper of the plantation slave" and therefore "construct a 'memory' to replace the one erased over generations of unrecorded and unvoiced slave lives" (190). Indeed, Dana does gain entry to the psychic territory of her slave forebears, but she does so with full cognizance of her status as a twentieth-century subject and, as a result, is able to make connections between her own experience within the American slave system and those of others who have been the subjects of racial persecution. Similarly, even as readers respond to the traumatic events in the novel with emotion, they do not lose sight of their own contemporary perspectives; rather than handicapping the novel's ethical mission, this sense of dual consciousness permits readers to recognize connections between slavery and traumatic events in more recent history.

Dana models such a connection to traumatic history following her third return to the present, a reverse journey precipitated by the whipping that Tom Weylin gives her for teaching slave children how to read. Reflecting on the terror and fear that initiated her return, Dana attempts to make meaning of her traumatic experience. Unfortunately, however, none of the books on slavery satisfy her need to understand: "I read books about slavery, fiction and nonfiction. I read everything I had in the house that was even distantly related to the subject—even *Gone With the Wind,* or part of it. But its version of happy darkies in tender loving bondage was more than I could stand" (117). Instead, it is a book about another cultural trauma, the Holocaust, that helps her make sense of her suffering:

> I got caught up in one of Kevin's World War II books—a book of excerpts from the recollections of concentration camp survivors. Stories of beatings, starvation, filth, disease, torture, every possible degradation. As though the Germans had been trying to do in only a few years what the Americans had worked at for nearly two hundred. The books depressed me, scared me. . . . Like the Nazis, antebellum whites had known quite a bit about torture—quite a bit more than I ever wanted to learn. (117)

For Spaulding (2005), this textual moment illustrates the failure of official historiography to accurately portray the brutality of slavery. Weylin's beating awakens Dana to an experience of slavery that has not been duplicated in texts. Indeed, the "only texts on slavery to which Dana has immediate access not only limit her understanding of her own experience but misrepresent the historical realities of slavery. As a result, Dana must turn to a more recent corollary to illuminate her own past: the torture of Jews in Nazi Germany" (Spaulding 2005, 50). Bernstein makes a similar connection, suggesting that Dana's identification with Jewish victims of the Holocaust helps her to better understand the experience of slavery, which illustrates the idea that "identification, a matter of relation, works by way of a 'detour through the other that defines a self'" (153). I extend these readings to argue that Dana's ability to recognize and acknowledge the suffering of other groups not only helps her to contextualize and make sense of her own history, but also models the kind of felt connection that Butler wishes her readers to experience.

Further, Dana's comparison is important for the way that it demonstrates the intercultural project of phantasmic trauma narratives, which is to foster in readers a deeper understanding of a specific traumatic event like slavery by recognizing the historical traumas of other groups. In this regard, the text itself becomes *ogbanje*-like by crossing over the boundaries of its own historical subject. For example, Kevin, who has time traveled with Dana to the early 1800s, confesses his belief that "this could be a great time to live in. . . . [W]hat a great experience it would be to stay in it—[to] go West and watch the building of the country, see how much of the old West mythology is true"

(97). For Kevin, the West is a clean slate, a safe remove from the horrible conditions of slave life that he witnesses daily on the Weylin plantation. Dana, however, knows differently, and points out that in the West, "they're doing it to the Indians instead of the blacks" (97). Where Kevin adopts a detached approach to history, Dana is able to make broader connections among different minority subjectivities as they relate to the dominant white power structure.

Just as Dana is able to physically transgress the borders of space and time thanks to her *ogbanje* capabilities, so too is she able to conceptually transgress the boundaries of her own experience and subjectivity in order to make important connections between the American slave culture and other systems of oppression. When Rufus forces her to destroy a history book because he is threatened by its subversive ideas, Dana likens this act to Nazi book burning because she recognizes that "repressive societies always seemed to understand the danger of 'wrong ideas'" (141). She carries this historical awareness with her when she returns to the 1970s and listens to a report on apartheid in South Africa on the radio. The newscaster's story about the "black rioting" and battles "over the policies of the white supremacist government" leads her to realize that although she is over a century removed from America's slave past, she still lives in a world plagued by racism and race-related violence (141). By relating slavery to certain aspects of the Jewish Holocaust, Native American genocide and dispossession, and South African apartheid, Dana recognizes the "omnipresence of oppression" (Varsam 2003, 219). Her experience of slavery does not blind her to the suffering of others; instead, it makes her more sensitive. As a result, Dana's *ogbanje* status positions her to make radical connections between her enslavement and the historical traumas of other groups that she was unable to perceive before. Moreover, her growing historical consciousness, particularly with regard to the suffering of other marginalized groups, is an important example of the kind of cross-cultural empathy that the phantasmic trauma narrative seeks to inspire in readers.

THE PERSISTENCE OF TRAUMA

The novel ends where it began, with the amputation of Dana's arm at the place where history and the present collide. Rufus, who governs her travel, is now dead. Dana feels compelled to revisit the geographical site of her trauma, but because she can no longer travel back through time, she journeys with Kevin to present-day Maryland to search for archival records of the Weylin plantation. Unsurprisingly, when they arrive in Maryland, Dana and Kevin are unable to locate anything but "incomplete" documents pertaining to the Weylins and their slaves (263). Touching her scars and empty sleeve,

Dana acknowledges her body's memory of her traumatic encounter with the past, and muses, "Why did I even want to come here. You'd think I would have had enough of the past" (264). Kevin reassures her that she has returned "to try to understand. To touch solid evidence that those people existed. To reassure yourself that you're sane" (264). Kevin's reply is a facile excuse for Dana's need to return to the site of her trauma and overlooks the possibility that her journey to Maryland is meant to replicate her previous journeys to the past. Dana's need to return to the historical site of her trauma—and that of her slave forebears—is symptomatic of the persistence of trauma and, hence, her *ogbanje* status.

Here, the *ogbanje* trope becomes particularly useful: in Igbo culture, the "born-to-die" are short-circuited spirits who return again and again in repetition of the life cycle. This repetitive loop of the *ogbanje* life cycle mirrors the cycle of trauma, which, unless addressed and worked through, returns time and again to inflict further pain.[26] Because Dana is now freed from her bond to Rufus and cannot physically return to the past, she substitutes archival research for time travel in an act of repetition compulsion. As a result, her return to Maryland is both a step forward and a step back, and while we hope, like Kevin, that Rufus's death means that the past will no longer beckon Dana, the novel leaves her fate undecided. What this means for the reader, who might share Dana's sense of disorientation, is that traces of traumatic history abound in the present, both in physical incarnations—like the "brick building of the Historical Society, itself a converted early mansion" (264)— and in our sociocultural and political institutions. By leaving us with this uncertainty, the novel argues that traumatic history can never be forgotten, but only concealed by a collective, often deliberate amnesia; paradoxically, to forget is to remain wounded.

However, Dana's final return is more than just a cliffhanger or narrative gimmick; rather, it sends an important message to readers. As Caruth (1996) explains, repetition signifies an attempt to overcome the traumatic event and yet is also, at the same time, an attempt to come to terms with having escaped death (63–64). Dana's persistent need to learn more about her experience and the historical narrative of her forebears—as well as her sense of guilt for her uncertain role in Alice's death—can be read as a "challenge [to the] power relations" that contributed to the creation of the traumatic circumstance (Vickroy 2002, 221). Further, her persistent quest to absorb more of the past speaks to the critical role that historical memory plays in self-definition, and it recalls Suleiman's (2006) assertion that "how we view ourselves, and how we represent ourselves to others, is indissociable from the stories we tell about our past" (1). For Suleiman, an individual's experience of trauma communicates important correlations to collective experiences of trauma, even when the individual testimony is a fiction, as in *Kindred* (134). Above all, she argues, we should strive to disclose trauma rather than submit to "the temptations of closure" (232) or "artificial forgetting" (226). Thus, *Kindred*'s conclusion drives home the pedagogical imperative of the novel, which is to challenge readers to excavate the past, consider its impact on the present, and, finally, to question the lingering effects of history on interethnic relations in contemporary society. The ending's untidiness communicates the sense that closure is not yet fully attainable.

The phantasmic trauma narrative provides readers a unique opportunity to develop a felt connection to cultural memories to which they might not otherwise have proximity. *Kindred* is just one in a number of contemporary African American texts that have turned to irruptions of the phantasmic as a means of facilitating a more intimate connection with history. Phyllis Alesia Perry's *Stigmata* (1998) and Gayl Jones's *Corregidora* (1975), like *Kindred*, invite readers to experience the trauma of history through the experiences of contemporary protagonists who share consciousnesses with their slave ancestors in a manner suggestive of Yoruba reincarnation beliefs. Other texts, such as Julie Dash's *Daughters of the Dust* (1997) and J. California Cooper's *Family* (1991), draw from Kongo cosmology to narrate the slave experience from the perspectives of ancestral spirits who provide readers with a way to experience multiple generations of African American history. Works such as Paule Marshall's *Praisesong for the Widow* (1983), Gloria Naylor's *Mama Day* (1988), and Tananarive Due's *The Between* deploy phantasmic irruptions to reaffirm connections to African American cultural values and traditions that have been forgotten or suppressed by postslavery generations. By emphasizing the importance of maintaining and reviving culturally specific spiritual and storytelling traditions, the phantasmic trauma narrative invites readers of all backgrounds to bear witness to the African American experience of history with empathy and to acknowledge the existence of a trauma whose resonances are still detectable in our nation's social, cultural, and political institutions.

NOTES

1. Lisa Long (2009), Marisa Parham (2009), and Lisa Woolfork (2009) address the significance of trauma and embodiment in the novel. Long (2009), drawing on the work of trauma theorist Cathy Caruth, argues that Butler and author Phyllis Alesia Perry utilize "the intimacy and immediacy of their protagonists' pain as strategies to obscure the distance of a traumatic history" (462). Woolfork (2009), by contrast, employs "a distinctly African American trauma theory" that attends equally to mind and body, arguing that what she terms as "bodily epistemology" functions as a representational strategy that uses the body of a present-day protagonist to register the traumatic slave past" (2). Camille Passalacqua (2010) links *Kindred*'s use of embodiment to that which is evidenced in novels such as *Corregidora* and *Stigmata*. Ashraf Rushdy (1999), Marc Steinberg (2004), Angelyn Mitchell (2002), Christine Levecq (2002), and Beverly Friend (1982) have significantly advanced scholarly discourse treating the novel's use of time travel as a vehicle for raising questions about the nature of historical memory. Kelley Wagers (2009) has contributed to our understanding of the way that the novel prompts us to consider the important intersections between historical knowledge and fiction.

2. There are a handful of scholars who have addressed Butler's incorporation of African traditions and spirituality in her fiction; these include Venetria Patton (2013), Christopher Okonkwo (2008), Gene Andrew Jarrett (2014), and Tonja Lawrence (2010).

3. Suzanne Keen (2007) argues that "empathy for fictional characters appears to require only minimal elements of identity, situation, and feeling, not necessarily complex or realistic characterization" (xii).

4. The *ogbanje* is only one manifestation of the phantasmic. Writing of hauntings in African American literature, Kathleen Brogan (1998) notes that "the figure of the ghost itself emerges from the cultural history of that group: one of the key elements of African religious thought to survive in syncretic forms of new-world religious practice and in slave folklore is the belief in ancestor spirits" (2). Thus, while "contemporary African-American writers often invoke the Gothic tradition, they tend to filter its conventions through African folklore and spirit beliefs" (Brogan 1998, 2). Contemporary African American texts such as *Stigmata* (1998), *The Piano Lesson* (1990), *Mama Day* (1988), and *Praisesong for the Widow* (1983) offer different models of the phantasmic ranging from spirit possession and haunting to communication with the dead.

5. I do not accuse Long of cultural insensitivity; indeed, it is clear that she is not reading the text through a culturally specific lens. However, I want to be clear in stating that my formulation of the phantasmic trauma narrative diverges from the narrative modes of science fiction and magical realism in its insistence on acknowledging the diversity of belief systems that do not necessarily align with Enlightenment principles of rationality.

6. It should be noted, however, that Woolfork is cautious about endorsing Butler's use of Dana as a vehicle for reader understanding of the slave past. In her estimation, Haile Gerima's *Sankofa* (1993) supplies a slightly more ethical model of reader/viewer empathy.

7. Similarly, Lawrence Blum (1980) suggests that because emotions of sympathy and empathy promote perspective taking, they may prompt stronger prosocial responses than rationality alone (122–39).

8. Although these journeys are preceded by dizzy spells, Dana cannot predict when they will occur. Woolfork (2009) argues that Dana's time travel is manipulated by Rufus, and describes her journeys to the past as "abductions" (20–21). However, Butler makes it clear that neither Rufus nor Dana are initially aware of how her time travel is governed, and it is in fact Dana herself who eventually manipulates the conditions of her time travel by attempting suicide.

9. Wole Soyinka's (1976) understanding of a "cosmic totality" is echoed in John Hanson Mitchell's "Ceremonial Time" (1999). Writing about Native American understandings of time, Mitchell defines ceremonial time as a moment "in which past, present, and future can all be perceived in a single moment" (227), usually during an important ritual or religious ceremony. Mitchell is adamant in insisting that ceremonial time is a tangible reality, and he decries Western thinkers who attempt to dismiss it as symbolic or metaphorical.

10. Antebellum America saw a staggering number of Igbo men, women, and children torn from their homeland and forcibly transported to the North American mainland. See Okonkwo (2008, xxi), Michael A. Gomez (1998, 30), and A. E. Afigbo (1981, x–xi).

11. The emphasis on the repetitiveness of the *ogbanje* cycle recalls the nature of traumatic repetition, which is underscored by the fact that Dana struggles with a form of post-traumatic stress disorder (PTSD) during her subsequent returns to the present. For more on the notion of a cultural form of PTSD, see Kirby Farrell's (1998) excellent introduction to *Post-Traumatic Culture*.

12. Okonkwo (2008) notes that the *ogbanje* is "assumed to engage in this scheme of transitory and transitive earthly returns with sinister motives" (xiv).

13. As a literary trope in African American literature, the *ogbanje* has been popularized as a way of examining the slave mother-daughter relationship, as in Toni Morrison's *Beloved* (1987) and *Sula* (1973), as well as a trope that interiorizes "the coexisting forces of or the dialectical tension between those phenomena we generally construe and separate as 'good' and 'evil'" that we see reflected in the slave experience (Achebe 1980, 33). Despite the fact that *Kindred* is among the first American novels to invoke the *ogbanje* figure, much of the scholarship that identifies the *ogbanje* as a trope in African American fiction focuses on the work of

Toni Morrison, most notably *Beloved* and *Sula*. Ogunyemi (2002) and Okonkwo (2008) identify the *ogbanje*'s mobility as the reason for its popularity in literature that examines the slave experience and the impact of slavery on American culture.

14. Nor, as Misty Bastian (2002) argues, do contemporary Nigerian novels: a number of "fictional accounts of ogbaanjism . . . are more sympathetic to the spirit child and . . . try to develop a more complex picture of life within the *ogbaanje* skin, perhaps seeking to advocate for these young people who feel themselves to be 'betwixt and between' worlds in modern Nigeria" (61).

15. In *Things Fall Apart*, Chinua Achebe (1998) describes the *ogbanje* as "one of those wicked children who, when they died, entered their mothers' wombs to be born again" (70).

16. Similarly, Lauren Berlant (2008) argues that the historical subjectivity of the reader is imperative, as our social, political, and social contexts play an important role in how we respond to the traumatic experiences of others. What I term "empathy," she refers to as "compassion." Where we agree is the idea that the sentiments of empathy/compassion "derive from social training, emerge at historical moments, are shaped by aesthetic conventions, and take place in scenes that are anxious, volatile, surprising, and contradictory" (7).

17. Keen (2006) notes that "narrative theorists, novel critics, and reading specialists have already singled out a small set of narrative techniques—such as the use of first person narration and the interior representation of characters' consciousness and emotional states—as devices supporting character identification, contributing to empathetic experiences, opening readers' minds to others, changing attitudes, and even predisposing readers to altruism" (213).

18. Following Spaulding (2005), I assert that Butler, like other African American writers who adopt nonmimetic devices in their representation of history, seeks to "reform our conception of American slavery by depicting a more complex, nuanced view of black identity in the context of American slavery" (4). In the case of *Kindred*, the postmodern black subject's liminality is mirrored in the liminality of the *ogbanje*. The fact that the *ogbanje* is rooted in Igbo spiritual beliefs, however, impels us to recall that the roots of African American identity extend further back into history than the period of American slavery.

19. Although these terms are used interchangeably in modern-day Nigeria to describe the spirit child phenomenon, their application varies from author to author and text to text. Connected by both linguistic and geographical proximity, the Igbo and Yoruba share a number of spiritual beliefs and practices in common, as has been noted by Bastian (2002), Okonkwo (2008), and Ogunyemi (2002). Because "both names describe the same phenomenon" (Chou 2011, 174), *ogbanje* and *abiku* are used interchangeably in Nigeria. The only real difference between the two is how they are deployed in literature and popular culture. Yoruba writer Niyi Osundare (1988) associates the *abiku* with divinity, "infant mortality," and "supplications" (97), while Igbo scholar Catherine Acholonu (1988) links the *ogbanje* with "violent death" and "reincarnation" (104). Ogunyemi (1996) elaborates on Acholonu's characterization of the *ogbanje*, describing it as a "traveler," one whose journey between worlds affords her a special "plurality of vision" (67). Because the *ogbanje* has been characterized as one who is "free yet bound," and because a number of Butler's other works—including *Mind of My Mind* (1977) and *Wild Seed* (1980)—draw on specifically Igbo traditions and locations, I have adopted the term *ogbanje* as a way of describing Dana's phantasmic status (Ogunyemi 1996, 67)

20. Although Dana's story is less concerned with the subject of mortality than it is with the idea of traveling between worlds and achieving a plurality of vision, her time travel does enable an important "rememorying" of the past for the reader.

21. The figure of Beloved has alternately been identified as an *abiku* (Ogunyemi 2002) and an *ogbanje* (Patton 2013; Okonkwo 2008).

22. While Dana's cycles of travel mirror that of the *ogbanje*, her freedom to choose between two worlds is far more limited. Where the *ogbanje* can die or be reborn at will, Dana cannot prevent her rebirths in the nineteenth century, and can only attempt an uncertain return to the present by attempting suicide in the hopes that her husband will be able to resuscitate her if and when she reappears in the world of 1976. Unlike the *ogbanje*, who revels in the anticipation of repeated life-death cycles, Dana is disconcerted by the experience of time travel, and by the fact that her journeys are precipitated by the threat of death. Because Dana's disappearances and returns occur abruptly and involuntarily, her experience of time travel recalls the historical

experiences of her ancestors during the Middle Passage. Crossley (2003) agrees, writing that "in her experience of being kidnapped in time and space, Dana recapitulates the dreadful, disorienting, involuntary voyage of her ancestors" (268) in a continuous, seemingly endless cycle. However, Dana's mobility carries with it additional significance. Ogunyemi (2002) notes that "as a mobile site, the ogbanje is the trope of migrations, thereby disquietingly scrutinizing the lack of social mobility of her constituency in the living world" (666).

23. See Bastian (2002, 59–60) for a discussion of the selfish qualities exhibited by children and adults who have been branded as *ogbanje* in present-day Nigeria. A number of scholars have commented on Dana's betrayal of Alice as a means of preserving her own existence in the present day. See Sandra Govan (1986), Robert Crossley (2003), Christine Levecq (2000), Linh Hua (2011), Stephanie S. Turner (2004), Angelyn Mitchell (2002), Marc Steinberg (2004), and Ashraf Rushdy (1999) for such commentary.

24. Mitchell (2002) comments that Butler's choice of 1976 as the novel's primary setting is calculated to reveal "inherent contradictions in American history. This duality of settings forces the reader to consider how integral the past is in understanding the present and in constructing the future" (53).

25. Interestingly, few other scholars have commented on Dana's role as a writer or her attempts to explain her traumatic experiences through narrative. Both Mitchell's (2001) and Govan's (1986) work on the novel, which examine the way that the text seeks to reframe the slave past, treat Dana's profession as an incidental by-product of the plot. See Mitchell (2001, 53) and Govan (1986, 88).

26. In using the phrase "cycle of trauma," I draw on Caruth's (1996) understanding of "the story of trauma" as "inescapably bound to a referential return" (7). Building on the Freudian roots of trauma theory, she argues that "the repetition at the heart of catastrophe—the experience that Freud will call 'traumatic neuroses'—emerges as the unwitting reenactment of an event that one cannot simply leave behind" (2). Dana's inability to fully integrate her *ogbanje*-ism—and the lived experiences of history that it facilitated—seems to indicate a possibility for future repetitions of her traumatic experience.

Chapter Two

Phantasmic Midrashim

The Midrashic Roots of Jonathan Safran Foer's Everything Is Illuminated

While the characters in *Kindred* (Butler 2003), *The Devil's Arithmetic* (1999), and *Sankofa* (1993) find their historical traumas forced upon them through mechanisms beyond their control, *Everything Is Illuminated* (Foer 2002) examines what happens when one goes in search of the past and finds nothing but absence. From this absence spring midrashim—in the form of epistolary exchanges between Alex and Jonathan; Alex's narrative account of the journey; and Jonathan's imagined history of the lost shtetl of Trachimbrod—that extend the genesis of that absence into the present moment. Jonathan Safran Foer writes elsewhere that his novel was "an experiential, rather than historical, record" of his ancestral shtetl (2011, xiv). Read as an "experiential" text, we can see the ways in which *Everything Is Illuminated* aligns with the other novels and films examined in this study. Rather than granting its characters (and readers) an experience of the past, *Everything Is Illuminated* communicates the experience of searching for historical understanding. This same quest for historical understanding is what drives Lena's *Miko Kings* to investigate the source of the mysterious journal she finds in the walls of her house (Howe 2007); it's also what compels *Older Than America*'s (2008) Rain to learn more about the reservation's boarding school and its historical legacy. What connects these works, then, is the sense of the experiential: whether voluntarily sought or violently imposed, each work describes an experiential journey, one that variously leaves characters wounded (*Kindred*'s Dana), awakened (*The Devil's Arithmetic*'s Hannah, *Sankofa*'s Mona, *Everything Is Illuminated*'s Alex), or hopeful (*Miko Kings*' Lena and *Older Than America*'s Rain).

The centrality of absence as a signifier of trauma is voiced by the narrator of *Everything Is Illuminated,* a descendant of survivors, who explains that "the origin of a story is always an absence" (230). The preoccupation with the notion of a generative absence, highlighted in the works of third-generation writers like Foer, Boris Fishman, Nicole Krauss, Andrea Simon, Molly Antopol, and others, arises from the sense of having grown up in the shadow of the Holocaust, with stories of the event perpetually on the periphery of their awareness.[1] As Alan Berger and Victoria Aarons (2017) observe,

> It is this periphery upon which the third generation trespasses in an attempt to capture memory and fill the ever-widening gap between those who directly suffered the events of the Holocaust and lived to recount their experiences and those for whom that particular history can only be imaginatively reconstructed from an approximation of that time and place, events excavated from the "shards" of memories, as one of novelist Ehud Havazelet's characters reveals, "refracting no more than their miserable incompleteness." (4)

For writers of the third generation, piecing together these shards of memory in order to make sense of the profound loss that continues to dominate their consciousnesses becomes the central focus of their works dealing with the Holocaust. Third-generation writers are less concerned with representing the Holocaust than they are with fashioning fragmented narratives that reflect the character of their inherited memories of the event. Using *Everything Is Illuminated* as a representative example, this chapter will show how third-generation novels have adapted the Jewish exegetical tradition of midrash to create narratives that extend the Holocaust into the contemporary moment, offering a kaleidoscope of phantasmically inflected stories that, when fitted together, communicate the burden of third-generation memory: to remember without knowing, and to feel without truly understanding. These texts are not only midrashic in form, but also include characters who read midrashim, compose midrashim, or both. In this way, these novels model what it means to read midrashically, "to read deeply and critically," in a way that gives rise to ethical thinking about the Holocaust (Osborne 2018, 130).[2] Through their literary invocation of trauma, these phantasmic midrashim—which incorporate elements of Jewish mysticism, folk beliefs, and irruptions of the supernatural—encourage an active discourse between writer, text, and reader that invites a felt connection to the Holocaust and a critical engagement with the way that it permeates our contemporary world.

The increasingly important role of the Holocaust in contemporary Jewish American literature has been noted by many scholars, including Alan L. Berger, Victoria Aarons, Jonathan Freedman, Dean J. Franco, and a number of others, such as Caroline Rody, Jenni Adams, and Aaron Tillman, have explored the increasing presence of what they characterize as magical realism in works about the Holocaust.[3] Of these, Rody has been the most interested in identifying culturally specific forms of the supernatural in Jewish American literature, and her important essay, "Jewish Post-Holocaust Fiction and the Magical Realist Turn" (2013), traces this thread through the works of Isaac Bashevis Singer, Bernard Malamud, and Cynthia Ozick to connect it to the work of post-Holocaust writers like Joseph Skibell and Jonathan Safran Foer. However, no scholarship to date has addressed the intersections of Jewish uses of the supernatural and the midrashic mode in third-generation works, despite the fact that such intersections are visible in works by Jonathan Safran Foer, Joseph Skibell, Nicole Krauss, Boris Fishman, Michael Chabon, and many more. I explore how the imbrication of the phantasmic and the midrashic offers a way to bear witness to trauma in the absence of memory and creates a space for cross-cultural engagement and ethical thinking about the Holocaust.

A number of third-generation Holocaust narratives have adapted the Jewish tradition of midrash, which is both a form of writing and a way of reading, to facilitate a felt connection to the Holocaust. In texts that use the midrashic mode, the felt connection is fostered not via a direct form of reader identification of the type we saw in *Kindred*, but rather through an indirect relationship with the trauma. This distance is established and maintained by the use of midrashim that, while preventing direct access to representation of the event, nonetheless create opportunities for a type of active reader engagement that privileges relational thinking between the Holocaust and the present moment. By inviting relational thinking between one's lived experience in the present and the trauma of the past, third-generation novels like Foer's encourage what Dominick LaCapra (2001) terms "empathic unsettlement" in a literary context,[4] a form of witnessing in which the reader responds empathically to the suffering of the historical other while at the same time engaging reflectively with his/her response. This mode of witnessing, in turn, gives rise to questions about what it would mean to engage with Holocaust history—and its lingering manifestations in the present—in an ethical way.

The chapter begins by distinguishing the literature of the third generation from that of the first and second generations: neither haunted by direct experience like the first generation, nor "witnesses to an uncompromising trauma" like the second generation, the third generation struggles to make sense of an incomplete narrative of the past, emphasizing the ways in which its shadowy legacy has engendered pressing questions about the shape of loss and what it means to bear witness to memory that is fundamentally incomplete (Rosenbaum 2002, 333). It then proceeds to place *Everything Is Illuminated* in the broader context of third-generation literature, which has adopted a variety of innovative narrative techniques that I read as phantasmic midrashim. The use of these midrashic strategies employed by these texts facilitates empathic unsettlement on the part of the reader and, in so doing, enables a felt connection to the traumatic impact of the Holocaust. Through an analysis of *Everything Is Illuminated*, I demonstrate how third-generation texts both perform and invite midrashic readings that extend the Holocaust into the contemporary moment, encouraging a felt connection that prompts readers to consider the lasting impact of the event in relation to the present. I also show how the exchange and analysis of these midrashim between Alex and Jonathan offer a model of cross-cultural empathy and ethical engagement.

GENERATIONAL SHIFTS IN HOLOCAUST LITERATURE

The relationship to memory—how it is accessed, understood, and represented—is what delineates the work of each generation following the Holocaust. The literature of the survivor generation, which often takes the form of the memoir, is characterized by an attempt to salvage from the "ruins of memory" narratives that follow the conventions of story with a recognizable beginning, middle, and ending (Fink 1987, 3). As a result, many works composed by survivors contend with the problem of memory itself and the way that the experience of trauma has distorted one's ability to recall, in a linear way, the lived experience of the event. These texts also express frustration about the limitations that these restraints place on one's ability to bear witness in a way that does justice to one's experience and to those who were lost. As Aharon Appelfeld (2004) explains, "When you're finally ready to speak about those days, memory grows faint and the words stick in your throat. So you wind up saying nothing of value . . . [as] the words flow, but they reveal nothing" (180). Elie Wiesel (1977) goes further: "He or she who did live through the event will never reveal it. Not entirely. Not really. Between our memory and its reflection stands a wall that cannot be pierced. . . . We speak in code, we survivors, and this code cannot be broken, cannot be deciphered" (7). Here, Wiesel articulates the central, twinned characteristics of survivor narratives, which are that they not only struggle against memory fragmented by trauma, but must also attempt to capture atrocity with words that ultimately fail. Yet, Berel Lang (2000) argues, the tropes of unspeakability that are pervasive in survivor narratives are also countered by "yards of writing that attempt to overcome the inadequacy of language in representing moral enormity at the same time that they assert its presence; certainly they hope to find for their own assertions of such inadequacy a useful—*telling*—place in its shadow" (18). Thus, even as survivor narratives struggle with the problem of unspeakability, they create an important space for remembrance. As Lang observes, "No Holocaust writing gives preference to silence" because the "cost [of] inviting the vacuum of forgetfulness—is too high" (18–19). Theodor Adorno's (1983) famous prohibition on representation aside, bearing witness becomes, for the first generation, an ethical imperative.[5]

If memory and representation pose a problem for the survivor generation, this problem is compounded by the one that follows. In his introduction to *Holocaust Remembrance: The Shape of Memory,* Geoffrey Hartman (1994a) explains that while Holocaust survivors are able to convey to their readers the sense of a direct relation to the event, the second generation—that is, the children of survivors, like Thane Rosenbaum and Art Spiegelman, among others—express "the trauma of memory turning in the void" (18) because they seek to represent an event that greatly impacted their own lives but that nevertheless exists for them at a remove.[6] The immediacy of the lived experience of the survivor gives way, in the second generation, to what Marianne Hirsch (1997) refers to as "postmemory," experiences that are "mediated not through recollection but through an imaginative investment and creation . . . the experience of those who grow up dominated by narratives that preceded their birth, whose own belated stories are evacuated by the stories of the previous generation shaped by traumatic events that can neither be understood nor recreated" (22).[7] For the children of survivors, the Holocaust is fundamental to who they are, as though their genetic makeup has been altered by their parents' experiences. As one of Rosenbaum's (1999) characters remarks, "my DNA may be forever coded with the filmy stuff of damaged offspring, the handicap of an unwanted inheritance" (63).[8] As a result, second-generation literature is characterized by a sense of "anger toward what is portrayed as an interrupted life, a life beholden to the past, and . . . fear of failure and inadequacy in response to their parents' trauma" (Berger and Aarons 2017, 30). This dual sense of fear and anger is expressed most famously in Art Spiegelman's *Maus* (1980), which imbricates the story of his father's survival—and Spiegelman's anxiety about telling that story—with anecdotes that reveal the extent to which growing up in the shadow of the Holocaust has exacted a toll, not only on Spiegelman himself, but also on his relationship to each of his parents. Often concerned with questions of theodicy and suicide,[9] second-generation literature moves beyond the event itself to explore what it means for the children of survivors to contend with the memory of the Holocaust within the context of their own experience of inherited trauma.

If the work of the second generation is marked by the paralyzing power of anger and regret at inheriting the unwanted responsibility of memory, the work of the third generation is defined, first and foremost, by the sense that these writers bear "an *indirect* relation to the original eyewitness[es]" (Lang 2009, 46). The term "third generation" typically denotes works written by the grandchildren of survivors, like Jonathan Safran Foer, Nicole Krauss, and Boris Fishman, "or by those, more broadly defined, who explicitly approach the subject of the Holocaust from a third generation perspective," such as Anne Raeff, Michael Chabon, and Thane Rosenbaum (Berger and Aarons 2017, 14). Joost Krijnen (2016) observes that "even as they attempt to approach the Holocaust," third-generation texts underscore the notion that "their engagement with this past is indirect, worked upon by separation in time and space, and therefore tenuous and highly mediated" (56). Jessica Lang (2009) goes further to explain that indirect relation of the third generation to the Holocaust is reflected in the way that the event is "both explicit and obscured . . . both as a memorial and a method" (46). As "witnesses through the imagination" (Rosen 1992, 10), writers of the third generation struggle to make sense of an incomplete narrative of the past and emphasize the ways in which its shadowy legacy has engendered pressing questions about the shape of loss.

Like the generation that preceded it, the third generation finds itself uncomfortably trapped in what Henri Raczymow (1994) characterizes as "the abyss between [the] imperious need to speak and the prohibition on speaking" (102).[10] Exacerbating the anxiety of this "double-bind" is the sense of urgency evinced by third-generation works (103). This urgency is not theoretical; it is temporal. Indeed, despite collective efforts to guarantee the preservation of Holocaust memory in America, there is still an anxiety that the terrible significance of the event will fade as survivors pass away.[11] Gary Weissman (2004) explains this concern by analogy, drawing on a historical trauma that is more distinctly American: "Americans do not deny that slavery is part of American history. At the same time, however, most know almost nothing about the histories of the Atlantic slave trade and plantation slavery . . . and even less about the plight of ex-slaves and their children following the Civil War" (7). This desire to prevent a similar historical amnesia with regard to the Holocaust is a driving factor in the works of many third-generation authors; indeed, they work against the possibility of a day when "the American people . . . will come to regard the Holocaust much as they do slavery—granting its facticity, even acknowledging its exceptional importance, but feeling no special commitment to commemorating or 'witnessing' this part of the distant past" (5). In the work of the third generation, Gerd Bayer (2010) observes, "memory takes on a different quality as it becomes transformed from direct witnessing and the resulting testimonials to archival and mediated forms of remembering that carry the responsibility of firmly embedding the Holocaust in the cultural memory of later generations" (116). In other words, the highly personal responses to the inheritance of trauma expressed in second-generation Holocaust literature give way, in the third generation, to texts that express a duty to memorialize while also drawing attention to the way in which those memories are mediated by what has been said—or, perhaps more to the point, by what has been left unsaid—about the event.

The task of third-generation authors, therefore, is to demonstrate the need to bear witness to the past, even as their knowledge of the past is mediated not by the survivors themselves, many of whom have since passed, but by fragments of memory in the form of photographs, documents, and the "scads of silent clues strewn about—closed doors, sorrowful glances, *yahrzeit* (memorial) candles" (Flanzbaum 2012, 13–14).[12] Hilene Flanzbaum, a scholar and the grandchild of survivors, explains that third-generation writers are compelled to "explore places they have never been, recover what they can and re-create what time has rendered irretrievable" (14). In the epilogue to her novel, *The Invisible Bridge,* Julie Orringer (2010) draws a similar portrait of third-generation memory:

> She'd learned about that war in school, of course—who died, who killed whom, how, and why. . . . She'd learned other things about the war from watching her grandmother, who saved plastic bags and glass jars, and kept bottles of water in the house in case of disaster, and made layer cakes with half as much butter and sugar as the recipes called for, and who, at times, would begin to cry for no reason. . . . There were strands of darker stories. She didn't know how she'd heard them; she thought she must have absorbed them through her skin, like medicine or poison. Something about labor camps. Something about being made to eat newspapers. Something about a disease that came from lice. Even when she wasn't thinking about those half stories, they did their work in her mind. (756)

Here, Orringer demonstrates that while the third generation possesses a sense of the overarching historical narrative of the Holocaust, what they lack are the particulars of their own family histories. In order to bear witness to the event, then, third-generation writers must both "rely on text and imagine text"; that is, they "work to represent a text of a text" (Lang 2009, 49). Sifting through what remains of memory, and reticent to represent what for them is unknowable, third-generation writers turn to midrash to fashion texts that highlight the profundity of loss and absence that they feel. As I show in my analysis of *Everything Is Illuminated,* third-generation texts use midrash and phantasmic elements adapted from Jewish folktales and mystical traditions to extend the ethos of Holocaust trauma into the present, creating opportunities for ethical engagement on the part of the reader by confronting the reader not only with fragments of the event itself, but also by modeling one possible form that such engagement can take in the exchanges between Alex and Jonathan.

THE THIRD GENERATION, THE PHANTASMIC, AND THE MIDRASHIC TURN

If the compulsion to bear witness is, as Victoria Aarons (1996) argues, a defining feature of Jewish American literature, so too is the use of fantastic and supernatural elements.[13] Howard Schwartz (1983) observes that "tales of magic and wonder can be found in every phase of Jewish literature, both sacred and secular" (3). Schwartz makes an important distinction between the Jewish uses of fantastic elements and what others might term magical realism, arguing that "what other fairy tales attribute to magical causes, the Jewish vision interprets as a demonstration of the power and beneficence of God" (3). Similarly, Caroline Rody, Tamara Kaye Sellman, and others have connected the decidedly fantastical qualities of Jewish American literature to its roots in Judaism. As a religious tradition suffused with deeply mystical elements,

> Judaism feeds root and twig and bud on stories steeped in vision and rapture and portent. . . . Tanach (the Jewish Bible) is one long narrative of wonders and crazy wonder-workers and visitations and miracles, woven all together with matriarchs and patriarchs and eerie strangers and towering heroes and idiot-savants. Our history has been a thriller of magical escape and immortal sorrow and deep study. A history designed to make its people fond of the fantastic. (Goldstein, qtd. in Sellman 2005)

As Daniel M. Jaffe's (2001) work further demonstrates, the Bible's fabulism has inspired a long history of Jewish literature that incorporates magical, mystical, and miraculous elements. These elements are similarly pervasive throughout the Talmud, Kabbalah, and Zohar, and their influence can be seen in the mystical practices of late medieval kabbalists. These religiously inspired uses of the supernatural, in turn, gave rise to the miraculous narratives associated with seventeenth-century Hasidism and the folklore common to Yiddishkeit, both in Eastern Europe and in the United States.[14] Indeed, the Jewish mystical and folklore traditions "[pervade] Jewish fiction in every era and language," and they are both the foundation of and impetus for the prevalence of the fantastic in contemporary Jewish fiction (Reisner 2004, 94).

Viewed historically, then, we can see "how integral fantastical modes have been in [Jewish] efforts to convey and to understand the complexities of our world and our places within it" (Tillman 2017, 122). Indeed, the fantastic in Jewish literature is often used to underscore Jewish religious and cultural values and to sustain the meaning of Jewish identity among the diaspora, and it assumes an additional importance in works that explore the traumatic legacy of the Holocaust. Michael Yogev (1993) agrees, noting that "not only is the fantastic appropriate for depicting the Holocaust, it may indeed be, paradoxically, the most 'natural' mode in which to re-present this age of extremity" (34). It should come as no surprise, then, that post-Holocaust writers who are at a remove from the event seek out phantasmic strategies for bearing witness to the trauma in a way that extends its impact into the present moment, creating opportunities for relational thinking and felt connections among readers.[15]

Here, it is important to clarify that most critics who examine texts that include magical elements and motifs from Jewish folklore and mystical traditions tend to classify such works as examples of magical realism. In so doing, they rightly connect such works with a "global, post-modern literary mode . . . that self-consciously mourns the horrors of the twentieth century" (Rody 2013, 57).[16] I agree with critics like Rody, Sellman, and others who argue that the use of supernatural and mystical irruptions enables post-Holocaust writers to imagine the worlds that were destroyed, and that such works "express the truths of a fissured, displaced culture against a conqueror's rationales and discourses" and "resurrect entire vanished worlds" (Rody 2013, 47). The incorporation of supernatural elements from Jewish religious and folk traditions in contemporary Jewish American literature is in keeping with what Christopher Warnes (2009) refers to as a "regional" "strand of magical realism . . . which strives to affirm specific cultural modes of perception" (8), thereby fashioning a "place for the cultural modalities of those who have been . . . excluded from the products and benefits of modernity" (Warnes 2005, 11). However, as I explain at length in the introduction, the appellation "magical realism" is problematic for the way that it seeks to graft rationalist Western ontologies onto non-Western, non-Christian texts.[17] Rody herself notes that "(Ashkenazi) Jewish literature . . . is after all a literature once but no longer European . . . declared in the Nazi era irrevocably 'non-European,' and so cast out or destroyed" (2003, 42). Thus, the use of "magical realism" to describe post-Holocaust texts that draw on the Jewish folklore and mystical traditions so reviled by not only Nazis, but anti-Semites throughout history, seems inappropriate. By using the term "phantasmic," we avoid replicating the hegemonic discourses that inevitably accompany the use of "magical realism" and therefore create a space within which we can read post-Holocaust texts that include supernatural irruptions as performing the important work of using cultural traditions to animate the trauma of the Holocaust for readers while at the same time avoiding the ethical pitfalls of realism. On a fundamental level, magical realism cannot inspire the kind of ethical reader engagement that the phantasmic trauma narrative seeks to achieve because it reinforces the hegemony of the self in the self/other binary.

The prevalence of the phantasmic as a mode of Holocaust representation in American literature has grown considerably over the past few decades, and has become even more pronounced in works of the third generation.[18] In Joseph Skibell's *A Blessing on the Moon* (1997), the murdered protagonist emerges from a mass grave to observe the pillaging of his home by Poles in a collage of Jewish mysticism and Jewish and Yiddish folktales. In a similar vein, Skibell's *A Curable Romantic* (2011) portrays the heavenly ascent of two characters in a scene that combines rabbinic thought and Jewish mysticism to explore the role of faith, both at the darkest moments of the Holocaust and, by extension, in its aftermath. Nathan Englander's "The Tumblers" (1999) draws on the fabled Fools of Chelm from Yiddish folklore to spin a tragicomic tale of escape from certain death at the hands of the Nazis, while Michael Chabon's *The Amazing Adventures of Kavalier and Clay* (2000) tells the story of Joseph Kavalier, a Jewish teenager who engineers his own daring escape from Nazi-occupied Europe by hiding inside a casket containing the legendary golem of Prague. Thane Rosenbaum's *The Golems of Gotham* (2002)—written by a second-generation author but dominated by a third-generation perspective—follows in this tradition by resurrecting the spirits of the dead as golems to teach the living important lessons about the Holocaust. In Boris Fishman's *A Replacement Life* (2014), a ghost emerges as an interlocutor to the fictional Holocaust testimonies penned by the story's protagonist, while in Foer's *Everything Is Illuminated,* the traditional fabulism of shtetl literature is rendered an inset phantasmic history that testifies to the existence—and destruction—of a Jewish village called Trachimbrod. Like *Everything Is Illuminated*, Dara Horn's *In the Image* (2002) and Nicole Krauss's *The History of Love* (2005) contain inset texts that abound with supernatural elements rooted in Jewish modes of perception and that ultimately work to extend the Holocaust—and the world it obliterated—into the present moment.[19] Although the variety and degree of phantasmic elements vary, each of these works combines Jewish religious, mystical, and folk traditions with midrashic strategies as a means of connecting readers to moments of trauma.

That so many third-generation texts structure their use of the phantasmic within the framework of midrashic narratives is unsurprising when we consider that "midrash is magical storytelling at its best, nesting Russian dolls of storytelling, story within story within story, as the unreal lives within the real, as reality lives in every dream, as dream in every day" (Goldstein, qtd. in Sellman 2005). Midrash began as a type of exegesis, the study and interpretation of Torah practiced by rabbis in the period of late antiquity. Although the term is still associated with the exegetical, midrash has assumed new meaning in literary studies as a "theoretical process of creating or critiquing texts, both sacred and secular" (Osborne 2018, xl).[20] It is its function as a secular hermeneutic that most interests me here, and this is of greatest relevance to a discussion of third-generation narratives. As a secular hermeneutic, midrash is a defining tradition in Jewish literary expression that comprises "stories that interpret and extend narratives and events in Jewish history" (Berger and Aarons 2017, 48). As Sara R. Horowitz (1998) explains, midrash acts as "an imaginative narrative commentary composed after the initial narrative of experience" to offer a "reading" that articulates the significance of the event in the Jewish cultural imagination (290). Sandor Goodhart (2008) describes midrash as a story that "is necessarily secondary in status; there is always a prior text to which it is a response" (18). He goes on to note "that to which it is a response in the prior text is a gap or tear or hole or discontinuity of some kind; a wound, or silence, or absence, or lack. The prior text is broken in some fashion; it lacks wholeness or completeness. Something is missing from it, and midrash is a response to that hole. . . . [It is] a response that in some way materially extends that prior text" (18). In the case of third-generation texts, the narrative to which their midrashic stories respond is the Holocaust itself. In its ability to take in minutiae as well as epistemology, midrash "is especially useful as an approach to thinking and writing about the Holocaust, which must be regarded as a historical as well as a philosophical and a personal cataclysm" (Rosenberg 1999, 3). For third-generation writers, who must confront the challenge of reconciling the overarching historical narrative of the Holocaust—who did what to whom, and when, and how—with the incomplete personal details of their family histories, midrash presents an opportunity for responding to those discontinuities.

However, even as midrash responds to discontinuities in the original narrative of experience, it "does more than just respond to a perceived gap in the text; it performs that dislocation itself; it echoes the dislocation that is already a part of the primary narrative to which it is responding" (Goodhart 2008, 20). In the context of Holocaust narratives, midrash works to destabilize the narrative experience to "create conditions for discomfort and unease . . . a language and a landscape of rupture, of discursive disequilibrium and of narrative disjunction" (Aarons 2014, 29). Consequently, midrash becomes what Goodhart (2008) calls "a material extension" of the original text, or in this case, the broader Holocaust narrative (18). As extension—rather than representation—midrash summons reader participation, what Horowitz (1998) describes as "moral and emotional engagement" (290), by asking us to read midrashically. Monica Osborne (2018) refers to this engagement as the "midrashic impulse," that is, the sense that one is compelled "to question, to interrogate, to fill in the gaps, to point out the inconsistencies, all the while maintaining continuity" (44).[21] Goodhart (2008) goes further, suggesting that to read midrashically is

> to read what is said as a continuation of its own subject matter rather than as a communication detached from that subject matter, to read the midrash as a performance of the text, but not one that mimics or echoes the text from a distance as much as a performance that continues the performance the text is already enacting. Midrashic reading is not something we bring to the text but something that we discover within the text, as an expression of what the text itself is already doing, even as the condition of the text's doing what it does. (20)

Thus, when we read midrash—and read midrashically—we find ourselves actively engaging with the original narrative that the midrash seeks to perform. It is within this engagement that ethical thinking arises. Osborne

(2018) agrees, noting that "midrash is an extension of the ethical . . . because its very existence implies an acknowledgment and ownership of the failures that precede it—that is, the failure of the primary text . . . to articulate a full and complete story. Midrash depends on the existence of failure" (xix–xx). When that midrash concerns the Holocaust, the text with which we engage is the narrative of traumatic experience. We are thus brought face-to-face, in the Levinasian sense, with the specter of the trauma.[22]

Because it does not seek to represent, midrash is particularly well suited as a tool for engaging the subject of the Holocaust. If, as Osborne (2018) contends, "traditional representational modes create greater distance between readers and the traumatic event," midrash, as an extensional rather than representational mode, creates unique opportunities for bearing witness (xvi). When midrashic form is combined with phantasmic elements, the opportunity for empathic unsettlement on the part of the reader increases substantially, creating the conditions whereby a felt connection can be achieved. The felt connection that the reader may then experience can be likened to Levinas's ethics of alterity, which requires that the reader acknowledges responsibility for the other and feels *with* the other, all the while recognizing his or her own otherness. Like midrash, the phantasmic works to disrupt the narrative in order to compel the reader to interrogate the inconsistences and discontinuities in the narrative, all the while reminding the reader of the very Jewish character of the phantasmic occurrences themselves. This reminder is both a response to oppressive Western belief structures and a reminder of the reader's own alterity. Thus, the midrashic and the phantasmic work together to foster a creative tension that at once enables the reader to respond empathically, but also ethically.

PHANTASMIC ILLUMINATION

Everything Is Illuminated returns to one of the geographical sites of the Holocaust, Ukraine, to expose the absent presences created by the genocide of Jews living in that region. Foer's novel shows us the Holocaust by inversion, locating in the conspicuous absence of physical traces of the event shards of memories that must be pieced together to reconstruct not only the story of Trachimbrod's destruction, but also the story of the shtetl and its inhabitants prior to that destruction. The urge to reassemble these fragments of memory is a response to "maladies of time and space" (Rothberg 2000, 172) that have precipitated the possibility of historical amnesia. In the face of tremendous loss arises an impulse to bear witness not only to the Holocaust, but also to the rich Jewish culture it extinguished. The novel both performs and invites midrashic readings of the event in its refracted dual narratives: those written by the fictional Jonathan Safran Foer, and those penned by his

Ukrainian counterpart, Alex Perchov. In their use of midrash, these narratives create opportunities for ethical engagement with the past and recognition of how that past continues to inform Jewish/gentile relations in the present.

Everything Is Illuminated is loosely based on an actual journey that Foer took to Ukraine during his junior year of college. He explains:

> I did not intend to write *Everything Is Illuminated*. I intended to chronicle, in strictly nonfictional terms, a trip that I made to Ukraine as a 22-year-old. Armed with a photograph of the woman who, I was told, had saved my grandfather from the Nazis, I embarked on a journey to Trachimbrod, the shtetl of my family's origins. The comedy of errors lasted five days. I found nothing but nothing, and in that nothing—a landscape of completely realized absence—nothing was to be found. Because I didn't tell my grandmother about the trip—she would never have let me go—I didn't know what questions to ask, or whom to ask, or the necessary names of people, places, and things. The nothing came as much from me as from what I encountered. (Foer 2012)

Confronted with the "absence" and "nothing[ness]" of a Ukrainian landscape divested of its once-thriving Jewish culture, as well as by his own dearth of historical awareness, Foer discovered that he could not write a travelogue of his heritage tour; quite simply, there was nothing to record. And the nothingness, Foer admits, threatened to silence him until he realized that the absence confronting him suggested more deeply philosophical questions about the nature of Holocaust representation itself: Is "the Holocaust exactly that which cannot be imagined? What are one's responsibilities to 'the truth' of a story, and what is 'the truth'? Can historical accuracy be replaced with imaginative accuracy?" (Foer 2012). Similarly, in another interview, Foer reflects that the "journey was really one hole: nothing was left. For me, writing this book was like filling this hole with lots of words. So not creation, but replacement: replacing the emptiness with words" (qtd. in Codde 2009, 65). What Foer describes here is characteristic of third-generation midrash, which "begins with the awareness that what is being examined suffers from absences, silences, voids—tears in the very fabric of both Jewish and non-Jewish history" (Osborne 2018, xxii). By "replacing the emptiness with words," Foer fashions a midrashic text that in its fragmentary nature opens up the possibility for ethical reading and, by extension, ethical engagement, with the historical and ontological voids engendered by the Holocaust.

However, in order for Foer to build a narrative bridge to the story of his ancestral home and the cataclysm that destroyed it, he needed to first develop a felt connection to his cultural roots. Like the fictional Jonathan, Foer failed to locate Augustine, the woman who saved his grandfather's life. However, he notes, "I'm not sure the purpose was to find her. I'm not even sure I wanted to find her" (Foer 2012). Driving his journey, Foer realized later, was a desire to locate himself. He explains:

> I was twenty when I made the trip—an unobservant Jew, with no *felt connection* to, or great interest in, my past. I kept an ironic distance from religion, and was skeptical of anything described as "Jewish." And yet, my writing . . . began to take on a Jewish sensibility, if not content. To my surprise, I started asking genealogical questions of my mother. . . . I was a closeted Jew. After 20 years of life, the feelings and the facts had begun to diverge. . . . There was a split—a strange and exhilarating split—between the Jonathan that thought (secular), and the Jonathan that did (Jewish). (Foer 2012, emphasis added)

The physical journey to the site of his ancestry and Holocaust trauma prompted the composition of *Everything Is Illuminated,* an amalgam of complex midrashim. The phantasmic qualities of these midrashim draw on a rich legacy of Jewish religious traditions and storytelling techniques to highlight the profound presence of absence in the geographical area where his forebears once lived and ultimately perished. Foer's novel calls on readers to bear witness to the Holocaust while also modeling empathic responses and ethical engagement. Further, while the novel applauds contemplation of the Holocaust (like that of the "Jonathan that thought"), it privileges active engagement in the form of midrashic reading (inspired by the "Jonathan that did") as a way of encouraging a felt connection to the event.

Everything Is Illuminated tells the story of a Jewish American writer (also named Jonathan Safran Foer) who travels through Ukraine with the aid of his Ukrainian translator and heritage tour guide, Alex Perchov, in search of Augustine, the woman who saved his grandfather, Safran, during the destruction of Trachimbrod by the Nazi *Einsatzgruppen.* What begins as a quest for a mysterious stranger and a place lost in time culminates in the discovery of a terrible secret about Alex's family history. Together, the young men discover that Alex's grandfather betrayed his best friend, a Jewish man named Herschel, to the Nazis, ultimately causing his death. What this revelation means for Jonathan and Alex, and how it relates to the way that the novel extends the traumatic past into the present through its use of phantasmic midrashim, inform the way that the text approaches the relationship between midrashic reading and empathy. In Foer's novel, the phantasmic operates not only in the midrash that Jonathan creates to tell the lost history of his grandfather's ancestral shtetl, but also in the midrashic opportunities created by the letters that Alex writes to Jonathan, which intersperse Jonathan's history of Trachimbrod and Alex's account of their journey together.

The novel consists of three narrative strands: Jonathan's history of Trachimbrod, which serves to anchor his understanding of his own ethnic identity roots, Alex's narrative of his encounter with Jonathan and their search for Trachimbrod, and Alex's letters to Jonathan. The refracted narratives move toward each other in time and converge at the Holocaust: the "Alex" chapters move backward from the present until they end at the moment of Grandfather's betrayal, while the "Trachimbrod" chapters begin with the shtetl's founding in 1791 and establish a quasi-chronological history that culminates in its destruction.[23] As we read on, we deduce that the sections of text that we are reading are being exchanged via mail after the trip, a suspicion that is confirmed by Alex's letters to Jonathan, which perform midrashic readings of the Trachimbrod chapters and respond to Jonathan's critiques and observations of Alex's travelogue that presumably accompany each edition of the Trachimbrod history. Together, these sets of chapters fashion midrashic narratives that bridge the fault line between "how things were" and "how things could have been," and, as Foer (2012) explains, measure "the difference between the two, and by so doing, [reflect] how things feel." Aware that he could not tell the story of Trachimbrod as it happened because he did not have access to that information, Foer instead crafted a narrative designed to make readers "feel" in response to that history, one that is at the same time human and phantasmic. The simultaneous movement forward and backward invests readers in the cataclysm at the heart of the novel, and therefore creates possibilities for empathic reader responses.

TRACHIMBROD: A PHANTASMIC HISTORY

The novel's reliance on the phantasmic is most conspicuous in the Trachimbrod chapters, which incorporate central tenets of the Jewish folklore tradition, such as using fantastic irruptions as a means of highlighting important Jewish religious and cultural values and underscoring the connection between memory and identity. The layered quality of the narrative here reflects the power of fiction to comment on itself as fiction. And while the phantasmic is not unique in its foregrounding of metafictional concerns—certainly historiographic metafiction and magical realism do the same—it is different from these other forms of postmodern writing because it articulates those concerns by drawing on culturally specific traditions and uses of the fantastic to emphasize the capacity of fiction to communicate one group's experiences and traumas to empathic readers.[24] Thus, the use of the phantasmic in *Everything Is Illuminated*—both in terms of the text's form as midrash, and in terms of the Chelm-like quality of the Trachimbrod chapters—enables Foer to create for the readers empathic pathways to Holocaust history while at the same time avoiding the attendant ethical debates that invariably arise where realist representations that implicitly lay claims to verisimilitude are concerned.

The Trachimbrod narrative begins with trauma and creation, death and birth: an unexplained accident causes Trachim B's wagon to overturn in the

Brod River, killing both Trachim and his expectant wife. From the depths of the river that claimed her parents' lives emerges the infant Brod, Jonathan's earliest ancestor: "In the middle of the string and feathers, surrounded by candles and soaked matches, prawns, pawns, and silk tassels that curtsied like jellyfish, was a baby girl, still mucus-glazed, still pink as the inside of a plum" (13). The remains of this disaster are the starting point of Jonathan's midrash about his ancestral shtetl. The objects he imagines floating in the river—which mark the beginning of Trachimbrod's chronology—anticipate the objects that, read metonymically, signal the moment of the shtetl's destruction in 1942 by the Nazis, when every citizen of Trachimbrod except Jonathan's grandfather, Safran, drowns in the Brod. As with Trachim B's accident, nothing remains to testify to the existence of the murdered Trachimbroders except the residue of their daily lives—"rings, and money, and pictures, and Jewish things" (152)—objects that are collected by Augustine, who shares them with Jonathan, Alex, and Grandfather.

Fragments—like the detritus amid which Brod is born, or the relics of shtetl life that Augustine shares with the narrators—assume a central role in all of the text's narrative strands, but most especially in the Trachimbrod chapters, which give readers phantasmic glimpses of prewar shtetl life that call to mind the Chelm folklore of Yiddish tradition, and, in turn, the kabbalistic myths and symbols of "cosmic brokenness, repair, and redemption" that gave them life (Rody 2013, 43).[25] Just as the fictional Jonathan grows up without knowledge of his family's history, so too is his imagined ancestor, Brod, sheltered from the story of her past: "She remembered, of course, nothing, and was told nothing" (48). Instead, her adoptive father Yankel combines fragments of his own life story with stories that he makes up about her mother, making certain to "[answer] the many questions that arose in the way he felt would cause [Brod] the least pain," in much the same way that Foer's own grandmother sought to shield him from painful knowledge. To underscore their shared identity, Yankel gives Brod "a string necklace of her own, with a tiny abacus bead" (47) that resembles the one that he wears "so she would never feel out of place in what would be her family" (48). Through Yankel's redemption of Brod, the novel communicates the idea that trauma is a rupture in history, a rupture that fragments the narratives that we need to tell about ourselves in order to know ourselves and to feel a sense of connection to others. Foer, too, is implicated in this task; indeed, we can see that "his role is to take fragments, in the form of words, representations, and memories of the past, and bring them together into a narrative" to not only document the past, but also suggest possibilities for healing, connection, and redemption (Feuer 2007, 38).

Informed by traditional Jewish forms of exegesis and storytelling, the Trachimbrod chapters are at once proleptic and analeptic, prophetic and reflective. As explained by narrative theorist Gérard Genette (1980), prolepsis can be understood as "any narrative maneuver that consists of narrating or evoking in advance an event that will take place later," while analepsis is defined as "any evocation after the fact of an event that took place earlier than the point in the story where we are at any given moment" (40).[26] The sense of simultaneously looking forward and backward is reflected in the Trachimbrod chapter titles, all of which include dates except the first and final chapters.[27] Working together, "analepsis and prolepsis interrupt linearity as well as the reader's sense of omniscience that would be reinforced by a strict chronology in which one sees everything unfold as it happens sequentially" (Rapaport 2011, 71). By confounding readers' sense of omniscience through the use of what Genette (1980) would term "anachronous moments," the text requires them to pay closer attention to disruptions in the narrative and to unpack the meanings of analepses and prolepses—in other words, to read midrashically—in order to connect the kaleidoscope of the shtetl's history to the absent presence of the Holocaust that is embedded, out of time, at its center.

Further, the proleptic and analeptic movement of the Trachimbrod chapters imitates the structure of biblical narrative, which unfolds by moving forward and backward in time, rather than proceeding in a directly linear fashion. The circularity of the narrative is underscored by the physical structure of the Torah itself, which, like a Möbius strip, has no beginning or end, but rather loops back upon itself ad infinitum. Thus, we can read the form of *Everything Is Illuminated* as yet another of its phantasmic qualities; that is, the text not only adapts Jewish mysticism and folklore traditions in its mode of storytelling, but also recalls one of Judaism's foundational texts in its very form as a mode of extending history through time and space, from the founding of Trachimbrod in the eighteenth century, to 1997, and back to the tale's traumatic center in 1941.[28]

The climax of Trachimbrod's embedded history occurs at its end, with invasion of the Nazis and their subsequent razing of the shtetl. The scene is narrated from the perspective of Safran and his pregnant first wife, Zosha, who have gathered with the rest of the villagers to celebrate the annual Trachimday festival. Rather than offering a direct representation of the trauma, however, Foer provides narrative juxtapositions that at once foreshadow the impending trauma and at the same time extend the moment of trauma into the present. We are told that Yankel, Safran's long-dead forefather, "turned in the earth" just as the "earth turned in the sky," presaging the inversion of logic and understanding that the impending trauma will cause (269). Imagining his grandfather and his young wife approaching the riverbank to get a closer view of the festivities, Jonathan interrupts his narrative with a proleptic aside: "Here it is almost impossible to go on, because we know what happens, and wonder why they don't. Or it's impossible because we fear that they do" (270). This metafictional aside serves two purposes. First, it functions as the narrator's meditation on the impossibility of directly representing such tragedy, what Brian McHale (1987) describes as one of the "dark areas" of history, "those aspects about which the official record has nothing to report" but that are nonetheless illuminated by phantasmic trauma narratives like Foer's (87). Second, Jonathan's aside also functions as an admonition to the reader to begin reading midrashically and to consider the ways in which the narrative, which becomes increasingly more fragmented as it progresses, extends a profound sense of the absent presence of the Holocaust into the present moment.

With the readers thus forewarned, the narrative continues as Safran and Zosha draw nearer to watch the Float Queen toss sacks into the river, at which point time stops. What follows is the actual bombing of Trachimbrod, which is not described with words, but rather is visually indicated by two pages of ellipses. Linguistically, ellipses signify "the omission of a word or phrase necessary for a complete syntactical construction but not necessary for understanding" (*OED*). As I have noted elsewhere, ellipses function in language in the same way that suture functions in narrative, constructing meaning where there is a fundamental omission or lack. Visually, ellipses resemble the puncture marks caused by stitches, prompting a recollection of the initial meaning of suture as the joining together the edges of a wound. A *breaking* of suture, then, signifies a reopening of the wound, or a reemergence of a trauma.[29] Such a breakage occurs in this scene when the ellipses are interrupted by sentence fragments that are meant to signify both the slow-motion movement of the sacks through the air, as well as what Jonathan imagines to be Safran's and Zosha's initial, shocked responses to the bombing: "They stayed there. . . . They hung as if on strings. . . . There is still time. . . ." (270–71). Although Foer does not offer a complete imaginative rendering of the shtetl's destruction, the shift in verb tense here in the final phrase extends the moment of trauma into the present, bringing us perhaps as close as we can be to witnessing the unencountered. If the ellipses metonymically signal the historical wound, they also stand in for what cannot be represented or even fully imagined; that is, they do not represent the catastrophe, but instead function as an extension of the catastrophe itself. Thus, the notion that "there is still time" can be read as a call to responsibility, an enjoinder to consider one's ethical responsibility to similar injustices in the present.

The total number of Trachimbrod chapters—eighteen in all—bears numerological significance in Judaism and further underscores their function as phantasmic pathways into the history that Foer seeks to tell in *Everything Is Illuminated*. According to the practice of gematria, which is "a complex hermeneutic technique in which numbers are used to reveal messages in texts and thereby derive insight into the order of the universe," the number eighteen is one of the most sacred numbers in the Jewish tradition (Dennis 2007,

104). As Geoffrey Dennis (2007) explains, "Eighteen is the value of the Hebrew letters *Chet* and *Yod,* which together spell the word *chai*" (חי), a word that translates as "living" (188). The word is thus a present participle that can be used in the context of the past, present, or future, and for this reason, the number eighteen bears special religious meaning for Jews and has assumed additional symbolic value in the aftermath of the Holocaust as a sign of the survival of the Jewish people (Milton 2001, 419). The symbolic value of the number eighteen therefore animates the phantasmic narrative of the Trachimbrod chapters in a meaningful way, extending the past into the present moment both for Alex, the textual reader, and for Foer's readers. The living quality of these chapters, in turn, compels us to interrogate and contemplate the significance of the Alex chapters, which build toward the revelation of Grandfather's secret in the same way that the Trachimbrod chapters progress toward Trachimbrod's inevitable destruction. The novel's phantasmic strategies guide both characters and readers and permit them to ascertain buried truths related to the past, not only to the drama of Jonathan's family history and the Holocaust, but also to Alex's family story. As readers, we are invited to consider the ending of the Trachimbrod narrative in conversation with the search for the site of the shtetl by Jonathan, Alex, and Grandfather, which I discuss at greater length in the next section. It is at the intersections of these narratives—rather than in representation of the event itself—that the opportunity for felt connections arise. Thus, while the Holocaust is not directly represented in the Trachimbrod narrative, the phantasmic strategies that these midrashic chapters employ prime Alex to respond empathically to the traumatic event when it is disclosed in Grandfather's testimony. In so doing, Alex models for the reader how to read and respond ethically to the dark histories that phantasmic trauma narratives convey.

MIDRASHIC RESPONSES

Although the text purportedly centers on Jonathan's return to his ancestral home, "Alex's own unintended pilgrimage of self-discovery . . . eclipses that of the fictional Foer" (Berger and Aarons 2017, 140). As Berger and Aarons (2017) observe, it is "Alex's family dynamic, including his grandfather's terrible secret, that illuminates the psychodynamic operating in the third generation of non-Jewish victims of National Socialism and their burden of traumatic inheritance" (140). Alex's chapters double and refract the themes of love, history, and memory that are introduced in the Trachimbrod narrative. In stark contrast to the Trachimbrod chapters, which draw on traditional Chelm stories as inspiration and are decidedly phantasmic, the Alex chapters are more realist in orientation,[30] with postmodern inflections that are manifested in their highly self-referential character. As Francisco Collado-Rodriguez (2008) argues, "the novel's structural experimentation . . . moves toward an ethical aim that tries to illuminate readers by transforming them into witnesses of a real tragedy that appears to have mythical dimensions: the Holocaust" (55). Thus, although the Alex chapters at first seem to be focused primarily on Alex himself—despite his references to Jonathan as his story's "hero" (1)—Alex functions as a witness to the Trachimbrod story, and it is through his position as witness that the stories of Trachimbrod and Grandfather intersect.

By refracting stories told by Ukrainian and Jewish narrators, the novel underscores the notion that the task of remembering the Holocaust is a collective, rather than solely Jewish, responsibility. Together, Jonathan's and Alex's respective chapters "embark on a shared project of mapping . . . the Holocaust's continuing effects," therefore underscoring the way in which the Holocaust has impacted Jews and non-Jews alike (Lemberg 2011, 87). However, this shared project of mapping is unequally balanced. Because the novel is structured as a call-and-response between Jonathan's phantasmic history and Alex's account of the heritage tour, we are encouraged to read the former as ultimately shaping the latter; that is, the text asks us to imagine that Alex is reading the Trachimbrod chapters in the same way that we are, so that each chapter he writes is undeniably shaped by the Trachimbrod chapter that preceded it. Thus, while the Trachimbrod narrative dominates the novel, it is Alex's narrative—and Alex's evolution as a narrator—that models empathic reading practices and offers pathways toward ethical thinking.

However, granting Alex the privilege of first-person narration does not necessarily encourage the reader to identify with his subject position, nor is it intended to redeem the Ukrainian perspective that he represents. By contrast, Alex's proximity to us as the first-person narrator is likely to inspire a sense of wariness in readers. Indeed, while his malapropisms are often funny and sometimes charming, his casual anti-Semitism and lack of historical awareness prevent reader identification, even though we know that his experiences with Jonathan over the course of the heritage tour cause a change within him: "I will be truthful," he writes at the outset of the novel, "and mention that before the voyage I had the opinion that Jewish people were having shit between their brains. . . . But then I met Jonathan Safran Foer. . . . He is an ingenious Jew" (3). While the adjective "ingenious" that prefaces the moniker "Jew" renders the phrase affectionate and humorous, it nevertheless underscores Jonathan's alterity and Alex's historical and emotional distance from the atrocities that took place in his country little more than fifty years earlier. Readers are encouraged to regard Alex's anti-Semitism—together with other incipient indications of anti-Semitism, such as a waitress's desire to see Jonathan's "horns" (107) and the rudeness that Grandfather directs at Jonathan, or as he refers to him, "the Jew" (7)—as humorous evidence of Ukraine's backwardness. However, as Lemberg (2011) observes, "lingering hostilities [among Ukrainians] are treated more seriously as the group drives into the countryside, where they are clearly unwelcome" (88). These hostilities are most pronounced in the way that the rural Ukrainians antagonistically dismiss Alex's queries about the location of Trachimbrod with anger and demand that he "go away" (116). Their recalcitrance in aiding Alex and his group on their journey stems from their desire to forget or obfuscate the past: "It was seeming as if we were in the wrong country, or the wrong century, or as if Trachimbrod had disappeared, and so had the memory of it" (116). The direct consequence of encountering this hostility on Alex is essentially the gradual dissolution of his latent anti-Semitic feeling toward Jonathan. By observing others react to Jonathan with antagonism and suspicion, and in response to their shared journey of discovery, Alex becomes more empathically responsive to Jonathan, which is manifested in letters where he repeatedly asks Jonathan for forgiveness, not only for his own transgressions, but also for his grandfather's.

In addition to seeing an unflattering reflection of his own anti-Semitism in the attitudes of his compatriots, Alex is also changed by the act of reading Jonathan's Trachimbrod narrative. As Menachem Feuer (2007) notes, Alex's written responses to the Trachimbrod chapters "indicate that Alex is reading the text in a self-reflexive manner, and that in so doing, he questions his own values and beliefs" (37). Indeed, as evidenced in his letters to Jonathan, Alex reads these chapters midrashically, interpolating in the Trachimbrod stories ethical questions that relate to the responsibilities of authorship and imagination and adding commentary that extends the lessons about love and loss into the present moment. What begins as surface-level commentary—*"There were parts I didn't understand, but I conjecture that this is because they were very Jewish, and only a Jewish person could understand something so Jewish"* (25)—gradually inspires philosophical responses that show Alex's growing awareness of his role as interlocutor and an active participant in the literary discourse as both reader and writer. This is demonstrated by Alex's recognition that his travelogue and Jonathan's history of Trachimbrod are interdependent texts that circle around the same void: *"We are talking now, Jonathan, together, and not apart. We are with each other, working on the same story, and I am certain that you can also feel it"* (214). Although this passage is written from one character to another, Alex's words also encourage the reader's participation, in a midrashic sense, in the narrative that is being relayed, and in this moment, the text seems to implicate the reader. Indeed, for Allard den Dulk (2015), this particular passage serves as evidence of Foer's treatment of fiction "as a dialogue between writer and reader" (259). Similarly, Collado-Rodriguez (2008) asserts that "the novel's use of two narrators serves to evaluate the power of fiction as an ethical instrument. . . . [It serves] to fix the meaning of his book and urge an ethical reading of it through a dual narrative structure" (54–55). The invitation to "feel" as a participant in the story can be read as a signal to read midrashically, to perceive the ways in which the narrative extends into the present moment, and to interrogate one's own response to the ethical summons that the text presents.

To underscore the notion that the text's engagement with the Holocaust past is extensional rather than representational, Alex goes on to articulate the ethical obligation of the post-Holocaust author: "*I would never command you to write a story that is as it occurred in the actual, but I would command you to make your story faithful*" (240). The text's emphasis on the connection between the problem of representation and the notion of ethical responsibility invites a Levinasian reading. As Levinas (1987) argues, the past "is not made up of re-presentations," but rather has "the signification of an inveterate obligation, older than any engagement, taking up the whole of its meaning in the imperative that commands the ego by way of the Other's face" (113). Thus, what Levinas terms the "immemorial past" is experienced as ethical responsibility. If, as Alex suggests, the duty of the author is to create a story that is "faithful" to the event without resorting to representation—which ultimately obscures the notion of ethical responsibility—then the duty of the reader is to engage, to take up the threads of the narrative that extend the Holocaust into the present moment and to face the disaster, bearing witness to it but not presuming to understand it. In the absence of language is feeling, and it is through this feeling—that which one may sense but not fully articulate or intellectualize—that ethical thinking arises. Given that the novel situates the fictional history of Trachimbrod in the context of written exchanges between Alex and Jonathan, we can see how Jonathan accepts the call to ethical responsibility in the way that he frames the destruction of Trachimbrod, which appears near the end of the text, presumably after he has read Alex's enjoiner to "make [his] story faithful" (240). And this is what Jonathan does: he creates a "faithful" representation that does not, in fact, presume to re-present the event, but rather solicits reader participation in its construction by way of ellipses. Thus, we feel our proximity to the void even as we are prevented from peering into it. In this way, the text demonstrates the ethics of reading, writing, and responding.

In addition to clarifying the ethical obligations of writer and reader, Alex also comes to understand the act of translation as a midrashic exercise itself, which is exemplified when he translates Augustine's testimony for Jonathan. Augustine's fragmented testimony emerges in the spaces created by Grandfather's persistent questions and is further obscured by the way that Alex translates the exchange for Jonathan. In a narrative aside, Alex explains to Jonathan, "You cannot know how it felt to have to hear these things and then repeat them, because when I repeated them, I felt like I was making them new again" (185). Here, we witness Alex develop a felt connection to the Holocaust experiences of Augustine. Dori Laub (1992) explains that "the listener to trauma comes to be a participant and co-owner of the traumatic event: through his very listening, he comes to partially experience trauma in himself" (57). But Alex does not stop at listening; he re-creates the testimony in a way that allows him to experience it in an even more meaningful way. As we can see, his translation is not exact, but it is *"faithful"* to the essence of Augustine's testimony (240). This moment provides both Jonathan and Alex the opportunity to ask questions that highlight the inevitable gaps in the stories they hear. Indeed, both become aware that Augustine's testimony is not only important for what it reveals, but also for how it highlights Grandfather's silence about his own role during the Holocaust. Thus, if this scene captures the impossibility of re-presenting the Holocaust, it also shows how, in the process of responding to gaps in the narrative, we respond with explanations—and perhaps even more significantly, with questions—"that allow us to see the ways in which the moment to which we are responding is extended into our present lives" (Osborne 2018, 6). The act of engaging with the text in this way facilitates the felt connection that is the necessary precursor to ethical thinking about the imbrication of past and present, self and other.

The act of writing, reading, and reflecting on his shared experience with Jonathan helps Alex to understand the way that he, too, is implicated in Holocaust history. This is emphasized when Alex finds himself confronting the task of telling the truth about Grandfather's betrayal of his best friend, a Jew named Herschel, during the war:

> Here it is almost too forbidding to continue. I have written to this point many times, and corrected the parts you would have me correct, and made more funnies, and more inventions, and written as if I were writing you this, but every time I try to persevere, my hand shakes so that I can no longer hold my pen. Do it for me. Please. It is now yours. (226)

Tracy Floreani (2001) observes that "Alex's unwillingness to commit to paper this testimony speaks of the difficulty of moving from the process of perception to that of documentation" (147). This failure, however, carries multiple meanings. Alex qua author articulates the struggle that Foer and other third-generation authors have confronted in their own attempts to bear witness to the Holocaust. On another level, we can read Alex's failure as the text's self-reflexive commentary on itself as an interwoven tapestry of midrashim in the sense that "midrash depends on the existence of failure" (Osborne 2018, xx). This failure, Osborne argues, is what makes midrash "an extension of the ethical"; indeed, "its very existence implies an acknowledgment and ownership of . . . the failure of the primary text . . . to articulate a full and complete story" (xix–xx). In this spirit, we can interpret Alex's plea as a signal to Jonathan, and by extension, the novel's entreaty to the reader, to begin reading midrashically. As a process that permits readers agency in the process of constructing narrative meaning by considering themselves in relation to the story, not as a subject or a stand-in for the subject, but rather as a participant in the process of bringing the failures of the original narratives into relief, midrash creates a space for ethical engagement with the past and the other. The novel's entreaty to read midrashically can be read, then, as a reminder of collective responsibility to actively remember. Alex's passing of the baton is one of the clearest examples of the text's investment in midrash as part of its broader phantasmic strategy: it "compel[s] the reader to respond to it in ways that enrich and extend it" (44). Indeed, Alex's plea to be excused from the task of rendering the ineffable obliges the reader to consider the ethical and philosophical quandaries posed by the text and, at the very least, to acknowledge the author's own struggle with these complexities.

Throughout his correspondence with Jonathan, Alex continuously voices the challenge of third-generation writers, who must "confront the past with the unpracticed, yet insistent resolve of the uninitiated," a past that is littered with events that "stealthily have come to have everything to do with them" (Berger and Aarons 2017, 64). Indeed, the "retrieval of the past for the third generation becomes central to identity formation; such stories—continuing memories—provide a framework for identity within which one might . . . give meaning to the future" (64). In one of his letters to Jonathan, Alex writes: *"Grandfather interrogates me about you every day. He desires to know if you forgive him for the things he told you about the war, and about Herschel. (You could alter it, Jonathan. For him, not for me. Your novel is now verging on the war. It is possible). He is not a bad person. He is a good person, alive in a bad time"* (145). It is clear that Alex wants Jonathan to absolve his grandfather, but despite his protestations about the unselfishness of that request, we know that Alex, in a sense a third-generation writer himself, also desires absolution: *"Everything is the way it is because everything was the way it was. Sometimes I feel ensnared in this, as if no matter what I do, what will come has already been fixed"* (147). Here, Alex fully articulates the spirit of the midrashic texts he has read, responded to, and created. In declaring *"Everything is the way it is because everything was the way it was,"* he acknowledges his newfound understanding of the way that these midrashim have extended the atrocity into the present moment in a way that direct representation never could. More importantly, this moment in the text is a profound statement of ethical awareness and a recognition of his responsibility to history. Indeed, Alex perceives that just as Jonathan carries the burden of the Holocaust as part of his familial and cultural legacy, so too does he carry the burden of guilt bequeathed to him by Grandfather.

The closer Alex's chapters come to the moment when Grandfather's dark secret will be revealed, the more the phantasmic elements of the Trachimbrod chapters spill over into his narrative sections; that is, the closer the heritage tour gets to the vacant site of Trachimbrod, the more surreal Alex's narration of the journey becomes. This narrative shift positions readers to read midrashically in the manner demonstrated by Alex earlier in the text. One of the most telling examples of this appears in his transcription of Grandfather's confession, which models the momentum of the old man's speech in translation, so that eventually punctuation and even spaces between words disappear as he recalls, in present tense, the last words of the friend whom he exposed as a Jew: "youaremyfriend do not let me die I am so afraid of dying Iamsoafraid . . . do something dosomething dosomething" (251). "I didwhatIdid," Grandfather cries, "I am I and Iamresponsible" (251). The shift from past to present tense extends the moment of Grandfather's complicity in the Holocaust into the present, capturing the essence of what it is that midrash does. At the same time, the omission of spaces forces the reader to slow down long enough to register "the most pressing and distressing moral questions of guilt and responsibility" (Krijnen 2016, 68). Alex struggles to bear witness to his grandfather's testimony, so much so that Jonathan seemingly disappears from the scene altogether as Alex ceases his real-time translation of Grandfather's words. As a result, Jonathan only learns the details of the story by reading Alex's narrative following his return to the United States.

What is significant here is not that Alex fails to translate for Jonathan in the moment, but rather that he recognizes the importance of bearing witness to the Holocaust. He explains: "When I listened to him, I did not listen to Grandfather, but to someone else, someone I had never encountered before, but whom I knew better than Grandfather. And the person who was listening to this person was not me but someone else, someone I had never been before but whom I knew better than myself" (245). This description of witnessing, and Alex's repeated use of the verb "to witness" as a substitute for the verb "to see" indicates the primacy of this act in Alex's story and in terms of how he perceives his role as the reader of Jonathan's Trachimbrod narrative. The transformative effect of bearing witness on Alex recalls LaCapra's (2001) understanding of empathy, which "is a form of virtual, not vicarious experience . . . in which emotional response comes with respect for the other and the realization that the experience of the other is not one's own" (40). Bearing witness, for Alex, takes him outside of himself and enables him to see himself, and his family, in relation to others.

More importantly, bearing witness to Jonathan's and Grandfather's stories also enables Alex to recognize his ethical responsibility for the suffering of the Jewish other as well as his responsibility to continue to bear witness. By recognizing the way that bearing witness takes Alex outside of himself, we see another doubling enacted: his repeated plea for forgiveness from Jonathan is a reversal of Herschel's plea to Grandfather to save him from death at the hands of the Nazis. This turning of the narrative in upon itself stands as an invitation to the reader to engage in ethical thinking, in particular because of the way that it suggests Levinas's (1989) ethical notion of the face of the other: "The Other becomes my neighbor precisely through the way the face summons me, calls for me, begs for me, in so doing recalls my responsibility, and calls me into question" (82). What the novel suggests, then, is that to think ethically about the Holocaust is to take responsibility for the Holocaust, whether we are directly implicated in it or not. The way that the novel uses midrash to extend the event at the center of all three of its narratives emphasizes the need to acknowledge collective responsibility not only for the fact that the event occurred at all, but also for the way that we tell and remember its history.

Everything Is Illuminated is one of a number of third-generation works that weave together the phantasmic and the midrashic to offer contemporary readers a new, and more ethical, avenue for confronting the enduring effects of Holocaust trauma. Future studies would undoubtedly consider the interplay of midrash and the phantasmic in Joseph Skibell's *A Blessing on the Moon*, Michael Chabon's *The Amazing Adventures of Kavalier and Clay*, Boris Fishman's *A Replacement Life*, and Nicole Krauss's *The History of Love*. Each of these works incorporates the phantasmic to reaffirm connections to Jewish cultural values while at the same time using midrash as a tool to extend the trauma of the past into the present, prompting not only an ethical engagement with the suffering of others in the past, but in the contemporary moment as well.

NOTES

1. The effects of the Holocaust on the grandchildren of survivors has been debated by psychologists and psychiatrists since the 1980s. However, as a literary designation, "third generation" is widely accepted.

2. In *The Midrashic Impulse and the Contemporary Literary Response* (2018), Monica Osborne has written definitively on the subject of contemporary midrash and the Holocaust, and she explains that what she terms "the midrashic mode" can be "discovered or utilized in both the creation and comprehension of literary and artistic expression" (xx). Citing Geoffrey Hartman, David Stern, Michael Fishbane, Gerald Bruns, and Daniel Boyarin, she argues that the midrashic mode is "a form of literary criticism and analysis, and in the context of Holocaust representation—what the French novelist and philosopher Maurice Blanchot calls the 'unrepresentable representation'—it provides a less compromised, and more ethical, path into conceptualizing the ineffable" (xx–xxi).

3. As I explain at length in the book's introduction and reiterate later in this chapter, I eschew the term "magical realism" because of the way that the term implies a hegemonic relationship whereby the reader essentializes and fetishizes the subaltern as an exotic object. Despite the problematic nature of the term, however, I have found the extant work on American ethnic uses of magical realism to be helpful in formulating my argument, especially the edited collection *Moments of Magical Realism in U.S. Ethnic Literatures,* edited by Lyn Di Iorio Sandín and Richard Perez (2013), and *Uncertain Mirrors: Magical Realisms in U.S. Ethnic Literatures,* by Jesús Benito, Ana Ma Manzanas, and Begoña Simal (2009). Included in the former is Caroline Rody's "Jewish Post-Holocaust Fiction and the Magical Realist Turn" (2013), which I address later in this chapter, and which engages in a substantial way the

historical uses of the fantastic and the supernatural in Jewish American fiction and provides important insights into how this body of work is reflective of a "transnational aesthetic," one that she traces to the broader uses of magical realism as a mode frequently employed by postcolonial writers (57). The other text specific to the historical use of the supernatural in Jewish literature is Tamara Kaye Sellman's "Jewish Magical Realism" (2005), which I also reference in this chapter.

4. LaCapra (2001) discusses the term at length in *Writing History, Writing Trauma*. See in particular pages 86–113.

5. Adorno's (1983) famous dictum reads: "Cultural criticism finds itself faced with the final stage of the dialectic of culture and barbarism. To write poetry after Auschwitz is barbaric. And this corrodes even the knowledge of why it has become impossible to write poetry today. Absolute reification, which presupposed intellectual progress as one of its elements, is now preparing to absorb the mind entirely" (34). However, Adorno (1992) later qualified his position, acceding that "suffering . . . also demands the continued existence of the very art it forbids" (88).

6. The use of the term "second-generation" in the context of Holocaust lineage can be traced back to 1973 with the publication of Sigal et al.'s psychology article titled "Some Second-Generation Effects of Survival of Nazi Persecution," which examined the "adverse physical and psychological effects" of concentration camp survivors on their teenage children, and the term has evolved to encompass all children of Holocaust survivors. Since that time, there has been substantial research on the psychological condition of the second generation, in particular the work of Helen Epstein, Aaron Hass, and Dan Bar-On. Notable studies on second-generation Holocaust fiction include Alan Berger's *Children of Job*, Marita Grimwood's *Holocaust Literature of the Second Generation*, and Efraim Sicher's edited collection, *Breaking Crystal: Writing and Memory after Auschwitz*.

7. While some argue that embracing postmemory is tantamount to embracing victimization, scholar and third-generation writer Hilene Flanzbaum (2012) argues that "the practice of postmemory" is in fact empowering: "My ancestry has given me a more informed, creative, and powerful present because like my writer counterparts I must combine memory with imagination to form a coherent narrative" (14).

8. Until recently, scholars assumed that the transmission of trauma between generations was the result of environmental factors, such as the parents' inability to cope with their own trauma, their approach to childrearing, etc. However, new research indicates that the children of survivors "may have been marked epigenetically with a chemical coating upon their chromosomes, which would represent a kind of biological memory of what the parents experienced. As a result, some suffer from a general vulnerability to stress while others are more resilient" (Kellerman 2013, 33). Fields such as epigenetics provide a more nuanced approach to the study of the transmission of transgenerational trauma by considering both environmental and hereditary factors.

9. See Berger 1997, 184.

10. Born in the 1960s and 1970s, third-generation authors "have either an actual or imagined kinship with those direct witnesses of the Holocaust" (Berger and Aarons 2017, 14). Berger and Aarons also stipulate that the reference to "generation" in this context is therefore "familial as well as cultural," and they suggest that the term might also "usefully encompass those writers who . . . create characters who are third-generation witnesses to horror" (14). See also Jessica Lang (2009, 46).

11. In *The End of the Holocaust*, Alvin H. Rosenfeld (2011) argues that while the general memory of the Nazi genocide of Europe's Jews will persist, such collective memory will lack historical awareness and moral outrage. Ominously, Rosenfeld predicts a time when "the immense historical and moral weight of the Nazi crimes [will be] whittled down into the familiar categories of a Sunday school sermon or conventional box-office spectacle" (3). The result of the end of Holocaust memory, Rosenfeld warns, will permit anti-Semitism to reemerge once again to threaten the Jews with destruction.

12. Most scholars who study third-generation literature agree that "there is a very distinct sense among the writing of the third generation that time is running out" (Berger and Aarons 2017, 7). See Berger and Aarons's *Third-Generation Holocaust Representation* (2017), Phi-

lippe Codde's "Keeping History at Bay: Absent Presences in Three Recent Jewish American Novels" (2011), and Jessica Lang, "*The History of Love,* the Contemporary Reader, and the Transmission of Holocaust Memory" (2009).

13. See the introduction to Aarons's *A Measure of Memory: Storytelling and Identity in American Jewish Fiction* (1996).

14. See also the introduction to Schwartz's *Elijah's Violin and Other Jewish Fairy Tales* (1983), Sellman's "Jewish Magical Realism: Writing to Tell the Tale" (2005) and Rody's "Jewish Post-Holocaust Fiction and the Magical Realist Turn" (2013).

15. In her book *Magic Realism in Holocaust Literature,* Jenni Adams (2011) argues that "magic realism . . . offers an important strategy in attempts to continue the project of Holocaust representation into the post-testimonial era, permitting a form of literary engagement with these events that nevertheless acknowledges its ethical and experiential distance from the real" (1–2). Of specific interest to me is her exploration of how the supernatural provides a vehicle for reconstructing "the events of the Holocaust" from a "postmemorial perspective" (2).

16. Similarly, Jenni Adams's *Magic Realism in Holocaust Literature* (2011) makes the important argument that magical realism is used by Holocaust writers as a means of circumnavigating the representational limits and ethical pitfalls of realism.

17. The difference between "magical realism" and "phantasmic" can be understood in the context of the debate about whether or not the spiritual folklore of Judaism should be considered "mystical" or "mythological." Tamara Kaye Sellman (2005) writes, "religious Jews, especially those from the Orthodoxy, are offended by the term 'myth' to refer to any part of Judaism. They consider it a pejorative denigration of . . . books of both classical Judaism and Kabbalah, [which] in their perspective, are uncompromisingly sacred and divine. . . . [T]hey hold that such fantastical tales, which move well beyond rationalism, are too difficult for modern Western people to grasp."

18. Although the focus here is on the increasing reliance in third-generation literature on phantasmic and midrashic strategies, it is important to credit Isaac Bashevis Singer as a literary progenitor of this kind of work. Singer's "The Last Demon" (in Singer 1966) is perhaps the earliest example of this phenomenon: in this story, a demon sent to tempt the pious finds his own evil intentions outdone by the Nazis who have destroyed the shtetl he intended to deceive. Cynthia Ozick's *The Shawl* (1989) continues in this tradition. This short work consists of two linked stories. In the first part, "The Shawl," a shawl assumes magical qualities as it protects and feeds Rosa Lublin's infant daughter Magda in the desolate world of a Nazi concentration camp (much like a tallit, which symbolizes life and symbolically protects the wearer). The second part, "Rosa," focuses on Rosa's life decades after Magda's murder in the camp, and in this part, the tattered fragments of the shawl summons Magda's ghost, staging a haunting reunion between mother and child. A number of scholars have read "Rosa" as an extended midrash on "The Shawl," and Joseph Alkana (1997) has gone further to argue that *The Shawl* can also be read as a midrash on Abraham's attempted sacrifice of Isaac.

19. Osborne's (2018) analysis of *In the Image* bears repeating here for the way that it reinforces the imbrication of witnessing and ethical response. Osborne argues that *In the Image* shows us "what it means to read and enact ritual in a world ravaged by terror and atrocities" (xxxv). In the exchange between the young American Jason and the aged immigrant Mr. Rosenthal, she contends, "The relationship between the storyteller and listener . . . is one in which pre- and post-Holocaust perspectives merge. . . . It is a midrashic moment—a moment in which a young person in a contemporary context is commissioned to respond midrashically" (xxxv).

20. The first substantive work to address the emergence of midrash in the field of literary studies was the aptly named *Midrash and Literature,* edited by Geoffrey Hartman (1986). In a collection of essays, Hartman and his colleagues demonstrate the growing importance of midrash as a mode of literary theory. Gerald Bruns (1987), in an essay titled "Midrash and Allegory," and David Stern, in a book-length study titled *Midrash and Theory* (1998), build on this work to map out the links between midrash and literary theory. Daniel Boyarin's *Intertextuality and the Reading of Midrash* (1994), although more invested in the original exegetical function of midrash, advances the critical notion of textual gapping that has informed subsequent literary critiques of post-Holocaust fiction written in the midrashic mode, including that of Sara R.

Horowitz, Meisha Rosenberg, Alan L. Berger, and Victoria Aarons. Monica Osborne's (2018) recent work, *The Midrashic Impulse and the Contemporary Literary Response to Trauma*, makes a valuable contribution to the study of midrash by connecting "the language of midrash" and the work of Emmanuel Levinas, whose philosophy of ethics is rooted in infinite responsibility: first, that we are infinitely responsible for the other; second, that we are responsible for the other's responsibility; and third, that we are ultimately responsible for the other's death.

21. As Osborne (2018) cautions, "it is not enough to suggest simply that certain texts have been written with a midrashic awareness; rather, to read a text midrashically is what allows its inherent midrashic components to materialize meaningfully" (6). In the texts I examine in this chapter, the phantasmic gives rise to midrashic reading.

22. Levinas's theory of ethical responsibility is most fully addressed in *Totality and Infinity* (1969), specifically sections III and IV, and *God, Death, and Time* (2000). I am deeply indebted to Sandor Goodhart's interpretations of Levinas. Goodhart introduced me to his works in a graduate seminar titled "Reading Levinas."

23. The novel's structural experimentation emulates the structure of trauma as a rupture in history and temporality (Caruth 1996, 4–6), or a resurfacing of the past in the present. Anne Whitehead (2004) goes further, suggesting that "if trauma is at all susceptible to narrative formulation, then it requires a literary form which departs from a conventional linear sequence" (6). Similarly, Laurie Vickroy (2002) argues that trauma narratives "internalize the rhythms, processes, and uncertainties of traumatic experience within their underlying sensibilities and structures" (3).

24. Philippe Codde (2009) challenges the categorization of *Everything Is Illuminated* as magical realism, arguing that it "is really closer to mythology" (65). While I take issue with the term "mythology" as a descriptor for spiritual and storytelling traditions that exist on the margins of mainstream Western (and Christian) ontology, I do agree with Codde that "in order to bridge the epistemological abyss that separates them from this inaccessible era, third-generation authors take the imaginative leap implied by the concept of postmemory . . . to fill in the blanks left by their absent history" (64).

25. Foer's depiction of shtetl life draws heavily on previous folklore representations of Eastern Europe, notably the Chelm stories recounted by American Yiddish writers such as Sholem Aleichem and Isaac Bashevis Singer. As Menachem Feuer (2007) argues, "Foer's fictional Eastern European space resembles the world of Chelm brought to us by I. B. Singer; although, admittedly, it is much more elaborate than Singer's world" (38). Joseph Boskin and Joseph Dorinson (1987) go further to argue that the Trachimbrod chapters, like the Chelm stories, parody "the Jewish preoccupation with learning bereft of common sense" (104). This tradition of humor—which both draws from and counters the "reverent stories about Talmudic scholars, who used reason and logic . . . [that] were in certain ways foolish" (Berger 1997, 89)—highlights the "unique tendency" of Jews to use irony and humor "to take the edge off tragedy" (Saper 1993, 82). Just as the Yiddish storytellers who used the Chelm tales as a way of coping with the grim fact of living in a land of pogroms and anti-Semitic sentiments, so does Foer use the tragicomic Trachimbrod chapters phantasmically, as a point of access into a rich yet painful cultural past.

26. Genette (1980) continues by "reserving the general term *anachrony* to designate all forms of discordance between the two temporal orders of story and narrative" (40). I suggest that such anachronous moments are the precise gaps in the narrative that encourage midrashic reading.

27. The novel further signals its nonlinearity by including dates in a majority of the Trachimbrod chapter titles. The timeline of these chapters primarily covers the years between March 18, 1791—the founding of Trachimbrod—and March 18, 1942, which marks the destruction of the shtetl by the Nazi *Einsatzgruppen*. Fourteen of the eighteen Trachimbrod chapters include date ranges in their titles: six of the chapters are linear, such as chapter 11, "Falling in Love, 1791–1803" and chapter 24, "Falling in Love, 1934–1941." Chapters 20 and 33—"The Dupe of Change, 1941–1924" and "The Beginning of the World Often Comes, 1942–1791"—reverse the chronology, while chapter 16—"The Dial, 1941–1804–1941"—moves both analeptically and proleptically. Two of the Trachimbrod chapters take the reader past the destruction of Trachimbrod: chapter 12, "Recurrent Secrets, 1791–1943," depicts the

arrival of Jonathan's grandfather, Safran, in New York City, and chapter 13, "A Parade, a Death, a Proposition, 1804–1969," offers a snapshot of Jonathan's mother as a young girl, watching the lunar landing on television.

28. For a thorough discussion of the way in which Torah's analeptic and proleptic gestures relate to the Möbius strip, see Goodhart's *Möbian Nights* (2017). See also Miriam Sivan (2009), who notes that the "Torah scroll [is] a strip" in its very structure (8).

29. As I show in "Haunted by the Past: Traumatica Rememory and Black Feminism in Gayl Jones's *Corregidora*" (Setka 2014) and "Bastardized History: How *Inglourious Basterds* Breaks through American Screen Memory" (Setka 2015), the strategic repetition of ellipses is a hallmark of works that narrativize historical trauma.

30. It should be noted, however, that Alex's attempt at realism is undermined both by his frequent malapropisms and by his correspondence with Jonathan, in which he often refers to embellishments he has made or alterations that he plans to make in order to offer a more flattering portrayal of Jonathan.

Chapter Three

A Phantasmic Tribalography

The Case of LeAnne Howe's
Miko Kings: An Indian Baseball Story

In her introduction to *Eating Fire, Tasting Blood: An Anthology of the American Indian Holocaust,* Marijo Moore (2006) explains that "for indigenous peoples, written history is concocted with lies that exacerbate our inability to be respected as an evolving race. Written history makes us more aware of the silenced truths concerning past and current deceit, theft, abuse, annoyance, decimation, murder, and racism toward our ancestors and ourselves" (xi). "Negation of the past," she continues, "allows the perpetuation of racial genocide to continue" (xiv–xv). If it is true that we "know ourselves through our history," then the act of correcting the historiographic record is, for Native writers, a "way of genetic ancestral healing" (xiii). In addition to agitating for political change and recognition of tribal sovereignty, many Natives have also turned to the indigenous tradition of storytelling as both a way of correcting the historical record and rebuilding tribal communities. Kathryn Lucci-Cooper (2003) speaks to the importance of this tradition for Native Americans, explaining that "it is the telling of stories . . . that brings forth tribal identity and defines purpose" (8).[1] Many contemporary Native American authors have adapted the spirit of oral storytelling in their writing, creating narratives that, though written, retain some of the aural quality of tribal stories by employing their Native languages, spiritual traditions, and a multiplicity of communal voices. By emphasizing these aspects of tribal culture, Native authors have found a new way to weave together tradition and innovation and communicate history as "living thought" (8).

This chapter examines the way that LeAnne Howe's *Miko Kings: An Indian Baseball Story* (2007) draws on Native spiritual traditions to create a type of "living thought" that connects readers to the past within the framework of Choctawan notions of time. In its efforts to reconstruct Choctaw history from a Choctawan perspective, this text also emphasizes more broadly the importance of indigenous languages and traditional stories as necessary elements of rebuilding and sustaining Native communities. Although the world into which Howe draws us is quite tribally specific, it offers important historical and linguistic contexts so that the novel is accessible to a diverse readership, and it creates opportunities for felt connections to Choctaw history through the use of phantasmic strategies culled from Choctaw tribal traditions and beliefs. Drawing on the structure of Choctaw linguistics, *Miko Kings* manipulates the space-time continuum to connect the worlds of the past and the present, enabling the unearthing of painful historical secrets and revealing historic alliances that present models for contemporary cross-cultural engagement.

While descendants of Holocaust survivors and American slaves must contend with temporal displacement from the experiences of genocide and enslavement, Native Americans, particularly those for whom home is a reservation, experience inherited memories of trauma—loss of population, land, and culture—accompanied by continuing forms of postcolonial trauma. The sense of cultural trauma as an ongoing experience is perhaps more acute in Native American literature, yet like the African American and Jewish American texts I addressed in earlier chapters, the Native American texts I examine here employ phantasmic irruptions for similar ends. In its use of time travel and its emphasis on the importance of written texts and language more broadly as conduits for bearing witness to the past, *Miko Kings* invites comparison to the other novels and films examined in this volume. Like *Kindred* (Butler 2003), *The Devil's Arithmetic* (1999), and *Sankofa* (1993), *Miko Kings* bridges the distance between past and present by bringing living characters together, although it does so by way of inversion: instead of sending its contemporary protagonist, Lena, into the past, the text summons her ancestor, Ezol, into the present. In so doing, *Miko Kings*, like Jonathan Safran Foer's *Everything Is Illuminated* (2002), extends the trauma of the past into the present moment, incorporating metanarratives that invite readers to consider the ways in which the past and present are mutually constitutive. If Ezol extends the past into the present, she also functions as a guiding ancestral presence similar to that which we encounter in *Older Than America* (2008); in both works, the ancestor figure educates and guides the present-day protagonist to facilitate healing and growth. Further, both *Miko Kings* and *Older Than America* emphasize the importance of a return to ritual and ceremony to enabling healing processes to occur.

Crucial to understanding these projects of recovery and resilience is what Irene Visser (2015) terms a "decolonized trauma theory," which revises classic trauma theory from a postcolonial perspective (258). Such an approach to trauma theory calls for a sensitivity to "indigenous literatures that situate trauma in the context of ritual and ceremony" (260). Where classic trauma theory tends to privilege a Western secularism that identifies itself with "ideas of modernity, progress, civilization, and the othering of religions that are different from Christianity" (Ratti 2013, 7), decolonized or postcolonial trauma theory recognizes the role that indigenous religious and spiritual modes can play in both the articulation of and response to cultural trauma. In so doing, postcolonial trauma theory challenges classic trauma theory's "'injunction' to regard malaise and melancholia, with their connotations of submissiveness and inaction, as the inevitable outcomes of traumatization" (Visser 2015, 255). Instead, this new approach to trauma theory builds on the work of Judith Herman's (1994) study of individual experiences of trauma in *Trauma and Recovery* by emphasizing the importance of storytelling and indigenous spiritual and ritual practices as fostering resilience and facilitating recovery. It is worth noting that even while she does not address the value of spirituality, even Cathy Caruth herself has moved away from her initial emphasis on melancholia and stasis as an inevitable response to trauma. In her 2013 *Literature in the Ashes of History*, she writes that "the experience of trauma is also the experience of an imperative to live" (7) and asserts that survival is linked to "an imperative that appears to have ethical force," such as in "the survivor mission to tell the story of the dead," as well as a relation to knowing and witnessing "as an awakening" (94). *Miko Kings* does indeed bear witness to the past, but it goes further to promote ethical, even activist thinking, first, by providing readers with historical models of cross-cultural alliances, and second, by showing how the act of storytelling itself may contain the seeds for reconciliation.

Miko Kings is just one of a number of Native American texts that use phantasmic strategies to teach readers about the past and the suffering—and survival—of America's indigenous peoples and their cultures. N. Scott Momaday's *House Made of Dawn* (1966) presents a complex Jemez Pueblo cosmology that maintains an interactive relationship between individuals, the community, and the land, one that counters the pervasive sense of alienation that one encounters in the mainstream, Eurocentric world. Throughout the novel, Momaday refers to the notion of "nothing in the absolute" (33), a phrase that suggests that everything is eternal, which allows for a being-ness that extends beyond the limitations of the physical world. Likewise, Leslie Marmon Silko (1977) refashions Laguna Pueblo and Navajo healing ceremonies for a contemporary audience in her 1977 novel *Ceremony*. Through the character of Tayo, she invites readers into a vision quest ceremony that features shape-shifting spirit guides. Silko imbues her novel with the power of indigenous spirituality and rituals to suggest Native strategies for achieving balance and wholeness in a fragmented, postmodern world. Both of these works emphasize the spiritual connection that exists between a tribe and its territory and show that healing can be achieved by reconnecting to both place and tribal traditions.

The connection between place and tradition has become an increasingly important feature Native American phantasmic trauma narratives. As Louise Erdrich puts it in her essay "Where I Ought to Be" (1985), the "unchanging landscape," a phantasmic setting for the stories that make up a tribe's history, forms the foundation of tribal identity: "People and place are inseparable" (1). Louise Erdrich's oeuvre in particular is deeply concerned with the relationship between place and tradition, and it is in the fictional reservation universe around which so many of her novels revolve that the phantasmic predominates. *Tracks* (1988) draws on Ojibwe cosmology by conjuring ancestral spirits not only as a way to illustrate the omnipresence of the past in the present, but also to suggest that the tools needed for cultural healing can be accessed by reconnecting to ancestral traditions. In Erdrich's narrative world, living characters encounter the spirits of the dead, and through this association forge a new, meaningful relationship to the living past. The coexistence of the living and the dead, and the sharing of ancestral knowledge that arises from this proximity, is present in a number of her other works as well, including *Love Medicine* (1984), *The Bingo Palace* (1994), and *LaRose* (2016). Several of her works, particularly *Tracks* (1988), *The Round House* (2012), and "The Flower" (2015) include *wiindigoo* spirits, cannibalistic entities that possess living humans, which illustrate the historical and ongoing loss experienced by indigenous peoples as the result of colonization, while others, such as *The Round House* and *LaRose,* emphasize the importance of traditional ceremonies as conduits for healing from historical trauma. In *The Round House* and *The Painted Drum* (2005), objects of great traditional significance (the drum, the round house) are imbued with ghostly characteristics, guiding the novels' characters to long-hidden secrets and enduring truths. In both cases, these objects underscore the connection between place and tradition.

Many contemporary Native American texts seem to share the notion that land itself encodes the tribal past and contains within it the roots of one's cultural identity. As Colleen E. Boyd and Coll Thrush (2011) observe, "ties to the land" have often been integral to the recovery of the past and the discovery of one's identity, "with sacred geographies, sites of historical conflict, and places that are haunted by the past being employed to weave powerful accounts of survival and persistence" (xx). Blake Hausman's underappreciated *Riding the Trail of Tears* (2011) carries this kind of engagement with place into the realm of virtual reality. Hausman's novel tells the story of Tallulah Wilson, a twenty-seven-year-old half-white, half-Cherokee woman who works as a tour guide "on a virtual Trail of Tears where everything is digital" in the Tsalagi Removal Exodus Point Park, or TREPP, a tourist attraction in north Georgia (13). Although Tallulah is well versed in Cherokee history and culture, she has been inured to the historical traumas of her people due to the "eleven hundred" tours she has guided on the virtual trail (15). Because the ride is geared more toward guaranteeing customer satisfaction than offering an experience that authentically represents historical suffering, the phantasmic emerges in the novel as a response to the exploitation and trivialization of the Cherokee past by white corporate interests. On one of Tallulah's tours, Tour 5709, strange events occur when the ride's virtual Cherokee characters—animated by spirit beings known in Cherokee tradition as the Nunnehi, or as they are referred to in the novel, the "Misfits" (6)—stage a rebellion to change the ride's programming and their own status as digital figures fated to endlessly repeat the experience of Cherokee removal. As a result of these "terrorist" acts by Cherokee spirit beings (38), the virtual ride becomes terrifyingly real in its sudden unpredictability, and Tallulah, along with Jewish tourist Irma Rosenberg, become attuned to the traumas of displacement and violence in a whole new way. Indeed, through Tallulah's interactions with Irma, and Irma's exchanges with the Misfits, readers are asked to consider the parallels between the historical oppression of the Cherokee and the Jews. Further, Tallulah's growth and self-discovery coincides with her newfound appreciation for both her ancestral home—rather than the virtual "place" that has exploited her—as well as her Cherokee traditions.

However, even when a connection to place is not particularly prominent, spectral presences permeate Native texts, both as reminders of historical wrongs and as advocates for positive change. Anna Lee Walters's *Ghost Singer* (1988) draws readers into the haunted spaces of the Smithsonian Museum of Natural History, where the ghosts of Native Americans guard their catalogued, objectified remains. The unspoken atrocities that resulted in this collection of human remains are alluded to by way of a comparison to the atrocities of Vietnam, a political indictment that connects America's history of Manifest Destiny to its imperialist endeavors in the twentieth century. Similarly, Susan Power's *The Grass Dancer* (1994), which tells the story of an ancestral spirit that returns to help the contemporary generation navigate their colonized existence and find pathways toward healing, shows how returning to the past can help one negotiate the political realities of the present. Likewise, Louise Halfe's book-length poem, *Blue Marrow* (1998), invokes the voices of the *kôhkomak*, the Grandmothers, to reconstruct the history of the fur trade from the perspectives of Cree female ancestral spirits.[2] In retelling this history, Halfe not only demonstrates the importance of maintaining a connection to traditional Cree beliefs by invoking the Grandmothers, but also shows how recovering traditional rituals can empower Cree women in the present. Warren Cariou (2006) asserts that while the ghostly Grandmothers' stories are meant "to heal the present generation," they also communicate an ethical imperative to the descendants of the colonizers: "to *do* something to acknowledge and to redress the wrongs of the past" (727).

By positioning their recovery and (re)vision of the past within tribal worldviews—and specifically, by using phantasmic elements as the means by which historical knowledge is recovered—these texts ask readers to take the tribal worldviews expressed within them seriously.

The tribal cosmologies and ceremonies that one encounters in Native American narratives imbue the process of recovery with political significance by providing "a pathway" that leads "readers to a more complete understanding of Native history, ideas, and rights" (Coulombe 2011, 19). Indeed, it is only by opening ourselves up to worldviews that differ from that which an Enlightenment rationality allows that we can fully understand, and respond appropriately to, Native American stories of trauma. The prosocial bent of such works is underscored by the fact that the phantasmic events in the texts, particularly those that are connected to spectral presences, do not simply function as reminders of the past; rather, "they very often demand something of the future" (Boyd and Thrush 2011, 14). This demand, Boyd and Thrush argue, is political in nature: specifically, they demand recognition of the "cultural and historical experience of colonialism . . . [and] the places and territories they inhabit" (xxxv). I would go further to add that these spectral presences, which manifest in myriad ways as phantasmic irruptions, also entreat reader engagement, not only in terms of recognizing the historical wounds that they communicate, but also as a summons to acknowledge our responsibility to past, present, and future generations of Native Americans.

THE ROLE OF THE READER IN PHANTASMIC NATIVE AMERICAN TEXTS

Reader engagement is paramount for Native writers. Catherine Rainwater (1999) writes that Native authors have made "deliberate efforts . . . to foster solidarity with a non-Indian audience" (36). Similarly, Joseph L. Coulombe (2011) argues that "contemporary [Native] narratives actively reach out to mold readers into better informed participants in a pluralistic world community" (7). Despite (or perhaps because of) the fact that "many readers of Native American fiction are non-Native," Coulombe explains, "[c]ontemporary Native authors address them in their own language—sometimes literally, often culturally. The experiences and philosophies they share with readers are expressions of self-definition and outreach, and they risk much . . . particularly considering the history of Native/white relations" (1–2). He adds that "for non-Indian readers, Native-authored publications represent both an invitation and a test" (2). In fact, "refusing to respond," Coulombe cautions, renders the reader "a type of enemy" (2). This is not to presume, however, that the Native experience exists for the consumption and edification of its non-Native reading audience. Certain aspects of Native tradition and ritual are always withheld from texts by indigenous authors so that they remain exclusively Native. Indeed, although many contemporary Native texts refer to or adapt sacred ceremonies, songs, and rituals, the extent to which readers are invited into tribal cultural worlds is limited, due in part to concerns that the disclosure of certain Native traditions to non-Native readers may lead to a repetition of "the cultural misappropriation and dispossession that has taken place over the past five centuries" (Coulombe 2011, 4). As a result, many Native people are wary of outsiders who seek to learn about traditional beliefs and sacred traditions. Sherman Alexie (1997) in particular is adamant in this regard: "We shouldn't be writing about our traditions, we shouldn't be writing about our spiritual practices. . . . [Y]ou also have to be aware that it's going to be taken and used in ways that you never intended for it to be. I think it's dangerous, and that's really why I write about day-to-day life" (15–16). Alexie's call for a prohibition on writing about indigenous traditions and rituals stems from a desire to prevent their appropriation and misuse by non-Native readers. However, as Coulombe and Rainwater show, a significant number of Native authors walk a middle line, providing general readers just enough information and context to understand the narrative worlds into which they enter (Coloumbe 2011, 6; Rainwater 1999, 36–37). In so doing, they foster solidarity with readers while at the same time protecting sacred tribal practices from appropriation by non-Natives.

By supplying important contextual information, Native phantasmic novels like Howe's *Miko Kings* (2007), Erdrich's *The Round House* (2012), and Hausman's *Riding the Trail of Tears* (2011) offer readers a new way of thinking about themselves in relation to indigenous history, as well as in relation to Native Americans in the present day. The effort of Native American authors to reach diverse audiences is important not only for the way that it contributes to the development of a cross-cultural dialogue (sometimes just between text and reader, but sometimes between Native and non-Native characters in the text), but also because it functions as a form of activism, a way of establishing what Jeffrey C. Alexander (2004) calls a "trauma claim," which functions as a call for recognition and reparation (12). In an essay commemorating the twentieth anniversary of his call for pan-Indian literary nationalism, Simon Ortiz (2004) writes: "By our acknowledgement and affirmation, we are empowered, basically and simply because knowledge shared with each other and gained from each other through communication is empowerment. We communicate with others because we need to empower ourselves, especially as Indigenous peoples" (113–14). Ortiz emphasizes the idea that such communication is not only intertribal, but also intercultural. By articulating their cultural and historical perspectives in literature that speaks to Native and non-Native readers alike, indigenous writers empower themselves and their communities, and reshape the historiographic record from an indigenous perspective.

Through her use of the phantasmic, Howe initiates readers into the Choctaw cosmological and cultural perspective. As a participatory audience—what P. Gabrielle Foreman (1995) calls "extended listeners"—readers become inclined to "imbibe the cosmology" of the indigenous community portrayed in the novel (298). Moreover, because readers are guided through the story from the perspective of a first-person narrator, they encounter the traumatic past at the same time and in the same way as *Miko Kings'* Lena does. By inviting readers to engage the world of the novel from Lena's perspective, Howe creates opportunities for empathic response and ethical engagement. Further, the Choctaw lens through which we encounter the narrative world of *Miko Kings* not only amplifies our awareness of Native culture and history, but also highlights the intersections among Native and African American histories of oppression and displacement.

For Howe, Native survival—and, more broadly, human survival—depends on our ability to make connections across monologic sociopolitical and cultural boundaries. Howe draws on a traditional Native understanding of being in the world to show that all things and peoples are fundamentally interconnected. She sees this "propensity for bringing things together, for making consensus, and for symbiotically connecting one thing to another" as a hallmark of traditional Native storytelling (Howe 2002, 42). Further, she argues that this Native tendency to highlight the interconnectedness of all things is best expressed for diverse contemporary audiences in tribalography, a mode of writing that "links Indians and non-Indians" (42). As Howe explains, tribalography connects multiple facets of Native life to the surrounding world and to time, the "past, present, and future milieus," and specifies that "present and future milieus mean non-Indians" (42). The tribalography provides a bridge both within and between cultural groups, pulling "together all the elements of the storyteller's tribe, meaning the people, the land, multiple characters, and all their manifestations and revelations" in a world that also includes non-Natives (Howe 2008a, 330). At the foundation of the tribalography, then, is the notion that historical and tribal events can be "synthesized" with "what is happening now" (Rader 2011, 76). In short, tribalography is a literary form that Native authors can use to show that "localized narratives of the past can contextualize—even if they don't explain—episodes of the present" (76).

When a Native text employs supernatural irruptions to highlight the intersection of the historical and the contemporary, we can see the project of the tribalography and the phantasmic narrative as intersecting and complementary. However, where Howe's conception of tribalography works primarily to highlight the interconnectedness of all things, the phantasmic trauma narrative takes this a step further to show how the fantastic intersections of past and present give rise to an ethical summons that emerges from the intersubjective counter of text and reader, self and other. *Miko Kings* represents an intersection of these two modes of writing; that is, it is a phantasmic tribalography. As I show in my analysis of the novel, the phantasmic tribalography facilitates the forging of connections between readers and tribally specific histories, and, even more importantly, provides ways for readers to reassess the past from a Choctawan cosmological and storytelling perspective to imagine a better future for Native/non-Native relations.

THE PHANTASMIC POWER OF LANGUAGE

> "She said, everything is related
> Everything is past and present
> Everything is future
> Something survives and endures, huh?"
> —LeAnne Howe, "The Unknown Women" (2005)

Howe (2002) defines tribalography as "a story that links Indians and non-Indians" (46). More specifically, she contends that Native stories "create" and "expand" tribal identities by showing the ways in which Indians and non-Indians are linked both historically and in the present. Because such intercultural encounters are often founded in a shared understanding of language, Howe infuses her primarily English-based texts with powerful Choctaw words and traditions, many of which when translated communicate to the non-Choctaw reader concepts sacred to the Choctaw people. Beyond highlighting the phantasmic qualities of the Choctaw language—such as the ability to permit time travel, or even construct reality—the novel uses the moments of its translation by Choctaw speakers to English speakers as a way of modeling intercultural communication to its readers. Moreover, the novel's translation of Choctaw into English invites non-Native readers to view the world through a Choctaw perspective, and in so doing creates opportunities for empathic engagement on the part of the audience. The novel's phantasmic elements—including Ezol and Lena's ability to exist in multiple dimensions as "moving bod[ies] in Choctaw space" (Howe 2007, 221)—suggest a permeability of history and time that reflects a Choctawan worldview, one that is intricately linked with the mechanics of the Choctaw language and the land itself. As Howe (2010) notes, "Choctaw language is almost always present tense and moving. . . . [T]he past is ever-present whether it's through the ceremonies, ghosts, or land" (219). Underscoring the connection between the language and the people, Howe continues, is the "land," which "is a wonderful space in physics that is all things at once—past, present, and future" (219). *Miko Kings'* emphasis on the spiritual significance of place and time for the Choctaw people, as well as its careful efforts to contextualize the fictional events of the novel within the broader scope of the Choctaw struggle for recognition and sovereignty, creates the conditions whereby ethical engagement with the suffering of the Native other—that is, feeling for the suffering of the other while respecting the alterity of the other—becomes possible.

The way that the novel connects Native and non-Natives in a phantasmic tribalography recalls the way that the Choctaw nation has traditionally viewed itself in relation to non-Choctaws. As Donna L. Akers (2008) argues, "Relations with outsiders were a fundamental facet of Choctaw being. . . . Relations with outsiders followed the precepts of kinship, and to Choctaws, these relations were not a parody of kinship relations, but were, in fact, actual kinship realized" (129). Just as tribalography seeks to "symbiotically [connect] one thing to another" (Howe 2002, 42), so too does the Choctaw worldview maintain that "everything in life—the physical, mental, abstract, and concrete—[is] of one functional whole, one system that tie[s] every being together in permanent yet ever dynamic relationships" (Akers 2008, 130). According to the logic of this belief system, Akers (2008) asserts, "if all were partners in an interconnected system, one could not act without affecting all others"; thus, "balance and harmony" were seen as fundamental to the survival of the community and the individual (130). Indian removal, as the white settlers called it, upset this sense of balance for the Choctaw, as a result creating "moral and spiritual crises intimately linked to fundamental Choctaw beliefs about place, origin, and identity" (130). Nonetheless, the Choctaws rebuilt their lives in Indian Territory by restoring their communities, reviving old stories, and creating new ones to face the challenges of life in a strange land. Howe's novel reflects this sense of indomitability in its excavation of the recent Choctaw past and the story of baseball in Indian Territory. Her critical use of history makes the past useful for the present by calling up forgotten ceremonies and traditions that were used, and can be used again or remade, to witness and resist oppression.

For Howe, the primary means of resisting the corrosive aspects of mainstream society is by telling stories that preserve and celebrate Native culture, language, and spiritual traditions. Echoing Umberto Eco, Howe (2008b) suggests that "the intangible power of stories—whether based on events or non-events—creates our cultural stories" (45). She argues that the "impact of [Choctaw] stories is still reverberating throughout [Choctaw] lands" (26). More important than the historical authenticity of a story, Howe maintains, is its ability to impact readers (or listeners) in an emotional way. However, unlike European stories, which focus on individual characters and circumstances, Native American stories "tell of certain epitomizing events," such as the creation of the world or the migration of a tribe (27). The significance of these "core narratives," Howe laments, has been diminished by mainstream culture's use of negatively charged words such as "myth," "legend," "lore," and "tale" to characterize Native stories. The prevalence of this dismissive attitude toward Native stories has permitted the dominance of white historiographic narratives of the Native past, accounts that, because they purport to be based on "evidence," have greater currency in the mainstream. For Howe, the dismissive attitude of the mainstream toward Native ways of preserving and telling history is ironic, especially given the developments in postmodern aesthetics that have begun to reshape the way that white mainstream writers (re)visit and (re)evaluate the past: "American novels in the last twenty-five years that began to use a splintered storytelling style with multiple characters and multiple points of view" are the result of "the land teaching people here how to understand and talk through that space" (Howe 2010, 216–17). She argues: "American literature is moving towards a more tribal [storytelling] space. . . . It's based on indigenous ways of telling, not the other way around" (Howe 2010, 217). Through tribalography, she suggests, we can use these indigenous modes of storytelling as a way of bringing people together across ethnic and cultural divides.

Like a growing number of contemporary Native American stories that return to the past intent on dispelling lies by uncovering painful truths, Howe's *Miko Kings* tells of the moment of allotment in Indian Territory from a Choctaw point of view.[3] Instead of presenting a single, totalizing view of the Choctaw past, however, the text offers a number of different perspectives to engage readers in a task that mirrors Lena's archival research: namely, to piece together stories about past events to gain a better sense of "everything that happened" (46). We gain access to these stories through Ezol, Lena's ancestor, who traverses the boundaries of time to teach her about Choctaw history and to challenge traditional historical accounts of that past. What permits Ezol's travel is the Choctaw language, which because of its rootedness in a nonlinear concept of time (it lacks verb tenses) acts as a quantum bridge that provides her passage through the boundaries of time and space. Although traditional Choctaw stories do not account for time travel in the way that Ezol performs it, the tribal narratives nevertheless convey a belief in supernatural occurrences. As Tom Mould (2012) writes, for the Choctaw, "[supernatural] creatures and events are unusual but not unexpected. Rather than relegate them to superstition, supernatural beings are integrally situated within Choctaw belief systems about power, medicine, and human nature" (94). Thus, while the recorded Choctaw stories do not reflect Ezol's experience, the Choctaw worldview does not exclude it as a possibility. In its function as a tribalography that connects "past, present, and future milieus" of the Choctaw people (Howe 2002, 42), *Miko Kings* "moves us away from colonialist habits of thought and toward a recalibration of our minds and hearts to see the science in a Choctawan way . . . a Native way of seeing science" (Meland 2014, 31). Because the text explicitly roots Ezol's time travel in Choctaw linguistics, we can read it as a phantasmic event, and further, a physical manifestation of the tribalography's fusion of past, present, and future.

True to its form as a tribalography, *Miko Kings* relies on multiple narrators from the past and present to tell the story of an early twentieth-century baseball team in Oklahoma Indian Territory: the Miko Kings. Although the novel's chapters present readers with a broad geographical range, from the Hampton Normal School for Blacks and Indians in Virginia down to New Orleans and even faraway Jordan, the primary action of the text takes place in present-day Oklahoma, the post-Removal homeland of the Choctaw people. Embedded within *Miko Kings* are the traumatic touchstones that dominated the Native American experience in the late nineteenth and early twentieth centuries: the struggles of reservation life, the further dispossession wrought by the Dawes Act, and the processes of deculturalization endured by those who attended Indian boarding schools. Even as it addresses these systemic issues, the novel also exposes more acute, but no less painful forms of oppression by juxtaposing the deceptive practices of politicians and bureaucrats who sought to acquire Choctaw land with the terrorism of the Ku Klux Klan. In so doing, the text reveals the myriad ways in which the Choctaw people struggled against forces of oppression as both individuals and as a tribe.

However, as a tribalography, *Miko Kings* "recounts not only the tensions that existed among these different groups, but also the political and familial alliances that continued despite, or at times because of, these tensions" (Romero 2014, 16). For example, the relationship between Choctaw pitcher Hope Little Leader and Justina Maurepas, his black Indian lover, suggests an intersection between Native American and African American histories of oppression and displacement: the characters meet at Hampton Normal School, and they are both terrorized by the Klan as the result of their interracial relationship. Yet even as the multiple narratives create a record of violence and loss, they also, in keeping with Howe's vision of tribalography, document positive alliances to "provide useful models for contemporary resistance" (23). Examples include the way that Choctaw characters welcome the multiracial Justina Maurepas and her cousin Beauregard Hash into their community, or the friendship that arises between Ezol and Mary O'Brien in response to their shared persecution by the Ku Klux Klan.[4] Through its use of multiple narrators and its emphasis on "making consensus" across cultural and ethnic lines, *Miko Kings* encourages cross-cultural engagement (Howe 2002, 42).

If the text's function as a tribalography and its emphasis on cross-cultural affiliations are most fully articulated in the relationships described above, the phantasmic core of the novel is located in the cultural education of its principal character, Lena Coulter, a Choctaw journalist who is disconnected from her Native heritage and, in particular, her own family history. It is through

Lena's encounter with the time-traveling Ezol Day—who teaches Lena about her tribal language and history—that we most vividly encounter Choctaw history. The story begins with Lena's return to her hometown of Ada, Oklahoma, after years living abroad in the Middle East. While refurbishing her grandmother's home, she finds an old leather pouch in the wall full of newspaper clippings, journal entries, letters, and photographs, all dated from around the turn of the last century. Intrigued by a photo of the all-Native Miko Kings baseball team, Lena puts her skills as a journalist to good use by conducting archival research to discover more about the team and its players. Soon, however, she finds herself assisted in this task by Ezol, who has time traveled from the early twentieth century to teach Lena about the Miko Kings and forgotten elements of her Choctaw heritage. In the process, Lena discovers that baseball, long considered the quintessential "all-American" pastime, locates its roots in the traditional Choctaw game of "base and ball" (39); more importantly, though, she discovers as the result of this experience the power of stories to connect people and cultures across the distance of time and space. As Lena gains knowledge about the history of Indian baseball, she also learns that the past, which in its distance from us seems abstract, is in fact deeply personal. Lena's phantasmic encounters with Ezol lead her on a journey of self-discovery and force her to confront her family's own traumatic legacy of discrimination, neglect, and assimilation.

Given Howe's faith in the power of stories to literally make the past come alive—"Our stories are unending connections to the past, present, and future" (Howe 2002, 47)—it is not surprising that *Miko Kings* hinges on written and spoken stories that are exchanged between characters from both the past and the present. Indeed, the novel's emphasis on the importance of storytelling is in keeping with a trend that Irene Visser, Susan Y. Najita, and others have observed in postcolonial trauma narratives: that is, that "postcolonial literature provides many examples that support the claim that trauma itself instigates a strong need for narrative," both oral and written, "to come to terms with the aftermath of colonial wounding" (Najita 2006, 257). In Howe's work, storytelling serves an additional function; it not only facilitates healing, but also provides an opportunity for connection across boundaries of time, space, and even cultures.

The sense of interconnectedness that arises from storytelling is most clearly expressed in the novel's emphasis on transformative abilities of language and "the dynamic nature of Choctaw time" (Howe 2008a, 337) as instruments of Native survival that transcend the oppression of mainstream American culture, as well as the artificial boundaries imposed by white notions of time and space. *Miko Kings* asserts that the Choctaw language, in both its written and spoken forms, has the power to "open a passage to another time and space" (43), and therefore renders "time ... at the mercy of the speaker" (139). In the world of the novel, the past exists not as a precursor to the present, but rather exists simultaneously alongside the present. The text's fascination with language and its emphasis on a Native understanding of time anchors the reader in the Choctaw worldview. For Chanette Romero (2012), the emphasis on chronological time works like Howe's can be read as an attempt to root "the temporalities of people of color within historical materiality. Continually recounting the year and time of day keeps the novels focused on historical conditions for people of color, presenting stories about ancestor . . . spirits as real to readers who might want to see them as fantastic" (59). Romero continues by suggesting that the presentation of non-Western notions of time provides an opportunity for readers to "reflect critically on how their concepts of time and the past relate to specific ideologies and actions based on those ideologies" (59). I would go further to add that the reader's initiation into a Choctawan view of time serves as both a reminder of the damage wrought by colonialism—that is, the wholesale discrediting by Western culture of indigenous belief systems—as well as a gesture toward how reparation and recovery can be aided by non-Natives, which is not by laying claim to an understanding of Native ways of being and knowing, but rather by appreciating and respecting that such alternatives to Western belief systems have value.

When Ezol explains the distinctions between Western and Choctaw notions of time to Lena, she invites readers to acknowledge the relativity of time as a cultural concept. This gesture is important on two levels: first, it facilitates reader engagement by positing the phantasmic events in the novel as possible, rather than fantastic. Second, it helps readers to reflect critically on the ways in which the Western understanding of time—which Jacqui Alexander (2005) characterizes as "constrictively linear and resolutely hierarchical" (189)—has been used to justify Native American dispossession and genocide. Vine Deloria, Jr., (1973) goes further to argue that "Western European identity involves the assumption that time proceeds in linear fashion; further it assumes that at a particular point in the unraveling of this sequence, the peoples of Western Europe became the guardians of the world" (62). Indeed, the circularity of the plot, which is manifested both in the recurrence of narrative voices and in the oscillation between past and presence, rejects Western constructions of linear time. Ezol, whose "Choctaw theorem of time" recognizes this disparity between European and Choctaw notions of time, insists that this is the way it should be; indeed, she "question[s] why we should expect our [Choctaw] ancestors to synchronize their time with our modern clocks, which are set and reset by the political whims of English speakers" (39). Much of the project of the novel, then, is to restore Choctaw valuations of time by connecting readers to a time when members of the tribe still adhered to traditional beliefs, beliefs that would soon be endangered by encroachments on the Choctawan way of life with the allotment of tribal lands and the admission of the state of Oklahoma into the Union. Further, by juxtaposing chapters from the past and the present, the novel encourages readers to see the continuity of history from a Choctawan perspective.

The refusal of Native history to be silenced, like the sudden appearance of Ezol, signifies an issue that lies at the heart of the phantasmic tribalography: the precarious relationship between the tribal past and the American present. Although Ezol does offer what would resemble, for the Western mind, something of a scientific explanation for her sudden appearance—hinting at one point that her presence could possibly be explained by her quantum physics theory of time, space, and culture propounded in a 1905 essay entitled "Moving Bodies in Choctaw Space"—the mechanics of her time travel are never explained (38). However, for Ezol, Choctaw ceremonies, rituals, and belief are not divorced from the laws of nature, but rather stem from the Choctaws' "deep spiritual and physical attachment to the earth," and their belief that the land—"the numinous presence of the divine, the sacred, the truly real by reference to which everything else found its orientation"—is the source of all power (Akers 2008, 130). Ezol tells Lena that "embedded in [Choctaw] rituals and games are mathematical codes that harness cosmic forces" (43). She elaborates: "Choctaw language doesn't distinguish 'science' from 'the sacred'" since both can be credited with the power to "split the clouds and open a passage to another time and space." And while Ezol never fully discloses the intricacies of her theoretical argument—which Lena describes as "elegantly reasoned" and thus appealing to Western sensibilities (38)—Ezol does cryptically reveal other secrets about the power of Choctaw words: "The logic I used in my Choctaw theorem of time is built around verbs" (39). Here, Ezol explains that because the Choctaw language lacks verb tenses that connote a linear progression of time, it permits speakers to experience other moments in time. This linguistic embodiment of a nonlinear, contiguous temporality is contrasted with the language of the Americans, who "live by the clock and the sword" (42) and "set and reset" clocks according to "political whims" (39). Ezol's characterization of American culture operates on two levels: first, it functions as a cultural-linguistic comparison by suggesting that English speakers are unable to move between different dimensions in the manner of Choctaw speakers because they are too consumed with the task of measuring, fixing, and enforcing time. Second, it functions as self-reflexive comment on the phantasmic quality of the text itself: just as Choctaw permits its speakers to transcend space-time boundaries and experience different periods of history, so do Choctaw cultural beliefs facilitate the connections between epochs that the tribalography seeks to forge.

Thus aided by Ezol, we move phantasmically through the novel's different temporalities, and like Lena, we learn about aspects of Choctaw history that have been occluded by official historiographic accounts. In the "the textual space" that she helps Lena to craft, Ezol creates a literary and literal past" for Native and non-Native readers alike (Howe 2002, 46). Because she restores Choctaw history, Ezol becomes what Kathleen Brogan (1998) calls a "reconstructive agent," both in the world of the text and in the mind of the reader (32). As Ezol tells Lena, "Choctaws and Chickasaws are renowned for their ability to rebuild. . . . We seem to manifest nature itself, as re-creators" (34). And it is through the novel's cycles of life and death, creation and destruction, that we see the power of this idea manifested. As the novel makes clear, however, it is by striving to learn about the past that these acts of (re-)creation are made possible.

For Ezol, as for Howe, language—specifically, the Choctaw language—is connected to experience. Ezol's easy access to the worlds of the past and present are made possible by her manipulation of words: "We have evidence in our language that our people experience other dimensions through our uses of particles and verbs which attend to specific movements in and out of spacetime" (39). Ezol makes clear that stories—and the words used to communicate those stories—contain the power to make different dimensions of being intersect. Because, Ezol explains, "the Choctaw language does not "distinguish between past and present" (37), she and Lena "are intimately linked by the motion of story" (221). Consequently, we can see how the use of Choctaw words in the novel functions as an important intersection between the past and present, made possible through a Choctawan view of physical laws that is inextricably linked to Choctawan linguistics. The "story" whose "motion" connects Ezol and Lena is that which they author together. Because the story they create is one that blurs the boundaries of time, one of the issues that the novel asks readers to consider is the role of narrative itself as a phantasmic force capable not only of preserving collective memories of the past, but also of making readers (or listeners) recognize the ethical implications of that past. In this equation, the author—whether Howe herself, or her literary doppelganger, Lena (whose name is an anagram of LeAn[ne])—functions as conduit for a type of cultural history that seeks to move readers beyond passivity into ethical thinking.

Lena describes her participation as a co-creator of the text that we are reading in this way:

> [Ezol] is the narrator; I the medium, intermediary, stenographer, and servant to the story. My work as translator feeds this apparition. . . . To be any good at translation, you have to do a kind of disappearing act. Teach yourself to become invisible by breathing life onto the page, and then exist there, side by side with the words and images. (24)

Lena's description of her responsibility as a translator echoes Howe's (2008a) preface to her story of Embarrassed Grief in "Blind Bread": "To be any good at translation, one must do a kind of disappearing act, which, in a way, signifies the trope of Native existence in America. We remain invisible.

Yet we continue" (325). It is this "disappearing act" that we witness when Lena's narrative abruptly switches in time and space to explore the present-tense perspectives of the novel's historical characters: Hope Little Leader (a Miko Kings pitcher), Justina Maurepas (Hope's black Indian lover), Henri Day (a Choctaw entrepreneur and owner of the Miko Kings), and even Ezol Day. Carter Meland (2007) points out that "it's critical to note that unlike most works of fiction, where the convention is to write in the simple past tense, Ezol's story is told all in the present tense, as is Hope Little Leader's—the past is in the present tense in their stories and memories, these dimensions are not separate but pump through the other" (229). These textual movements through time gradually render Lena an invisible presence in the narratives of the other characters, a silent observer who only resurfaces when the narrative returns to the present.

Further, if time, as Ezol informs Lena, is "like a majestic dance" moving "forward or backward or sideways . . . form[ing] multiple patterns that intersect" (44), then Lena's story, which forms the text of *Miko Kings,* is the phantasmic point of access, the wormhole through which we access the different narratives and historical periods of each of the novel's characters. Just as Ezol is able to time travel into Lena's present "but also [be] in another time and space" (44), so too are readers able to occupy the site where the past and present "intersect" (45). Thus, while it is unclear whether or not Lena is able to literally replicate Ezol's journeys through space-time, her submersion in the stories of the past obfuscates our view of her present-time consciousness. The seeming disappearance of Lena from the narrative does not alienate readers, but rather provides them the opportunity to engage the text's historical narratives without the mediation of her perspective; that is, we do not witness her witnessing, but rather become witnesses ourselves. Indeed, if Lena's invisibility as writer/translator is meant to signify the broader invisibility of Native Americans, our association with her as the present-day "intermediary" in the phantasmic trauma narrative means that we, too, are asked to experience that invisibility during the act of reading. Read another way, the unobtrusive posture that the text asks us to assume is an ethical orientation that carries with it acceptance of ethical responsibility, which "turns us toward [the trauma], allows us to face it and bear witness to it without proposing that we understand it" (Osborne 2018, 96). We, as readers, are invited bear witness to the trauma of the Choctaw past, even to feel for the suffering of others while doing so, while being reminded of the other's alterity and our inability to truly understand.

If we agree with Jill Robbins (1999) that "ethics is something that 'happens' in language," we can read Howe's extensive illustrations of the temporal, spiritual, and coalition-building capacities of the Choctaw language as a strategy for summoning the reader into an ethical orientation with the characters and the history that they, through writings and interactions with one another, convey (54). The novel charges Ezol, whose equal knowledge of Choctaw and English renders her linguistically liminal, with the task of bearing culture across language divides. For Ezol, the act of linguistic translation is also an act of cultural translation, and vice versa; indeed, language and culture are inextricably linked in the Choctaw imagination. For example, in response to Lena's desire to learn more about the Miko Kings than the scant historical record can reveal, Ezol shares what she knows about the team, but does so by emphasizing particular Choctaw words and concepts.

In fact, it is when Ezol attempts to emphasize the crucial importance of baseball as a tribal ritual and a site of Native resistance and identity that she introduces her radical theory connecting Choctaw linguistics and physics, so that the two become symbolically linked in the reader's imagination. As Ezol explains to Lena, the Choctaw language offers avenues of access to the past and ways of thinking about the world that the English language is not capable of expressing:

> "I was right about analyzing language as the way into my theorem of time. The laws of physics do not distinguish between past and present. Neither does the Choctaw language, at least not in the way that English does. Choctaw verbs have a much broader application, which shades the meaning in ways that English verbs cannot. Take for instance the word *chifitokchaya*."
> "I don't know what it means."
> "Run and live," she says.
> "That's a hard one to imagine," I say.
> "Not if you're a batter on third," says Ezol. "Now what do you see when I say *chifitokchaya*?"
> "A baseball player running for home plate!" I say, excited. (37)

Here, Ezol introduces Lena to the complexities of the Choctaw language system and philosophy by way of analogy, drawing on common knowledge that spans their two temporal dimensions. This illustration is important because it demonstrates the highly figurative qualities of the Choctaw language, and the way in which this specialized linguistic form constitutes an integral part of a shared tribal identity. Indeed, "language, rules of grammar, and meaning are the agreement of a particular group based on their practiced experience" (37). Ezol continues by explaining: "I theorized that Choctaws didn't have the same experiences with time as those of Europeans because we speak differently" (37). To "speak differently," perhaps, is to come from opposing backgrounds and cultures. Ezol argues that the English and Choctaw languages are "in conflict." Here, Ezol does more than teach Lena the Choctaw language; she shows Lena the symbolic importance of language in relation to Choctaw identity and history, and demonstrates what would be lost if it did not survive. By translating the words and concepts into English,

Ezol creates spaces for non-Native readers to engage and learn about Choctaw beliefs and customs.

However, it is important to note that the novel does not "redeem" Choctaw customs and language "through explanation" (Meland et al. 2005, 401); rather, what traditions and translations the novel discloses to non-Native readers are communicated by way of a limited invitation into the Choctaw worldview.

When Lena struggles to grasp the sophisticated interrelation between Choctaw cosmology and linguistics, Ezol offers another example:

> "Consider this. *Okchamali* is the Choctaw word for both blue and green.... Its roots appear in the Choctaw word *okchanya,* meaning 'alive.' Now, where did our people originate? Answer: a world of blue sky and green swamplands, a watery place. So perhaps *okchamali* relates to 'place' as 'alive.'"
>
> "Or 'lived,' as in past tense?" ...
>
> "Not past tense, exactly," she says. "*Okchamali* could be a description of a place name of a primeval epoch when the sky and sea were so close that there was almost no atmosphere in between. In Choctaw it is the subtle shading, the intensity and grayness, the dullness or brilliance of a thing that determines how it is spoken of. Our language marked the dullness of the sky *in that place* at that particular time.... *Okchamali* then becomes a descriptive remnant, the color of a time that the ancient Choctaws experienced, or, most likely, knew of. *Okchamali,* then, signifies *life*." (38)

Ezol does not simply refer to the Choctaw language's economical use of color signifiers, but rather emphasizes how for Choctaw speakers linguistic signifiers connote cosmological significations. As Ezol explains, *okchamali* is not just a word that denotes two colors, but also recalls the "primordial" moment; for the Choctaw, then, the word for "blue" and "green" evokes their place of origin and signifies their very existence. Because of its indubitable association with a moment in time, Ezol describes *okchamali* as a "space-time term" (39), one capable of linking the speaker to the source of Choctaw identity and cosmology. Further, by translating this term for Lena, Ezol communicates an origin story, and, perhaps most importantly, offers Lena the words to share it with others. In this act of storytelling, Ezol demonstrates the importance of not only using the Choctaw language, but also recognizing the deep cultural and spiritual meanings attached to Choctaw words. As Ezol shows us, "equations" contained in the speech act connect individuals to history and words (or, by extension, texts) to experience.[5] The idea that the equations embedded in language can "connect us to other dimensions" is illustrated in the way that Ezol's story, like those of all the other historical figures in the text, is narrated in the present tense. Further, by offering the reader a small but significant insight into Choctaw language and history, the novel involves the reader more fully in its phantasmic world, and in so doing opens up spaces for ethical thinking about Native American experiences.

LANGUAGE, HISTORY, AND BASEBALL

Lena, perhaps like the reader, is perplexed by the complicated web of connections that Ezol illustrates between Choctaw cosmology, language, and ritual: "I don't really understand physics, the etymology of our language, or moving bodies in space" (39). And anticipating a likely reader response, she struggles to understand how Ezol's Choctaw theory of time relates to the novel's central story, the history of the Miko Kings baseball team. "What," Lena asks, "does all this have to do with the Miko Kings and baseball?" Ezol explains that baseball is a sacred game, one not to be confused "with the one that's been assimilated into America's consciousness" (43). It contains, she continues, "sacred geometric expressions," the same "spacetime terms" as those embedded in the Choctaw language (39). The symbolic meaning of the game is crucial to the novel's ethical project: as Howe argues, baseball is "an Indian creation story" that "demands the participation of everyone," regardless of racial difference (Meland et al. 2005, 392). As the intertribal makeup of the Miko Kings suggests—there are Choctaw, Chickasaw, Cherokee, Creek, and Seminole players on the team—baseball is a game that unites people across tribal and cultural divides and predates European contact (modern baseball locates its roots in the traditional Native American game of base-and-ball, sometimes referred to as stickball).[6] "Base-and-ball," explains Ezol, "was a game that was played on every ancient square ground in the southeast.... Natives played variations of the game all over North and South America long before white people ever arrived in the New World. From the mound, a pitcher was the embodiment of the center pole that could access the Middle, Upper, and Lower Worlds" (39). And though entertaining, the sport also held political significance by "help[ing] with diplomacy between tribes" (40). Like tribalography, the goal of baseball is "to bring people together from diverse backgrounds to produce knowledge. To create" (391). Thus, the sport plays a crucial role in helping Howe to illustrate the kind of cultural synergy that the tribalography suggests because it functions both as a site of cultural exchange and as a site of resistance.

To understand how baseball gradually assumed importance as a site of Native resistance, it is important to understand its changing cultural significance over the course of the late nineteenth and early twentieth centuries. Although Natives from the Southeast had been playing the game generations before the incursion of white settlers, renewed hostilities "between the U.S. Cavalry and tribes on the Great Plains" in the 1880s inspired "tribal nations in Indian Territory" to form baseball teams and "[battle] it out on the prairie diamond" (Meland et al. 2005, 409). A few decades earlier, the game, stripped of its Native associations, had gained popularity with whites, and with a few tweaks to the rules, was gradually transformed into a tool of assimilation. Greg Ahrenhoerster (2004) explains that by the early part of the twentieth century, "Native American children were *forced* to play the sport at the boarding schools many were required to attend" (57). Ironically, for Hope Little Leader, playing baseball becomes a means of survival at Hampton Normal School for Blacks and Indians, where "Indian students are trapped" and "teachers discourage personal beliefs, rituals, and traditions" (62). As we learn, Hope "was placed at Hampton" because, as the nephew of the famous ballplayer Ahojebo Little Leader, the school's administrators wanted him "to play on Hampton's baseball team" (63). And true to Hope's declaration that he will "get out of [Hampton]" and "play ball like [his] uncle" (66), he returns to his tribal lands in Indian Territory and, like his uncle before him, learns how to harness the sacred power of the game, stepping out of time and moving between worlds to "collaborate with nature" when assuming his position on the pitcher's mound (44). Thus, baseball provides Hope with both psychological and spiritual support. Further, this sacred game, in which Hope participates and which Ezol explicates, is important for the way that it links people and cultures. While American baseball was founded on exclusionary principles ("The first thing whites did during their civil war was exclude blacks from playing on their baseball teams. Later they excluded Jews" [43]), Native base-and-ball "was created so that we could include everyone. . . . [It was] played [in order] to collaborate with other tribes, the stars, and with the great mystery" (43–44). If the white version of baseball is a "pastime," the Native game is *past time*, a sacred ritual that brings the past and present together and offers the possibility of intercultural collaboration across ethnic and ideological divides.

Despite the appropriation of the game by white mainstream culture, Howe shows that for Natives living in Indian Territory at the turn of the century, baseball was both a way of earning recognition and respect in the white mainstream as well as a declaration of tribal solidarity. As Hope's early mentor, Wild Buck, reminds his team of adolescents, "We aren't just a baseball team—we represent the Choctaw Nation, and whether we win or lose we are the diplomats of our people" (94). However, for Natives in Indian Territory at the time of allotment, tribal solidarity was often realized through intertribal cooperation. This idea is underscored by the intertribal Miko Kings' close affiliation with the Four Mothers Society, described in the novel as "a vibrant, vocal organization opposing the allotting of their lands" (126). Comprising Cherokee, Creek, Choctaw, and Chickasaw members, the Four Mothers society worked together as an intertribal coalition to "find a solution to get out of their [Dawes] allotments and return to traditional ways" (Fixico 2004, 169). Although the organization had been active for the greater part of the nineteenth century,[7] the "Four Mothers incorporated as a dues-paying organization to raise the funds necessary for the relief of the desperate poverty caused by the Dawes Act and to underwrite its most audacious effort yet: the attempt to create a pan-Native American state called Sequoyah out of the Oklahoma Territory" (Mann 1998, 100). Donald L. Fixico (2004) goes further to note that the Four Mothers Society even went so far as to send "a delegation to Washington to try to convince the federal officials to change federal plans to allot the lands . . . and instead to sell [them] so that they could instead purchase lands in Mexico and reestablish the tribes there" (169). Instructed by Ezol to research the society, Lena learns that her family was "heavily involved in the activities of the group, often arranging their meetings at stickball games and tribal baseball games" (126). Further underscoring the connections between the baseball team and the organization is the fact that the "Indian baseball league seems to be a model of the Four Mothers society," with its democratic structure and its emphasis on intertribal cooperation for the greater good of all.

By introducing readers to alternative rituals of diplomacy and political practices by way of stories about the Miko Kings and the Four Mothers Society, the novel asks us to consider how we can learn from these democratic, intertribal models and how we might apply this knowledge in the present. In this way, Howe presents a phantasmic Native history that "seek[s] out Indian agency as a main determinant in America's shared story" (Meland et al. 2005, 392). To fashion a story that features Native characters that are subjects rather than objects, she brings the past forward into the present to show that these figures are truly the agents of their own stories. Although some of what Lena learns about her tribal past is tragic, the novel moves us beyond grief into hope, and, in so doing, renders the past truly usable for future generations of Natives and for interracial readers. The need to move beyond trauma toward recovery and healing that dominates so much of postcolonial trauma fiction also drives this phantasmic narrative, and is ultimately manifested in the novel's emphasis on the idea that language has the power to determine reality, an idea that is deeply rooted in the Choctaw worldview.[8] In keeping with this cosmological tradition, Howe has been clear that this view is not limited to the realm of fiction: "I'm saying flat-out that speech acts create the world around us" (Howe 2010, 219). Ezol echoes this when she informs Lena that "reality is manifest from what we see and how we speak of it" (219). What this suggests for readers, then, is that the world of the novel creates both a metaphorical and literal space within which they can encounter and (re)examine the Choctaw past from a fresh, non-Eurocentric perspective, and to imagine brighter possibilities for the future.

For Howe, empowerment and healing are predicated on reconciliation. Noting that too many Native stories transmit "historic grief," Howe (2006) urges us to "reconcile our past, for peace, for the future." Similarly, Romero

(2014) writes that in order to "create healing in the Americas, we must knead together knowledge of historical atrocities with the material and spiritual significance of people of color's temporalities" (81). Such synthesis, she continues, allows texts to act as metaphoric spaces for healing. This sort of textual healing is modeled for us when Lena rewrites, in a gesture reminiscent of the midrashim we encountered in chapter 2, the ending of the fateful baseball game that the Miko Kings play against the Seventh Cavalry on October 5, 1907. The historical outcome of this game is the mystery that propels the novel's historical plot; as we learn, Hope Little Leader, succumbing to outside pressure, throws the game and sets off a fateful chain of events that include the dissolution of the Indian baseball league, Ezol's tragic death in a fire, and the amputation of his hands by his vengeful teammates when they discover his betrayal. Heeding Ezol's insistence that "words are power" (16), Lena offers us an alternate ending. In Lena's rewriting of the story, instead of throwing the game by "[throwing] a big easy pitch down the middle of the plate" to the opposing team's batter and thereby ensuring their win with "four runs" (198), Hope Little Leader

> winds up, looking straight up into the sun as if in prayer to *Hashtali,* the Choctaw's source of power. He disappears inside it. When he pulls out of the light he throws everything he's got at the Cavalry. Hugh Scott swings again but just tips the ball, and it flies straight into Hope's glove.
> And the roar of Indians can be heard all the way back to Fort Sill, where, after twenty-two years, Geronimo, honored leader of the Apaches, is still a prisoner of war. (218)

In this moment, Howe juxtaposes a moment of Native victory with an important reminder of white oppression in the figure of Geronimo to show that the truth of the Native past is not effaced in the phantasmic writing of Native history. Nor is the story that Lena writes an alternative or substitute history. Indeed, whereas an alternative history is often interpreted as a *counter*narrative that replaces or corrects a substitute history, Lena's story is both real and not real, just as Schrödinger's cat can be both alive and dead at the same time; in short, Lena's story is a parallel history that exists in another dimension.[9] Significantly, she does not keep this history to herself, but rather shares it with others on "the new Miko Kings' weblog" where "dozens of new posts about their historic victory over Fort Sill's Seventh Cavalrymen" have surfaced (220). For this, Ezol applauds her: "You have truly turned back time" (220). Here, Ezol expresses the ethos of tribalography, which posits that we must (re)write and (re)visit the past—"turn back time"—in order to move forward. Significantly, Lena's final act of storytelling takes place on the World Wide Web, a cyber-realm of intercultural encounter that by its very name suggests the ethos of tribalography, an intricate web where "past, present, and future milieus" are linked and comingle. Viewing Lena's story in this tribalographic context demonstrates for readers how reconsidering Native history can provide useful insights for creating a future of mutual acknowledgment, respect, and recognition.

Miko Kings draws on Choctaw beliefs about the power of language to connect people across space and time, and shows how telling and sharing stories are powerful tools for helping people to access stories not documented in historiographic accounts. Although the historical witnessing that occurs in the novel takes place between two Choctaw women, it is evident that Howe is keenly aware of her diverse, potentially non-Native audience in the way that she takes pains to define terms and recount historical events. Just as Ezol leaps forth into Lena's world through her diary, newspaper, and clippings, so too are we invited to think about the text as a phantasmic link into the past, and to consider how reevaluating the past can foster ethical thinking about the Native other in the present. In so doing, *Miko Kings* asks us to explore not only the "ethical consequences" of narration but also the "reciprocal claims binding teller, listener, witness, and reader" and the actions that arise from them (Newton 1995, 11). The simultaneity of past and present that this novel imagines emphasizes the influence of the past in the present, both in terms of oppression and strategies for resisting oppression. Because it permits a present-day character who is disconnected from her tribal past (Lena) to *feel* history in very dramatic and real ways, *Miko Kings* illustrates the impact of history's causality in the present, and invites readers to make connections between the histories that the protagonists are made privy to and the social, cultural, and political institutions of the contemporary moment. As a result, when readers imagine the future unfolding in the context of the novel, it is a broader, more inclusive future.

For Howe, as for the African American and Jewish American writers that I discuss in the previous chapters, the phantasmic trauma narrative offers readers not only felt connections to traumatic history, but also a space in which they can imagine possibilities for social justice. As Jessica Berman (2011) suggests, "Narrative can play a crucial role in bridging the gap between ethics and politics, connecting ethical attitudes and responsibilities—ideas about what we ought to be and do—to active creation of political relationships and just conduct—what is right and possible within the power structures and discourses of our social life and institutions" (5–6). The highly relational character of the phantasmic trauma narrative creates opportunities for readers to take account of alterity and to not only engage in ethical thinking about the subaltern other, but also to imagine social justice. "The ethical demands of alterity," Berman argues, "infuse the narrative situation and the process by which we attempt to respond to it even as the narrative itself takes place as an ethical event between writers and readers that responds to, intervenes in, and changes its rhetorical and social situation" (6). Thus, when readers encounter the "living thought" that Howe recovers in her phantasmic tribalography, they also encounter ethical obligations to the Native past, present, and future.

NOTES

1. Storytelling is central to the development of both the community and the individual. Indeed, as Lee Francis (2003) argues, "for Native People, story was and continues to be essential to an individual's identity construction" (77).

2. Halfe (1998) makes it clear that the Grandmothers are no mere literary device, stating instead that the writing of *Blue Marrow* was guided by their powerful spectral presences: "The prairie is full of bones. The bones stand and sing and I feel the weight of them as they guide my fingers on this page" (2).

3. The Dawes Act in 1887 turned Indian allotment land into private land, which broke up homesteads and left many landless; this, in turn, endangered Choctaw tribal life. See Lambert's *Choctaw Nation* (2007, 19–60).

4. Howe uses this term in her documentary, *Indian Country Diaries: Spiral of Fire* (2006), when she argues that an overemphasis on "historic grief" precludes healing. She proposed that "for healing we must forgive. Together we can reconcile our past for peace, for the future."

5. While English speakers are connected to the world of Choctaw language and thought in *Miko Kings*, this is not to suggest that the Choctaw terms are included solely for the benefit of English speakers. Not all Choctaw terms found in the novel are defined, and some only partially so. Howe is, in fact, quite vague when offering the English equivalents to Choctaw words and concepts. *Ohoyo Holba* is elaborated, but with care. The associations with this word range from "woman-like," to "healer," to "one who is brave or powerful," and it can even be used to describe homosexuality (90). The word is never directly translated for Howe's readers. Choctaw outsiders, at times, seem to be invited to read and learn about specific cherished Choctaw practices and phrases. At other times, they are kept at arm's length. Implying that the Choctaw language is as powerful as Ezol says, Howe seems to suggest that it should be shared with caution.

6. See George Eisen's "Early European Attitudes toward Native American Sports and Pastimes" (1995).

7. There are several minor historical inaccuracies in Howe's account of the Four Mothers Society. Howe quotes Angie Debo's assertion that "the organization began around 1895 and lasted through 1915, roughly the same length of time as the heyday of Indian Territory" (qtd. in Howe 2007, 126) However, Barbara Mann (1998) provides compelling evidence that the group was active for most of the nineteenth century, and suggests that the reason for Angie Debo's belief that the group was not founded until 1895 was due to the fact that the group did not formally incorporate until that time. Further, Donald L. Fixico (2004) indicates that the group lasted well into the mid-1930s (169–70).

8. See Susan Y. Najita's *Decolonizing Cultures in the Pacific* (2006), in which she argues that recovery and redress, often facilitated by political activism, are dominant themes in postcolonial trauma narratives (18).

9. Developed by Erwin Schrödinger, Schrödinger's cat was a thought experiment that attempted "to compare the indeterminacy of the quantum system to the determinism of the classical or macroscopic system we interact with everyday" (Stephenson 290). The experiment imagined a cat in a "sealed box chamber with a flask of hydrocyanic acid . . . a Geiger counter, a hammer, and a tiny bit of radioactive material. . . . If, after an hour, an atom from the radioactive material decays and [is] detected by the Geiger counter, the hammer would be released, striking the flask which would discharge and kill the cat." If the atom decay remained undetected, however, the flask would not be shattered and the cat would remain alive. Schrödinger maintained that "until someone looked, the cat was both dead and alive simultaneously. Only when someone looked did the state of the cat become known as either one or the other" (290). Carter Meland also references Schrödinger's experiment in "Talking Tribalographies" (2014), where he offers an interesting close reading of the relationship between Ezol and

her illustration of the Eye Tree. Meland writes, "Ezol sees the universe in all its angles and all its possible iterations through the medium of the Eye Tree; for her, the eyes on the branches of the tree allow her to track potential resolutions to superposed states across space. She see the alive-cat in the alive-world and the dead-cat in the dead-world" (34).

Chapter Four

Projecting the Phantasmic

Even more powerfully than written narratives, films—particularly those that seek to convey history—have the power to bestow on spectators experiences through which they have not lived and therefore offer them new perspectives regarding the relationship between past and present. The impact of the cinematic experience on the spectator is a dominant theme in film analysis,[1] and much of the scholarship focuses on the way that film can be used as an apparatus to "suture" viewers into unfamiliar worlds (Silverman 1986, 219). In this way, the cinematic process of suture parallels that of the phantasmic trauma narrative, which encourages in readers and viewers the development of a felt connection to the suffering of others. Further, the power of cinema to enfold viewers in new perspectives and immerse them in unfamiliar historical narratives provides compelling opportunities for thinking about the reach of the phantasmic in the space of the cinema.

The characters in the films that I examine in this chapter, like those in the texts that I address in previous chapters, are asked to confront the traumatic events of collective and cultural pasts. Following the chronological and ethnic organization of my previous chapters, I begin by examining *Sankofa* (1993), directed by Haile Gerima, which draws on African beliefs—such as that signified by the Akan *sankofa* symbol—to bridge the temporal divide between the present day and the antebellum past. *Sankofa* tells the story of Mona, a present-day African American woman who, like Dana in *Kindred,* is transported to the traumatic past. Once she returns to the past, however, she is deprived of her postslavery consciousness and instead becomes what the film describes as "a bird of passage," or a *sankofa*, through which the spirit of a dead slave bears witness to her experiences. Next, I turn to the Showtime production of *The Devil's Arithmetic* (1999), which rewrites the Elijah ritual commemorating the Exodus from Egypt as a lesson in Holocaust remembrance and adds new significance to the rituals of remembrance that characterize the Passover holiday. Unlike *Sankofa, The Devil's Arithmetic* permits the protagonist to retain her present-day consciousness as she struggles to survive the Holocaust, and she carries the memory of her experience with her when she returns to the present. The final film, *Older Than America* (2008), transports viewers to the Native past through Rain, a young Ojibwe woman who experiences disturbing visions of the abuse suffered by Native American children in Indian boarding schools where the motto was "Kill the Indian, Save the Man," and the official policy was cultural genocide. Rain's visions bear witness to attempted cultural extermination and help her testify against present-day encroachments on Native sovereignty. In closing, I arrive at some provisional conclusions about the potential of phantasmic trauma narratives—text and film—to inspire political activism rooted in ethical engagement.

Like the novels I discuss in the preceding chapters, *Sankofa, The Devil's Arithmetic,* and *Older Than America* are concerned with what Pierre Nora (1989) has described as *lieux de mémoire* (sites of memory), places "where memory crystallizes and secretes itself . . . at a particular historical moment" (7). For Nora, *lieux de mémoire* can take the form of places, objects, or texts, and as sites of collective memory, they are imbued with a symbolic value that is regenerated by ritual. The specific *lieux de mémoire* that initiate the protagonists' entry into the world of the past—a slave fortress and a *sankofa* bird, a Seder table, and Ojibwe ceremonial spaces—become "a turning point" for the characters "where consciousness of a break with the past is bound up with the sense that memory has been torn—but torn in such a way as to pose the problem of the embodiment of memory in certain sites where a sense of historical continuity persists" (Nora 1989, 7). However, whereas Nora sees social memory and historical memory as disconnected, I echo Kathleen Brogan's (1998) contention that "different forms of memory, including those that Nora describes as the collective and the historical, can and do exist side by side" (141). In each of these films, *lieux de mémoire* concretize memory by serving as portals to historical experience for both the protagonists and the viewers. By witnessing the physical and emotional pain that results from these characters' phantasmically charged encounters with the traumatic past, and by occasionally inhabiting the protagonist's point of view, spectators develop a felt connection to the suffering of others and are challenged to think about their own ethical responsibility for the wounds of history. I explore the potential of these films to take the project of the written phantasmic trauma narrative a step further by constructing "transferential spaces" in which viewers might gain access to sensually processed memories of the past (Landsberg 2004, 23). The power of seeing images and hearing sounds of historical trauma, I suggest, makes the development of felt connections even more likely and may further encourage ethical thinking. I further probe the ethical dimensions of the phantasmic as a mode of narrating trauma by examining how the films use the transferential experience to foster viewer identification with the experience of the protagonist.

SANKOFA

Haile Gerima's 1993 film *Sankofa* was considered a commercial success for an independent film of its time, grossing more than three million dollars by 1995, which was no small feat for a film project that no one in America wanted to produce, let alone distribute (Rhines 1996, 171). This lack of interest in Gerima's project was not limited to the mainstream film industry in the United States; indeed, as Mark Reid (2005) notes, the international press reporting on film festivals in Berlin, Montreal, and Toronto was similarly disinterested in *Sankofa* and avoided mention of it entirely, a "rebuff" that Gerima interpreted as a "form of censorship" that he attributed to both the film's style and its content (115). Unlike other films from the 1990s that addressed slavery, most notably Steven Spielberg's *Amistad, Sankofa* eschewed a linear narrative that would likely have been more appealing to a mainstream audience. However, Gerima saw the American film industry's unwillingness to promote and distribute the film more as a reluctance to face history than a resistance to his creative direction. He explains: "In America, slavery is a very sensitive topic. The moment I wanted to make *Sankofa* my credentials in the USA vanished, because I was venturing into forbidden territory. . . . I couldn't get funding. Censorship became a reality" (qtd. in Reid 2005, 115). Undaunted by this commercial resistance, Gerima began a grassroots distribution campaign, screening his film in "churches, community spaces, and rented theaters" in thirty-five cities across the United States (Reid 2005, 114). What drove Gerima to overcome these obstacles was his desire to offer an alternative to mainstream portrayals of American slavery such as those seen in *Gone with the Wind* (1939) and *The Birth of a Nation* (1915) (Sidhu 1999). Rejecting the image of happy, contented slaves, Gerima set out to depict "an African race opposed to this whole idea, by making the history of slavery full of resistance, full of rebellion" (Gerima 1994, 92). Because these narratives have been occluded by mainstream historiographies, Gerima (1994) asserts that films like his are charged with the task of "creat[ing] monuments, healing symbols, Nat Turners: they have to convey their variety and the truth of their history" as a means of amending dominant historical accounts. (102) *Sankofa* amends the historical record by sending a present-day African American woman, Mona, back in time, where she becomes Shola, a slave woman driven by her desperate circumstances to insurrection. The film uses an African slave fortress, the Cape Coast Castle in Ghana, as a *lieu de mémoire* to mark both the literal site of departure for millions of enslaved Africans headed for the New World as well as the symbolic site of embarkation for Mona's phantasmic *sankofa* journey.

The concept of *sankofa*, from which Gerima's film takes its name, comes from the Akan tribe of West Africa; the *sankofa* bird, commonly illustrated in Akan iconography, is depicted as a bird with its head turned around so that its beak rests on its back (Reid 2005, 112). Together, the term and the symbol mean "*se wo were fi na wosankofa a yenkyi*," which when literally translated reads, "it is no taboo to return to fetch something which has been forgotten" (Grayson 2000, 26).[2] The film expresses the idea that one must return to the past in order to move forward in the character of Mona, a contemporary fashion model visiting Ghana for a photo shoot, who becomes Shola, a slave on an unidentified New World plantation. In its collapsing of the boundaries between past and present, slavery and freedom, *Sankofa* shares common threads with both *Kindred* and Phyllis Alesia Perry's *Stigmata* (1998). Indeed, the film's complete temporal shift from the present to the past resembles *Kindred,* although unlike Dana, Mona loses her twentieth-century consciousness when it is replaced by that of Shola. Rather, Mona becomes "a vessel, or what the film describes as a 'bird of passage' through which the spirits of the dead tell their story" (Woolfork 2009, 34). To a certain extent, Mona's consciousness shifting recalls *Stigmata*'s Lizzie, who although she retains some degree of present-day awareness becomes, like Mona, overpowered by ancestral memories of enslavement. Further, just as Lizzie's phantasmic encounters are grounded in Yoruba reincarnation beliefs, so too is Mona's consciousness exchange with Shola rooted in an Akan cosmology that is closely aligned with ideas of reincarnation.[3] The phantasmic elements in *Sankofa* can be traced to the Akan belief system known as *cra*, which is still observed in present-day Ghana. Gerima (1994) explains *cra* as "a belief in spirits, a belief that people who have died but are not yet settled roam the village, trying to find a living body to enter, to go back into the living world to repent their crimes or avenge injustices done to them. All of this was on my mind while working on the story for *Sankofa*" (103). The film invites us to make connections between *cra* and the relationship between Mona and Shola; indeed, if we regard Shola as one of these spirits, then we read her presence as a possession of Mona's consciousness, one that enables the telling of a story that has been obscured in mainstream histories.

Another important link between *Kindred, Stigmata,* and *Sankofa* is the fact that our point of entry into their neo-slave narratives is through the perspective of a contemporary protagonist. Some, like Lisa Woolfork (2009), have argued that the primacy of present-day characters in novels such as Butler's *Kindred* and Perry's *Stigmata* is potentially problematic for the way that their presence acts as a "prism [that] obfuscate[s] our vision of the actual slave characters" (34); such prismatic interference, Woolfork contends, presents an "empathic difficulty" because of the way that it distracts the reader/viewer's attention from the real victims in the story, those who cannot escape the system of slavery by returning to the present. However, what Woolfork views as an impediment to reader empathy I read as a conduit for it; indeed, by reading these texts as phantasmic trauma narratives, we see that the contemporary protagonists function as the reader's point of entry into a potentially unfamiliar history. That is, if we can argue that the project of phantasmic trauma narratives like *Sankofa, Kindred,* and *Stigmata* is not only to help readers and viewers connect to the trauma of slavery, but also to provide opportunities for empathy and to offer models for intercultural encounters, then we see that inclusion of a contemporary protagonist is often helpful for facilitating a felt connection for readers/viewers.

Interestingly, Woolfork does not believe that *Sankofa* presents the same kind of problem; rather, she argues that Gerima "circumvents this empathic difficulty by using his time-traveling protagonist as a receptor for a female slave character's story" (34). I go further to assert that the means by which *Sankofa* superimposes Shola onto Mona is not a departure from works like *Kindred* and *Stigmata,* but is rather the application of the phantasmic in film. The present-day subjectivities of *Kindred*'s Dana and *Stigmata*'s Lizzie play an important role in how those novels facilitate reader identification; in fact, what makes these works unique among phantasmic trauma narratives treating the subject of slavery is the way that they use a time-traveling protagonist to solidify this felt connection. Gerima's film shifts this strategy somewhat: Mona becomes Shola when she goes back into time and does not retain her present-day consciousness. However, the film retains viewer identification in a different way: it uses the same actress to play both characters, so that when we see Shola, we see Mona as well, even if the characters remain unaware of their shared consciousness. That Mona, Lizzie, and Dana are not slaves themselves but are granted access to the slave experience does not make them "time-traveling impostors" (Woolfork 2009, 43), but rather offers new ways for the reader/viewer to connect to the historical moment of slavery in a way that does not elide differences in historical and temporal subjectivities. That is, readers/viewers are always cognizant of the different perspectives of the present-day protagonists and historical subjects in these works, even as they feel for the characters' experiences, and it is this sense of distance that preserves for readers/viewers a healthy sense of the alterity of the historical subjects.

Through its reference to the African belief system of *cra* (expressed in the film's *sankofa* imagery), and its use of extradiegetic narration and calculated point-of-view shots, the film asks all of its viewers, black and nonblack alike, to look at enslavement through different eyes.[4] However, as crucial as viewer identification with Mona is, the film's first shots do not center on her, but rather focus on African statuary: a *sankofa* bird, a mother and child, and a man struggling to free himself from the chains that bind him. By animating these inanimate figures through camera movement, the film imbues these *lieux de mémoire* with phantasmic qualities before we meet Mona. In a series of three shots, the camera rotates around each statue in such a way that seemingly imbues them with the power of motion. As Mbye Cham (2004) observes, these images are further animated by a combination of extradiegetic sounds: Kofi Ghanaba's rhythmic atumpan drums and a cacophony of chanting and wailing voices (60). Gradually dominating the drums and chanting voices is a voice-over reciting Gerima's poem "Spirits of the Dead," a work that links the African diaspora and calls on the dead to assume agency by claiming and bearing witness to their traumatic history:

> Spirit of the dead, rise up and possess your bird of passage! Those stolen Africans step out of the ocean from the wombs of the ships and claim your story.... Lingering spirits of the dead, rise up and possess your vessel.... [P]ossess your bird of passage! Those lynched in the magnolias, swinging on the limbs of the weeping willows, rotting food for the vultures, step down and claim your story.... [Y]ou African spirits.... [R]ise up!

The recitation of the poem, together with the relentless call of the drums and the movement of the camera, seems to impel the statuary into being. Moreover, the poem introduces the phantasmic project of the film: namely, to revive the spirits of the dead so that they can "claim" their stories.

The film's opening sequence is important not only because it establishes Gerima's historical recovery project, but also because it prepares viewers for Mona's transformation into Shola: following the logic of Gerima's poem, viewers immediately understand that Mona has become Shola's "vessel," or "bird of passage." After a brief shot of the ceremonial drummer, who we later learn is named Sankofa, we meet Mona, who is modeling at the Cape Coast slave fortress, garbed in a suggestive tiger-striped bathing suit and wearing makeup and a wig that figure her as "savage and exotic" (Gourdine 2003, 19). Mona's sexual objectification is heightened by the high angle of the camera, which is positioned in such a way that when the viewer encounters her, it is from the photographer's perspective. The photographer, a white man, encourages her to pose with erotic expression, offering prompts such as "Mona, more sex. That's it," and "Let the camera do it to you." The film heightens the visual dialectic of viewer/object with reverse shots that focus on the white photographer as he calls out direction. As Angeletta Gourdine (2003) observes, this scene "recalls the intersection between economic and sexual exploitation of black women during slavery" (19–20), a figurative rape that anticipates the literal rape of Shola by a white slave owner in a subsequent scene. Perhaps even more important is the fact that Mona not only permits the photographer's objectification of her sexuality, but also actively participates in her own commodification and unknowingly reproduces racist stereotypes of black women as sexually rapacious beings.

Mona's ignorance demonstrates her own historical amnesia, which is only repaired when Shola possesses her.

The process of restoring Mona's historical awareness begins when Sankofa interrupts her photography shoot, carrying a staff topped with a wooden *sankofa* bird. Glowering, he admonishes Mona and other nearby tourists for desecrating the sacred ground of the slave fortress. When Mona giggles nervously from behind her white photographer—a position that suggests her identification with the culture of her ancestral captors—Sankofa issues the command that initiates Mona's phantasmic journey: "Go back to your past. To your source." In the subsequent scene, Mona descends into the bowels of the fortress, where she furtively follows a tour group on their exploration of the dungeon. The camera follows Mona's movements down the stairs, and as she moves deeper into the fortress, the framing gradually "tightens into a close-up, creating a sense of progressive entrapment as Mona is wedged visually against the wall" (Petty 2008, 31). Just as the tour guide's voice fades away, confirming Mona's solitariness, a huge crash sounds, and Mona is transported in time, so that she instantly finds herself surrounded by Africans in chains. The camera alternates between close-ups of the despondent faces of the bound Africans and Mona, as she shrieks with fear and tries vainly to escape the dungeon. As the enslaved move toward her with their hands outstretched, the audience assumes Mona's point of view, so that their mute pleas are directed not only to her, but to us as well, imploring our acknowledgment of their suffering. This brief moment of viewer identification with Mona is broken, however, as she runs for the exit and encounters the cruel European jailors. We view this escape attempt not from the position of the Europeans, who are outside of the dungeon, but rather from over Mona's shoulder, from the point of view of the Africans. Our association with their viewpoint is sustained as Mona is dragged back into the dungeon, shrieking that she is "not African," but "an American." When the slave traders strip Mona of her clothes in order to brand her, the camera shifts between Mona's viewpoint and that of the Africans; this movement between perspectives not only signals Mona's transition from an "American" to a slave, but also prepares the audience for the shift in subjectivity that will follow when Mona becomes Shola. In this way, the film sustains the identification that the viewer would have with Mona as a contemporary figure, or even more specifically, an American, and transfers that identification to the enslaved historical character of Shola.

Our identification with Mona/Shola is made complete when she is branded with a hot iron. At the moment of her branding—the intense pain of which is made evident by her heart-wrenching screams—the extradiegetic music shifts abruptly, African drums giving way to the gospel hymn "Precious Lord," an aural transition that marks her phantasmic transformation from Mona into Shola. Gerima (1994) confirms the phantasmic significance of the branding as a liminal moment, one that "allows an exploration of the past. It unleashes the collective memory of people who had certain identities and characters and beliefs" (100). Further, Mona's branding marks an important moment of viewer identification, one that leaves a corresponding imprint on the viewer's psyche. Indeed, Gerima contends that "it's [the viewer's] mind that is branded when Mona is branded" (100). To underscore our connection with Mona, the camera follows her as she falls to the ground writhing in pain, and then shifts upward to look at the ceiling from below, as though assuming Mona's position on the floor. By making us privy to the dramatic sights and sounds of Mona's time travel experience, we not only experience the shock of her shift in temporality, but also gain a sense of the brutality of enslavement.

The viewer's association with Mona/Shola's perspective is sustained through the next sequence, which though focused on the sky is punctuated by sounds of water and creaking, and fleeting, shadowy images of Africans in chains; taken together, these sounds and images are redolent of the Middle Passage. Although here *Sankofa* is almost certainly recapitulating the transAtlantic voyage that sent millions of Africans into New World enslavement, this moment is also one of phantasmic transition, a metaphoric Middle Passage that solidifies Mona's transformation into Shola. The shift in temporality is important because it underscores the film's reliance on Akan cosmology as a phantasmic vehicle. As Sheila Petty (2008) observes, "Mona's journey from contemporary to past times, aided by mystical forces, decenters Eurocentric narratives of slavery by transforming her from an object/slave to a subject/human through an African cosmological viewpoint and an African sense of time" (35). Further, the film's strategy for moving across character subjectivities permits the viewer to consider temporalities as they intersect, providing an opportunity for ethical thinking about the relationship between the trauma of slavery and post–civil rights racism that plays out in Mona's interaction with her white photographer.

The majority of the film is narrated by Shola, a "spirit of the dead" who carries the spectator through her experiences as a slave on the Lafayette plantation. Like Mona, Shola is disconnected from her African heritage, and the trajectory of her narrative focuses on her cultural education and psychological awakening. As the film progresses, Shola, nurtured by her African mentor Nunu, begins to draw on Akan spiritual symbols and rituals as "a means of personal empowerment, subversion, and resistance" (Mayer 2002, 233). This spiritual foundation provides Shola with the courage to stage acts of resistance, and together with a group of slave insurrectionists, she helps to burn the plantation, kill several white men, and attempt an escape. In particular, the film asks us to associate Shola's acts of resistance with the *sankofa* symbol, which acquires additional significance when Shola's lover, Shango, carves a *sankofa* amulet for her and places it around her neck. It is following this exchange that Shola takes part in the slave uprising, and as a result, "the symbol becomes associated with rebellion and resistance, as well as Shola/Mona's transformations" (Grayson 2000, 30). In this way, the film expands on the phantasmic significance of the *sankofa* bird: that is, it not only permits us access to the past, but also demonstrates what it sees as its ethical project, which is both to ask viewers to feel and acknowledge the pain of the past as well as to recognize that achieving positive change often necessitates acts of resistance. That the film is punctuated by repeated references to the bird further underscores the idea that the strength required for such resistance can be located in traditions and beliefs systems that were all but erased by systems of slavery and colonialism. And although Mona does not have to risk her life for change, as Shola must, she nevertheless returns to the present with a need to free herself from the shackles of mental enslavement and exploitation, and she, like Shola, will locate strength in symbols of Akan—and more broadly, West African—culture.

The final transformation of Mona/Shola occurs when Shola, having participated in the uprising, attempts to run away from the plantation after killing her master. As she flees through the fields, we hear the sounds of gunshots close by. However, in a phantasmic twist, Shola is lifted into the air by a giant bird, which carries her across the ocean back to Africa, a journey that we are invited to similarly experience when the film offers us panoramic aerial shots of the ocean and the Ghanaian coastline.[5] Gradually, Shola recedes and Mona reappears, naked and chastened, feebly groping her way upward from the darkness toward a bright light in a scene meant to evoke her spiritual and historical rebirth.[6] Her emotional response to emerging from captivity in the dungeons—she weeps uncontrollably—clearly indicates that although her consciousness was not integrated with that of Shola, she has nevertheless retained the memory of Shola's experience and hence of her own bodily captivity. Woolfork (2009) argues that "Mona's stark transformation is the film's greatest achievement: the reeducation of a black woman so corrupted by Western or European ideas that she cannot properly respect the sacred ground of the slave castle" (43). This is demonstrated, in part, by Mona's dramatic shift in attitude toward her white photographer at the film's end: where her unwitting acceptance of the photographer's commodification of her at the film's beginning communicated her initial "state of ignorance and her racial oppression," her refusal to pose or even acknowledge him at the film's end "symbolizes her enlightenment and her racial resistance" (Tillet 2012, 125). Further, where she once shied away from the drummer Sankofa, she is now drawn to him and the hypnotizing rhythm of his drums. Having assumed African dress, she sits among a crowd of black people outside the slave fortress, whose disparate costumes are suggestive of the African diaspora. Shots of this diasporic assembly are interspersed with images of the *sankofa* symbol and flying birds.

By juxtaposing images of the diaspora with the phantasmically charged bird motif, the film situates the Cape Coast Castle in Ghana as a *lieu de mémoire* that not only bears witness to the past, but also functions as a generative site for the African diaspora. In this way, the fortress becomes like the *sankofa* symbol itself, connecting viewers to the African ancestral past while also prompting them to think about the way that their newfound knowledge of this past challenges them to deal with this history in an ethical way. This message is affirmed by the physical positions of the diasporic community members, each of whom faces forward and who, when framed by close-ups, does not look directly into the camera (as the enslaved Africans did at the film's beginning), but rather look off into the distance toward the future. In this face-to-face encounter with these figures, nonblack viewers are charged not only to acknowledge the multigenerational impact of slavery, but also to reconsider the way that this historical trauma has ultimately shaped the state of contemporary race relations. We cannot, the film argues, continue to reinforce political, commercial, and social systems of oppression, such as that symbolized in Mona's shoot with the white photographer at the outset of the film. Resistance to these systems is not only the responsibility of black people, but also the ethical responsibility of nonblack people. It was entirely appropriate, then, that President Barack Obama, as a mixed-race representative of a country that played a significant role in the institution of slavery, toured this same fortress while visiting West Africa, descending into the bowls of the fortress amid the sound of drumbeats in a way that echoed *Sankofa*. Obama's message to the press following his visit was that such acts of commemoration "help to teach all of us that we have to do what we can to fight against the kinds of evils that sadly still exist in our world" (Obama 2009). Like Buchenwald, he continued, places like Cape Coast Castle "remind us of the capacity of human beings to commit great evil" (2009). However, while Obama's symbolic gesture of collective responsibility was powerful, it is crucial that individuals, too, accept responsibility for the past. As Rachel Wittmann (2019) has argued, "An official, national admission of guilt is not enough. When individuals refuse to accept responsibility for crimes that were committed with their tacit consent, the crimes can easily be repressed, forgotten and, ultimately, repeated." By facilitating felt connections to the sufferings endured by such crimes, phantasmic trauma narratives create opportunities for this kind of acknowledgment of responsibility.

THE DEVIL'S ARITHMETIC

Like *Sankofa, The Devil's Arithmetic* was a long time in the making. The film is an adaptation of Jane Yolen's best-selling young adult novel, which garnered the National Jewish Book Award in the category of children's literature in 1989 and is a popular favorite on middle school reading lists.[7] However, despite the book's popularity, the struggle to make the film was a long one. At the time of the film's release, Yolen told reporters from the *New York Times* that her novel "had been under option for more than 10 years but that no one had been able to get a film made" (Applebome 1999). Robert J. Avrech (2011), who adapted the novel as a screenplay and described it as "the best, most fully realized work of [his] long Hollywood career," admits that it took him seven years to get the film produced. "Every studio and network in town declined until Mimi Rogers and Dustin Hoffman came aboard as producers, championed [his] script and made a deal with Showtime" (Avrech 2012). Even with Hoffman's formidable star power associated with the picture, the film "probably would not have been made without a marketable star like [Kirsten] Dunst" playing the lead role (Applebome 1999). Despite its long journey from adaptation to small screen, the film was well received and earned Avrech an Emmy for Best Screenplay.[8] Like *Sankofa, The Devil's Arithmetic* met with resistance from Hollywood because studios feared that the story was too depressing to be marketable, and it was only through the influence of the film's producers and the broad appeal of its teen leads, Kirsten Dunst and Brittany Murphy, that the film gained exposure.

The film tells the story of Hannah Stern, a teenager from New Rochelle, New York, who is distanced from her Jewish heritage and disinterested in her elders' stories about their experiences in the Holocaust. When Hannah flaunts her willful ignorance of Jewish history and culture at her family's Passover Seder, she is transported back in time to 1941 Poland, where she must struggle to survive in Auschwitz. However, while the film is almost exclusively regarded as a Holocaust movie, Avrech (2011) contends that it is just as much "a Passover story, a story of slavery . . . to mindless trends and secular humanism" that communicates the "need to . . . remember Jewish history or risk a descent into . . . nothingness." In its efforts to contextualize the Holocaust within the broader spectrum of Jewish history and culture, the film shares a thematic emphasis with *Everything Is Illuminated,* which not only cultivates phantasmic connections with Holocaust history, but also recovers and reconstructs threads of the pre-Holocaust Jewish narrative that are often overshadowed in works that approach or seek to represent the traumatic event.

However, whereas Jonathan Safran Foer's novel eschews direct representations of the Holocaust, *The Devil's Arithmetic* propels Hannah directly into the past, staging a return to the moment of trauma that most closely resembles that of Dana in *Kindred.* Thus, while the protagonists of Foer's novel can only access the Holocaust through its traces—the phantasmic midrashim that Jonathan spins to replace a lost shtetl history—Hannah experiences the Holocaust directly, retaining her contemporary perspective, and like *Kin-*

dred's Dana, she makes comparative observations about her two worlds that remain with her when she returns to the present. Further, Hannah's direct experience of the concentration camp world endured by her forebears provides viewers with a greater degree of access to the historical moment of the Holocaust than does *Everything Is Illuminated*. However, what gains the film makes in terms of viewer identification come at the expense of intercultural exchange; that is, while *The Devil's Arithmetic* may be more successful in fostering felt connections to Holocaust history in its viewers, it does not directly provide the same models of cross-cultural communication and empathy as those proffered by Foer's novel. Despite these differences, the film, like the text, is rooted in Jewish cultural and religious history, and locates its phantasmic interface in these traditions. *The Devil's Arithmetic* focuses on the Jewish festival of Pesach (Passover)—and in particular the ceremonial practices of drinking wine and opening the door for Elijah—as Hannah's phantasmic point of access into Holocaust history. The film establishes the Seder table as its *lieu de mémoire,* and situates the Holocaust within a larger Jewish narrative of bondage, suffering, and, ultimately, redemption.

While *The Devil's Arithmetic* has been widely criticized by Holocaust scholars for its redemptive quality,[9] I contend that its emphasis on freedom does not stem from a desire to ameliorate the trauma of the Holocaust, but rather testifies to the film's greater didactic purpose, which is that we must not only remember the past, but also actively and willingly engage in rituals of remembrance for the sake of passing on felt connections to the Holocaust to future generations. The film reinforces this idea by framing Hannah's time travel experience within the context of the Passover ritual, a weeklong festival when all Jews are commanded to tell the story of the Jewish Exodus from bondage in Egypt in first person, as if they were there. Indeed, the Talmudic rabbis, interpreting the Torah, conclude that "in every single generation, one is obligated to look upon himself as if he personally had gone forth out of Egypt" (qtd. in Sender 1991, 189). By commanding that every Jew retell the Exodus story in this way, the Haggadah formalizes the preservation and transference of felt connections to history for present and future generations.[10] However, the ritual of Passover is not simply one of commemoration, but also one that gives rise to felt connections to the Jewish past. Indeed, the Passover Seder is a profound moment in the Jewish calendar when historical and liturgical time collapse, providing people in the present access to the trauma of enslavement in Egypt and the moment of Exodus. "[T]hroughout the Haggadah, we find past and future uniting; the worlds of old and young coalescing around a common narrative, yesterday and tomorrow meeting at one another's door" (Levine 2011, 6). Further, Rabbi Yosie Levine writes, Passover is special because it emphasizes "a constant: A timeless and ageless enemy of the Jewish people bent on [their] destruction. On Seder night, the sweep of Jewish history collapses into a single moment—as if we could really envision a Crusader and an Inquisitor arm in arm with a Cossack and a Nazi" (7). Thus, the film's staging for Hannah's time travel could not be more appropriate: the Passover Seder both connects observers of the holiday to the ancient Exodus and provides access to every other tribulation in Jewish history. *The Devil's Arithmetic* therefore asks the audience to view Hannah's Holocaust experience in the broader context of Jewish history and invites us to regard the Seder ritual—its *lieu de mémoire*—as a constitutive site of identity for the Jewish people, because in Jewish liturgy the Exodus marks the moment of "the creation of Israel," a community of people devoted to the worship of one God (Enns 2000, 45). More importantly for the gentile viewer, the fact that Hannah's story begins and ends at a ritual of remembrance underscores the importance of actively commemorating the trauma of the Holocaust.

Like *Sankofa*'s Mona, Hannah is detached from her cultural history, and we as viewers are meant to identify her disinterest in the Jewish past as the impetus for her time travel. The film begins with a close-up of Hannah in profile against a backdrop of blinking neon lights, a shot that establishes our identification with her as the protagonist of the story and presages the phantasmic time travel experience she will undergo. We soon discover that she is in a tattoo parlor, trying to decide which tattoo to get as her friends receive theirs. This moment underscores Hannah's distance from Judaism, which expressly forbids tattooing.[11] It also functions as a deliberate point of contrast for a subsequent scene in which we see glimpses of the tattooed forearms of Hannah's elders at the Seder and foreshadows Hannah's arrival at Auschwitz, where she is forced to submit to having a numerical identifier tattooed on her arm. Before Hannah can commit to a design, however, she takes note of the time and rushes out, telling her friends in an exasperated voice that she has to go to her "Aunt Eva's for Passover," or the "cracker thing," as one of her friends describes it. The next few sequences depict Hannah expressing her reluctance about attending the Seder, which she dismissively deems "a waste of time." Her parents do not defend the ritual or even bother to justify it: indeed, her father offers only a passive tautology by way of explanation ("Some things you have to do because you have to do them"), which her mother echoes by snapping, "We're going because it's important. . . . It's important because I say it's important." In highlighting her parents' refusal to take responsibility for educating their daughter about the significance of the Passover holiday, the film partially absolves Hannah from responsibility for her lack of historical awareness. Whereas *Sankofa*'s Mona and *Older Than America*'s Rain are adults, Hannah is only an adolescent, and we are therefore invited to see her as not wholly responsible for her cultural ignorance. Further, the fact that the film implicates Hannah's parents in her lack of appreciation for her own culture emphasizes the importance of intergenerational transmission of memory; without this deliberate effort, the film suggests, the communal memories of the past become empty signifiers.

Unable to grasp the historical and religious significance of the Passover ritual, Hannah is equally incapable of understanding the symbolic relationship between Passover, a story of survival, and the survivors sitting around her at the Seder table. Hannah brushes off her uncle Morris's attempts to share stories of the family's ancestral shtetl, and she becomes visibly uncomfortable when her uncle Abe attempts to tell her a story about the attempted escape by and execution of Yeshiva students in the concentration camp. A characteristically self-centered adolescent, she is much more interested in stories that she perceives as having a direct connection to her. For example, when Hannah's aunt Eva compares her to her namesake, a relative named Chana who died at Auschwitz, Hannah pleads to hear more about her. This query, however, is rebuffed; Aunt Eva shushes her, saying, "You wouldn't understand. . . . [W]hat it was like in the camps. What we lived through, if we lived. What it was to be a Jew. This experience is so far from your world! I am afraid, though I so want to tell you what happened, [that] it will mean nothing to you. And that would hurt me very much, see?" Here, Aunt Eva expresses an anxiety common among survivors. As Lawrence Langer (1991) writes, "From the point of view of the witness, the urge to tell meets resistance from the certainty that one's audience will not understand" (xiii). In her elderly relatives, Hannah encounters the extremes of survivor responses: the earnest, somewhat intimidating Uncle Abe who threatens to reveal too much, and the reluctant Aunt Eva, who withholds because she fears that Hannah cannot comprehend the atrocity. Hannah has access to the past in the form of these eyewitnesses but lacks the maturity and the motivation to understand how their experiences have affected them, or how they relate to her and the ritual in which they are all about to participate. Indeed, she views herself as disconnected from both ritual and history, and as viewers, we are primed to regard this disassociation as the catalyst for the historical reckoning that follows.

Hannah's disinterest in her Jewish culture is demonstrated by the way she is discernibly annoyed by the rituals of the Seder as they are performed. These rituals are replicated in careful detail for the viewer: the lighting of the candles, the blessing of the wine, the chanting of the Four Questions, and the narration of the biblical story of how God freed the Jews from Egyptian bondage. Throughout the Seder, close-ups of the tattooed forearms of Hannah's elders provide visual links "between the bondage of the Jews in ancient Egypt and their status as nameless slaves under Hitler" (Baron 2005, 188). Although the Seder is a participatory ritual, one that requires each person present to engage by reciting from the Haggadah, Hannah refuses to cooperate. In fact, the only part of the ceremony that she does embrace is the ritual drinking of wine, which she consumes to the point of intoxication. At the close of the meal, Aunt Eva volunteers Hannah for the final ceremonial task of the night, the practice of opening the door for the Elijah, whose return to the world of the living is prophesied to herald the coming of the Messianic Age. Hannah reluctantly complies, and as she steps through the doorway into the hall of Aunt Eva's apartment building, a bright flash of light and the haunting sound of wailing wind signal her journey back in time to her ancestral Polish shtetl where her family, including Aunt Eva, lived until they were deported to Auschwitz. We view Hannah's chronoportation from over her shoulder, as though we are asked to imagine that we are accompanying her on her journey. Our association with her perspective is sustained as she walks forward into the past, assessing the unfamiliar scene of the 1940s shtetl from a window. The anachronistic sights we see beyond the window—chickens in the street, a horse and cart—confirm that we have been transported to another time, and Hannah's initial shock at the impossibility of such a temporal and geographical shift reflects any concomitant feelings of disbelief shared by the audience.

The film's choice of the door-opening ritual as the moment for Hannah's phantasmic transition into the world of the past is significant for a number of reasons. First, the act of opening the door and crossing the threshold signifies Hannah's entry into her liminal status as a person who is at once a subject of both past and present; indeed, the door itself functions as a phantasmic portal, signaling her entry into the realm of the past. The symbolic value of the door is heightened by its association with the entry of the prophet Elijah, who is arguably a phantasmic figure in Jewish folklore history in his own right. Elijah is esteemed as "the personification of optimism" by the Jewish culture because his presence is regarded as a symbol of God's promise for the final redemption of the Jewish people (Olitzky 2002, 76). At Passover, as at circumcisions and weddings, Elijah is a supernatural guest, one who not only heralds redemption, but also is regarded as a guardian of the Jewish community in exile (Lindbeck 2010, 164).[12] Further, he is regarded as a "supernatural mediator," one who "connect[s] humankind to God" (ix) and is "as much or more a teacher and ethical guide than a savior" (xiv). Talmudic stories recounting Elijah's visitations to Jewish communities in disguise teach the importance of "ethical behavior" and "human responsibility" for the other (x). Because of his association with Jewish ethics, which emphasizes empathy for those who have been othered—"the stranger, the widow, the orphan, the poor"—Elijah's invisible presence at the outset of a phantasmic journey functions as an ethical call to the audience to bear witness to and feel empathy for the suffering that will soon be displayed on-screen.

As Hannah steps into the unfamiliar landscape of 1940s Poland, she is informed by women who introduce themselves as her cousin Rivka and her aunt Mina that she is Chana Stern from Lublin, Poland, and that she has just recovered from the typhus that claimed the lives of her parents. Hannah, alarmed, exclaims, "Something is wrong! I'm not crazy . . . and I'm not dreaming! Please believe me!" Rivka, who will later rename herself Eva upon immigrating to the United States following the war, gently excuses Hannah's insistence that she is from New Rochelle and queer references to the future as side effects of her recent illness by confirming Hannah's worst fears: "No, Chana, this is real." This moment clarifies for Hannah that she is experiencing a phantasmic process by "introjecting" into Chana and "being transformed into/by her" (Tribunella 2010, 120). The film's efforts to establish viewer identification with Hannah mean that it invites the viewer to enact the same transformation; that is, we occupy Chana's subject position while sharing Hannah's consciousness. Just as Hannah becomes Chana, so too is the viewer encouraged to share Hannah's contemporary perspective in this journey into the past.

The following scenes solidify this transformation. We observe the unfamiliar quotidian events of shtetl life along with Hannah, who consistently reconfirms her present-day consciousness for the audience by making anachronistic references and by asking Rivka to explain things to her, particularly Jewish customs (such as the tradition whereby a groom unveils his bride in a ceremony known as a Bedeken that precedes the wedding rites). By reaffirming Hannah's contemporary subject position for the viewer, the film sustains the identification it establishes at the outset, so that Hannah's sense of alterity from the historical period in which she finds herself anticipates that which the viewer likely feels. This sense of historical distance quickly becomes one of horror when the idyllic scene of the Jewish wedding at which Hannah and Rivka are guests is disrupted by the arrival of SS officers, who begin herding the Jewish community into trucks. Many viewers will likely recognize the portent of such a roundup, given the fact that it is a familiar convention in popular mainstream Holocaust films such as *Schindler's List* or *The Pianist*, and even viewers with a more limited knowledge of Holocaust history will recognize how the shattering of the shtetl idyll by archetypal villains in Nazi dress augurs a sense of imminent doom. In like manner, it is this moment that triggers Hannah's vague historical knowledge. "What year is it?" she frantically asks Rivka. On learning that it is October 1941, Hannah predicts that six million Jews will be murdered, but no one in the community, including Rivka, believes that anything so terrible could happen.

As the film carries the girls into the concentration camp, where we see the typical signifiers of the concentrationary universe, Hannah's ability to distinguish between past and present becomes increasingly unreliable. Hannah rues her previous unwillingness to learn about the Holocaust because she recognizes now that her historical ignorance is a liability, telling Rivka, "I was thinking about how much help I could be. . . . I had a history teacher who spent a whole semester talking about the Jews during the war. . . . [And] I have no idea what my teacher said. The only thing I remember was that no one paid any attention." Gradually, she becomes both Hannah and Chana; at times she "remember[s]" with clarity the awful truth of her predicament with the full knowledge that she is bearing witness to the Holocaust as it happens, while at other times she is as ignorant as those around her about what is happening. As Eric L. Tribunella (2010) observes, "She is the contemporary child who knows or recalls bits of information about the Holocaust but for whom that knowledge remains murky or uncertain" (119). At one point, she asks Rivka, "Which is worse? Knowing or not knowing?" For Hannah, as for the viewer, the past is suddenly rendered unpredictable in its predictability; that is, we know that Hannah and Rivka's journey in the cattle cars will lead them to a place of death, but death for whom? Unlike traditional Holocaust films, we cannot be assured of the protagonist's survival and redemption.[13] Because Hannah's survival in the world of the past is not assured, viewers are likely to share her fear and uncertainty, the sense that history has suddenly been rendered a dangerous unknown and that she cannot be guaranteed survival.

The Devil's Arithmetic continues by portraying aspects of the concentrationary universe that are likely familiar to many viewers: shorn heads, striped uniforms, and starving inmates alternately standing in line for inadequate food rations, toiling in barren fields, and huddling together for warmth in overcrowded, unsanitary barracks. Just as Shola turns to Akan spiritual traditions as a source of personal empowerment and resistance, so too does Hannah find meaning and emotional sustenance in Judaism. She learns from a Yeshiva student how to pray, and she even risks her safety to bribe an SS guard for flour to make matzo for Passover. Together with Rivka and a few other women, Hannah organizes a secret Passover Seder in the women's barracks, performing with reverence and devotion the rituals that she previously found meaningless. By returning us to its *lieu de mémoire* in the context of the Holocaust, the film underscores the connections between remembrance and Jewish identity that were lost on Hannah at the beginning. However, where for Shola resistance is signified by rebellion and escape, for Hannah resistance comes in the form of substitution. On discovering that Rivka is her aunt Eva (she confides in Hannah that she will change her name to Eva if she survives), Hannah trades places with her when the commandant condemns Rivka to the gas chamber. This selfless act signifies the ethical project initiated by the film's phantasmic turn to the past, one best explained by Emmanuel Levinas's (1996) notion of "substitution," whereby one recognizes her infinite responsibility for the other, which gives rise to a process where the concern for the other takes primacy over concern for the self. Substitution signifies "expiation," responsibility for "the other (*autrui*)—for his distress *and his freedom*" (145, emphasis added). As Anna Strhan (2012) explains it, "In substitution, my being is in question to an infinite degree. I am totally exposed to the wounding of the other . . . in an asymmetrical relation" (52). In the film, Hannah renders this symbolic substitution literal, and, in so doing, clarifies for viewers the film's two-part ethical mission: first, that we are always already responsible for the suffering of others, and second, that ethical thinking about the plight of the other must always be accompanied by corresponding ethical action. This ethical mission is confirmed by the fact that many "involved in the film's production considered it a tribute to the lost world of European Jewry, as well as a warning against contemporary racism" (Baron 2005, 190). *The Devil's Arithmetic* bolsters its didacticism with the phantasmic, using Hannah's act of substitution—and hence her death in the gas chamber—as the phantasmic means by which she is transported to the present, where she bears witness to the atrocities of the Holocaust and vows to "always remember what happened. Always."

When Hannah returns to the present, sensitized by her experience of the Holocaust, she returns to the Seder table with a new sense of purpose. Joining her family in a rendition of the Passover song "Chad Gad Yad," Hannah demonstrates a profound sense of belonging to her Jewish community, which is represented not only by her family, but also by the Jews whose murders she witnessed while in the camp. The fact that Hannah's journey to the past results in the cultivation of her Jewish identity suggests parallels with *Everything Is Illuminated,* in which Jonathan's creative efforts to (re)imagine his family history bring him closer to his cultural identity. Further, by returning us to its *lieu de mémoire,* the Passover Seder, the film again underscores its efforts to integrate the Holocaust story into the broader fabric of the Jewish diasporic narrative. In the final frames of the film, which feature a close-up of a chastened Hannah, we observe as she looks thoughtfully around the Seder table, taking in the scene around her with appreciation and wistfulness. She has been reintegrated into her Jewish community and now possesses a newfound understanding of her place in her cultural history. In viewing Hannah from across the table, the camera invites the viewer to share a seat at the table, not as a Jew, perhaps, but rather as a participant in a broader human community committed to remembering the Holocaust. Thus situated at the table, we are asked to see ourselves reflected in Hannah and her commitment to remembrance, as well as to heed the voices of the now-unseen survivors at the table. As the survivor generation passes on, the film suggests, we are still charged with remembering their voices and heeding their pleas that we never forget what happened to them.

OLDER THAN AMERICA

Inspired by stories passed down to her by family members and friends who were forcibly enrolled in Indian boarding schools, Georgina Lightning wrote, directed, produced, and starred in the 2008 film *Older Than America,* which uses phantasmic irruptions in the form of ghosts and visions to connect viewers to the trauma endured by students who attended Indian boarding schools. Filmed on location at the Fond du Lac reservation in Minnesota, *Older Than America* testifies to the physical and psychological abuse suffered by many Native American children from the nineteenth century until well into the twentieth century. The need to tell this story is great, Lightning says, because "there is not one Native American here [on the reservation] who hasn't felt the impact of boarding schools." The intent of these boarding schools, Lightning explains, was to enforce "mandatory assimilation," which resulted in "a cultural genocide" that for many survivors manifested itself in alcoholism, drug addiction, or suicide. The primary motivator for telling this story was Lightning's father, whose suicide led her to the discovery of the fact that his depression had been driven by the trauma he endured at a parochial Indian boarding school (Hearne and Foat 2014, 72). Following this revelation, she "made a personal journey to that very school," where she saw the graveyard where the corpses of Indian children were buried ("Older Than America," 2006). The cemetery was so vast, she said, that she "couldn't see the far end of [it]." As Lightning explains, her commitment to making *Older Than America* was fueled by a desire to bring healing "not just to Native Americans, but to everyone, in every community." She asserts that if the film can create a productive cross-cultural "dialogue across the country," it will have been a success (2006). *Older Than America* encourages this kind of dialogue by featuring a non-Native character who bears witness to the boarding school experience and who actively campaigns for recognition of and reparations to those who suffered this trauma.

Unlike *Sankofa* and *The Devil's Arithmetic*, *Older Than America* does not have a clear tripartite structure whereby the protagonist expresses historical ignorance, is thrust into the past, and returns with a new historical and cultural sensitivity. Rather, it begins en media res and therefore expresses the sense of historical immediacy that Lightning intended when making the film. Compared with the Holocaust and African enslavement, the Native American boarding school experience is a lesser-known trauma, perhaps because it is one that has yet to be confronted on a broad public scale. As recently as the 1970s, the US government still mandated the enrollment of Native American children in boarding schools, and the last of the Canadian First Nations boarding schools was closed in 1984.[14] In 2003, a "$25 billion class-action lawsuit was filed against the US Federal government . . . for the physical, sexual, and psychological abuse suffered by the Native American claimants while attending boarding schools" (Stout 2012, 130). That the case was filed and summarily dismissed indicates the need, on the part of the Native Americans, to have their experience of deculturalization acknowledged by mainstream American political and social institutions. The film demonstrates this need not only by bearing witness to this trauma and indicting those responsible, but also by offering an example of a non-Native witness who addresses these injustices and intervenes on behalf of the Native community to see that justice is done.

The film tells the story of Rain, a young Ojibwe woman who is contemplating marriage and children with her fiancé, Johnny, who is a tribal police officer. However, on the verge of embarking on this new life and bringing new generations into the world, Rain begins receiving frightful visions of the child abuse suffered by students at the now-defunct Indian boarding school. As we soon discover, Rain's mother, Irene, who was enrolled in the boarding school during the 1960s, is now confined to a mental hospital. Because Rain's mother is nearly catatonic from the relentless barrage of the shock therapy treatments to which she was subjected as a young woman, Rain knows nothing of what she suffered in the boarding school. As we discover over the course of the film, Irene, together with her brother Walter Many Lightnings, was physically and psychologically abused by the priests and nuns who ran the school, a trauma that was compounded by the fact that she witnessed the deaths of six of her schoolmates who, after being locked in the school's basement as punishment for trying to speak their Native language, were buried by rubble caused by an earthquake.[15] Because Irene is unable to communicate her story, Walter Many Lightnings—who we discover was murdered by white people for his involvement in the American Indian Movement as an adult—tells it for her by imparting visions of the school to Rain and by summoning the ghosts of the dead schoolchildren. Guided by her uncle's spirit, Rain gains a new purchase on the systematic psychological torture and physical abuse suffered by generations of Indian children at the hands of white clergy and educators who ascribed to Richard Henry Pratt's infamous motto, "Kill the Indian . . . and save the man."[16]

In its use of the phantasmic as a source of cultural identity reclamation, *Older Than America,* like Howe's *Miko Kings,* emphasizes the importance of reviving and sustaining Native traditions, as well as the need to reclaim the Native past by narrating it from a Native perspective. Although devoted to recovering a Native story that has been occluded in official historiographies, the film, like Howe's novel, is also interested in engaging a non-Native audience to foster the felt connections on which cross-cultural empathy is premised, and thus offers a strong model of intercultural collaboration. However, while *Miko Kings* locates the phantasmic in a tribally specific context in order to relate the history of the Choctaw, *Older Than America* is more pan-tribal in focus because it seeks to tell the story of a historical trauma that affected Native Americans of many different tribes. Thus, just as the trauma impacted Natives across tribal lines of difference, so too does the film's phantasmic solution. *Older Than America* locates its use of the phantasmic in Sun Dance and Big Drum ceremonies, as well as sweat lodge rituals, all of which, though traditionally associated with tribes of the Great Plains, assumed broader spiritual significance for Natives across tribal boundaries with the rise of the Native American Church and the American Indian Movement in the twentieth century.[17] Although we assume that Rain is Ojibwe because she lives on the Fond du Lac reservation, the past that she experiences through phantasmic flashbacks and visions is a pan-tribal story, one that conveys the devastating impact of cultural genocide for a group of people whose historical and cultural roots on this continent make them "older than America."

However, despite these differences, the film does share important links with *Miko Kings*. Both works draw on indigenous spiritualties as phantasmic strategies for connecting their audiences, both Native and non-Native, to specific events in the Native American past. Like Howe's novel, *Older Than America* emphasizes the importance of ancestors as forces capable of repairing gaps in individual and cultural memory. Although Walter Many Lightnings does not time travel in the manner of Ezol Day, he does serve as a source of guidance, leading Rain on a quest for historical knowledge that parallels the one that Lena takes in *Miko Kings*. Moreover, both *Older Than America* and *Miko Kings* offer positive examples of intercultural encounter, showing how cross-cultural communication can lead to helpful interethnic alliances. In so doing, the film clarifies its ethical project as one that seeks to encourage productive encounters between Natives and non-Natives. As we will see, Lightning's film resembles Howe's project of tribalography because of its interest in uniting "past, present, and future milieus" in telling its story (Howe 2002, 42). Indeed, the film's emphasis on renewing the practice of Native medicine and spirituality in the presence of non-Native witnesses who affirm and acknowledge those reconstruction efforts pushes the collaborative potential of the tribalography even further.

The phantasmic agents in the film—Walter Many Lightnings and the ghost children—are closely associated with sacred Native ceremonial spaces, which function as its *lieux de mémoire*. These ceremonies simultaneously enable Rain's connection to the world of the past and reaffirm the film's cultural reclamation project. The film opens with a scene of the Sun Dance, which Lightning describes as "the kind of ceremony used before the white people came and made it illegal for us to practice our ceremonies and incorporate our medicine into our way of life. . . . The ceremony at the beginning shows who we were when we were 'older than America'—a strong, vibrant people, with a lot of pride and power" ("Older Than America," 2006). The figure at the center of the scene is Rain's uncle, Walter Many Lightnings, an American Indian Movement activist who was murdered for trying to raise awareness about the crimes that took place at his boarding school. Although it is Rain, and not Walter Many Lightnings, who acts as the film's protagonist, this initial scene is important for establishing the phantasmic character of the story. Indeed, because we are made privy to Walter Many Lightnings's vision quest, we are invited to read the action of the film as the phantasmic fulfillment of that quest, one whereby Rain, guided by Walter Many Lightnings's spectral insights, exposes the truth about her mother and uncle's abuse and indicts those responsible for those crimes. In so doing, Rain initiates a healing process that, though personal, implicates the entire tribal community.

The Sun Dance ceremony that opens the film sets the tone for the film's emphasis both on a shared tribal history of colonial oppression as well as the power of pan-tribal unity. Practiced by many Great Plains tribes, the Sun Dance has become a syncretic, pan-tribal expression of Native identity and spirituality over the last century (Gagnon 2007, 426). Indeed, although Lightning sets her film in an Ojibwe tribe, the principal ceremonies that she reenacts are those that the Ojibwe adopted from other tribal cultures. As Kade M. Faris (2004) notes, the Sun Dance practiced by the Ojibwe is a "variation . . . learned from the Dakota Sioux" (336) while the sweat lodge ceremony that Rain participates in shares similarities with that of Lightning's own Cree tribe (Dusenberry 1968, 61). Generally considered a purification ritual, the Sun Dance has historically been performed by individuals wanting to "break through their small selves in order to serve as clear vehicles for the energy of the Great Spirit" (Fisher 1997, 64). The scene, shot with a yellow lens filter, possesses a timeless quality: in separate shots, we are shown figures dressed in traditional ceremonial costumes from the Great Plains region, dancing around a forked tree from which Walter Many Lightnings is ceremonially suspended, and shots of a drum circle, in which the drummers wear costumes associated with a more contemporary time.[18] Indeed, because we are not given an establishing date, we are free to imagine that the ceremony is occurring in a collapsed temporality that represents both past and present and therefore unites figures from different tribes and periods of Native American history. The supernatural quality of this opening scene is important for the way that it establishes Walter Many Lightnings as the phantasmic channel through which the film's historical secret is transmitted. The space of the Sun Dance ceremony collapses temporalities and is what permits him—as a "clear [vehicle] for the energy of the Great Spirit"—to access Rain's consciousness, both teaching her about the past and helping her to connect with Native traditions and spiritual beliefs.

As the focus of the ceremony, Walter Many Lightnings is suspended by two metal rings that pierce each of his nipples; the rings, in turn, are connected to ropes secured to the forked tree that occupies the center of the ceremonial circle. This particular form of "self-torture" (492), Leslie Spier (1920) writes, "characterizes the quest of a vision by an individual" (492–93). As the drumming and chanting crescendo, we see glimpses of his vision: a circle within which is a cross with rays of equal length. Generally referred to by plains tribes to as the Sacred Wheel or medicine wheel, this iconography is often associated with Sun Dances and, like the dance itself, has assumed pan-tribal significance for Native Americans in the twentieth and twenty-first centuries (Spier 1920, 515). As Walter Many Lightnings falls into a trance and collapses, wrenching the metal rings from his flesh, the camera flashes to a close-up of the Sacred Wheel, this time in the form of a pendant around his neck. It is the image of this pendant that becomes emblazoned on Rain's mind and wrenches her from sleep in the following scene.

Following tradition, the film depicts the Sacred Wheel as comprising four color-coded quadrants.[19] The quadrants—red, white, black, and yellow—unite to signify an indigenous belief system based on the idea of a balanced natural and spiritual world, a form of indigenous medicine that was forcibly displaced by Christian systems of belief. In the context of the film, a world in which past and present collide in powerful ways, the symbol signifies these intersections, and, more broadly, the interconnectedness of all things, the notion that everything is encompassed in the circle. This idea of interconnectedness is an important one for the film, which expresses the need to confront the wounds of the past in order to effectuate healing in the present and form productive intercultural alliances in the future. As Walter Many Lightnings explains to Rain at the film's end, "the important thing about coming full circle is that it allows us to see not only the past, but also the future, a brighter one." The Sacred Wheel image recurs throughout the film in various ways as a phantasmic signifier of the connection shared by Rain and Walter Many Lightnings and as a sign of cultural protest, a reminder to Rain that she must learn about her tribe's traditions and rituals to undo the active deculturalization processes forced on her family. The Sacred Wheel and the Sun Dance not only initiate our introduction to Rain—who, witnessing them in a dream, is awakened from her sleep—but also signal the intersection between the phantasmic spirit world of Walter Many Lightnings and the ghosts of the boarding school victims on the one hand and the earthly existence of Rain on the other. Further, images of the Sacred Wheel appear throughout, affirming the notion that Rain's visions are driven by the need to bring history "full circle." Aided by the phantasmic interference of Walter Many Lightnings, with whom we associate the Sacred Wheel, Rain is armed with the knowledge necessary to bring the crimes of the parochial boarding school to light. Just as the Sacred Wheel figures significantly in solidifying the phantasmic bond between Rain and her uncle, it also presages the appearance of the ghost children.

The ghost children appear several minutes into the film, and their impending arrival is heralded by an image of the Sacred Wheel. Rain, circulating through her elementary school classroom, notices one of her pupils illustrating the symbol. When she asks the student about his drawing, he smiles cryptically and hands it to her, saying simply, "I made it for you." Heightening the connection between the symbol and Rain's vision for the viewer is the next scene, when Rain, observing the children outside her school, suddenly has a vision of children from the boarding school era, crying and bruised. After the flashback ends, we resume our status as observers, from which vantage point we see Walter Many Lightnings standing just behind her. During this vision, as in all the others that permeate the film, the viewer and Rain become one: that is, we see everything that she sees just before, during, and after the flashbacks from her perspective. Thus, the phantasmic reach of the narrative is twofold: just as Rain is psychologically transported elsewhere when her flashbacks occur, so too are we transported when the camera shifts our focus *from* Rain *into* Rain. In this way, we witness what she witnesses: the physical and sexual abuse of young Native children, the active efforts of priests and nuns to abolish indigenous spirituality and languages, and, as the film reaches its climax, the deaths of children trapped by the rubble of the school's crumbling foundations, and the shock therapy treatment forced on Rain's mother in her adulthood when she threatened to reveal her knowledge of the school's crimes. Because she is phantasmically transported into the past, the sense of pain and fear that permeate these scenes is vivid for both her and the viewer.

Although Rain's encounters with the phantasmic and the historical secrets these encounters uncover are central to the film's historical reclamation project, *Older Than America* features an additional character who is key to the film's interest in intercultural collaboration: a white geologist named Luke. In his capacity as a geologiest, Luke visits the Fond du Lac reservation to investigate the recent, phantasmically triggered earthquake centered on the grounds of the abandoned boarding school, which functions as a phantasmic reminder of the earlier earthquake that killed Irene's classmates. Luke befriends Rain and her fiancé, Johnny, and soon comes to have phantasmic visions of his own that are validated by the tribal community. Significantly, it is Luke who identifies the now-closed boarding school as a "site of repressed energy," and it is through his exploration of the grounds, together with Rain's guiding visions, that the secret mass grave of the school's pupils is discovered. Through his interactions with the tribal community, Luke learns about a part of history he had never been taught in school: that those who did not die of malnourishment, disease, and abuse were left "broken and confused, with scars that will not heal." On learning this from the tribe's medicine man, Luke admits that it "sounds like a holocaust." "How come," he asks, "I never learned about this in school?" Fueled by curiosity, and angered by the resistance of the white municipal government, Luke delves into the local historical archives and uncovers evidence of the boarding schools' unconscionable treatment of its Native pupils, treatment that led to the death of these students due to negligence and abuse on the part of the school's parochial staff. Luke's active participation in Rain's historical reclamation efforts, coupled with his own receptiveness to phantasmic historical visions, demonstrates for viewers an ethical model of intercultural engagement; that is, we must be receptive to history and willing to take ethical action to make reparation on behalf of others who have been wronged. Indeed, the film suggests that just as the mainstream culture must be held accountable for its crimes of cultural genocide, so too is it responsible in helping to restore the communities that were damaged by the systematic acculturation policies established and enforced by the US government. As a representative of that mainstream culture, Luke expresses empathy for Native trauma and respect for tribal traditions, and he translates these ethical *feelings* into ethical *actions* by working with the tribe to see justice done and engaging the Native community in a ritual of healing.

When Rain's visions become public knowledge, her conservative, assimilationist aunt, together with a parish priest associated with the boarding school cover-up and the one responsible for silencing Irene, have her committed to a mental institution where she, like her mother before her, is subjected to shock therapy treatments. With phantasmic intervention of Walter Many Lightnings, Rain escapes from the hospital and seeks out the guidance of her tribal elders, who agree that she is in need of a healing ceremony. As one elder explains to Luke, "Rain needs to go back to her traditional ways. The seventh generation prophecy teaches that if we go back to [the] teachings of our ancestors, if we go back to our traditional ways, that we will gain wisdom and knowledge—those things that are older than America." This exchange is significant on two levels: First, it underscores the importance of returning to indigenous rituals as a means of healing for contemporary Native Americans. Second, it communicates to a diverse viewership—represented in the film by Luke—that the only way forward for American society is via a redemption of its historical sins.

In a subsequent scene, we are taken into the sweat lodge, where Rain, seeking a renewed connection to her Native identity and spiritual cleansing, engages in the traditional ceremony with the elders. The sweat lodge serves a "very sacred function through the ritual healing or cleansing of the mind, body, and spirit, while also serving as a way of bringing people together" (Garrett 2004, 174). Melissa Pflug (1996) further notes that the communal aspect of the ritual is crucial to its success:

> Through the sweat lodge, the elders . . . guide the person and the group to encounter the . . . power persons. . . . Personal power is enhanced through group solidarity. Each person emerges from the lodge with a changed state-of-being and identity. For those who receive a vision during the ceremony, solidarity is established with the group. . . . The ritual concretizes power as a gift that transpires between a community of ethically empowered persons. (489)

In returning us to a ceremonial space, the film returns us to an important *lieu de mémoire,* the place that gives rise to the phantasmic "power persons" represented by the ancestral spirits who have helped Rain to discover the truth about her past. However, where Rain's previous phantasmic encounters were intended to impart historical knowledge, her final phantasmic episodes offer her an important felt connection that prompt her to engage in cultural and spiritual practices that facilitate healing for the broader tribal community.

As the medicine man initiates Rain into the ceremony, he transforms into Walter Many Lightnings, who directly addresses Rain for the first time and informs her that he is her uncle. He continues:

> I am here to look over you, to help you understand your place in our family and our people.... [W]hen [the white people] came, they did everything they could to end our traditional ways of life. But there were things they couldn't take: our dreams and our spirits.... You have been shown through these visions the truths of the past.... Now ... we have to learn to forgive these people for what they do not understand about our good way of life. We can't expect them to understand, but pray that one day they will. Then we can all heal together and get back to being a nation of strong, traditional people.... Continue to dream of healing and unity amongst our people, and one day, it shall come to pass. (*Older Than America*)

Walter's words further underscore the idea communicated earlier in the film to Luke that the ability to imagine a positive future is predicated on a deeper and more meaningful understanding of the past, not only for Native Americans, but for non-Natives as well. Although it tells the story of a Native woman, the film creates space for the non-Native viewer to bear witness as well, and nowhere is this invitation more explicit than in the sweat lodge scene. Within the ceremonial space of the sweat lodge, the spectator is invited to participate in a limited capacity, weighing Walter Many Lightnings's earnest expression against Rain's visibly emotional one. Our status as a spectator in this community is confirmed by interspersed glimpses of the elders' faces, which, lit from below by firelight, express sadness and convey a mute understanding of the phantasmic event taking place. Thus, the sacred space of the sweat lodge, a *lieu de mémoire,* becomes both a space of historical witnessing as well as a place of cultural affirmation. Because we are invited to observe the ceremony, we are asked to acknowledge the tribe's trauma claims and serve as empathic witnesses. Through this ritual, Rain experiences an emotional and spiritual catharsis that permits her to reconnect to her Native identity and gain clarity of vision that helps her to solve the boarding school mystery.

The secret of that mystery is imparted in Rain's next vision, which occurs shortly after the sweat lodge ceremony. Where her previous visions of the boarding school children were fragmented, she is suddenly able to perceive the events that led to the mass burial of the anonymous schoolchildren in a clear, linear way. Together with Rain, we witness the screams and fear of the children, who huddle in a group as the foundations of the school crumble on top of them and kill them. Rain eventually locates the unmarked grave of these child martyrs, which results in charges of corruption against white officials who silenced reports of abuses at the boarding school. The film's closing scene depicts a Big Drum ceremony in which Rain and Irene—who has just been released from the mental hospital following the revelation of the parish priest's attempts to silence her—are fully reintegrated into their tribal community. Also in the crowd, quiet and unobtrusive, is Luke, who looks on respectfully. As the drums and chants crescendo, the ghosts of the schoolchildren and the spirit of Walter Many Lightnings slowly walk away from the tribal group into the forest as the community looks on. In this closing scene *Older Than America* brings its narrative full circle, the drums of the Sun Dance ceremony at the film's beginning echoed in the sounds of the Big Drum ceremony at the end and the traumatic visions that arose at the first *lieu de mémoire* receding in the space of the second *lieu de mémoire*. By linking trauma and healing in this way, the film reinforces the idea that Native traumas must be remembered and worked through with Native traditions and rituals. However, while emphasizing the importance of these culturally specific strategies for healing, the film also suggests that such repair cannot be fully effectuated without the willing cooperation of non-Natives. Thus, the fact that Lightning invites viewers to observe, in a limited capacity, sacred ceremonies such as the Sun Dance and the sweat lodge is important because for those of the audience who are not Native, these *lieux de mémoire* also function as sites of cross-cultural exchange meant to inspire collective healing and cooperation (Lightning).

Sankofa, *The Devil's Arithmetic*, and *Older Than America* each underscores the value of ceremony and ritual as a means of healing for inheritors of traumatic legacies, and each also demonstrates the importance of collective memory, not only for the viewer who shares the ethnic heritage represented on-screen, but for all viewers. These three films invite viewer identification in ways that enable the development of a felt connection to the historical suffering depicted on-screen. Just as Morrison's *Beloved* throws readers "ruthlessly into an alien environment as the first step into a shared experience with the book's population" (Morrison 1987, xiii), so too do these films disrupt viewer expectations by deliberately juxtaposing past with present, prompting more meaningful reflection on how these traumas reverberate—and are repeated—in contemporary life. In this way, the felt connection to historical suffering that the viewer may experience finds a logical outlet—and opportunity for activism—in the context of present social justice issues.

NOTES

1. Much of this scholarship, which is referred to in the field as "apparatus theory," is grounded on the work of Louis Althusser and Jacques Lacan. In a sense similar to reader response theory, the work of scholars engaged in apparatus theory is based on the idea that the cinema posits the spectator as subject. See, for example, Browne (1976), Silverman (1986), and Mulvey (1975).

2. Angeletta Gourdine (2003) further explains that the *sankofa* proverb not only "warns one to know the past," but also reflects the notion that "one must always look to the ancestors, to those who came before, for guidance and information" (19).

3. In "Yoruban Visions of the Afterlife in Phyllis Alesia Perry's *Stigmata*" (forthcoming), I argue that the Yoruban concept of matrilineal reincarnation, or *yetunde*, serves as an interface between the slave past and postslavery African American identity in *Stigmata*. Specifically, the novel adapts the Yoruban notion of the *yetunde* to frame the corporeal and emotional connection that the protagonist, Lizzie, shares with her female ancestors. In its transgression of geographical and temporal boundaries, the novel highlights the inextricable ties between past and present and demonstrates how the painful consequences of slavery's legacy reverberate today. However, the consciousness that Lizzie shares with her foremothers is more than just a conduit for memory; it also provides her with the tools necessary to begin working through the weight of historical trauma. By infusing her novel with a Yoruban understanding of the connections between the afterlife of ancestors and the world of the living, Perry not only rejects the primacy of Western, specifically Christian, ontologies, but also insists that a reappraisal of the slave past be framed within a non-Western cultural context.

4. In this, the film shares Toni Morrison's beliefs that works about slavery should communicate across racial boundaries by inviting both black and nonblack readers to inhabit memories of slavery. See Morrison (1994, 96).

5. This return to the African homeland also refers to the ubiquitous "flying African" stories found in African American folklore in which slaves were suddenly imbued with the power of flight, which carried them back across the ocean to Africa. Such tales were "shared among enslaved people" to give them "hope that they could escape bondage and return to their African homeland" (Caruana-Loisel 2010, 198).

6. The DVD version of the film confirms this, identifying this scene on its menu as the "Re-Birth Canal."

7. For example, a Google search of the terms "*The Devil's Arithmetic*" and "reading list" yields over one hundred required and suggested reading lists for American grade schools all across the country.

8. See Avrech (2012).

9. See in particular Gubkin (2007, 168–69) and Bernard-Donals and Glejzer (2001, 151–52).

10. The Haggadah is the ritual text that sets forth the order of the Passover Seder.

11. See Leviticus 19:28: "You shall not make any cuts in your body for the dead nor make any tattoo marks on yourselves: I am the LORD."

12. See Kristen H. Lindbeck's *Elijah and the Rabbis*, particularly "Elijah from Rabbinic Times to the Twenty-First Century" (136–70) for a historical overview of the Elijah figure in Jewish folklore and liturgy.

13. The two most popular examples of this are probably *Schindler's List* (1993) and *The Pianist* (2004). *Schindler's List* in particular has been criticized for its "redemptive message." See Novick (2000, 214).

14. See Andrea Smith (2007).

15. While the first earthquake appears to be a natural event, the second earthquake that reignites interest in the boarding school site is implied to be of phantasmic origins.

16. Richard H. Pratt's famous motto was first articulated in the *Official Report of the Nineteenth Annual Conference of Charities and Correction* in 1892, and the speech was later reprinted under the title "The Advantages of Mingling Indians with Whites" in *Americanizing the American Indians: Writings by the "Friends of the Indian": 1880–1900*, edited by Frances

Paul Prucha (Cambridge: Harvard Univeristy Press, 1973). The version that I am citing here was published as "Kill the indian . . . save the man."

17. See in particular Gagnon (2007, 426–27) and Glass (2009, 163–65).

18. This detail lends added authenticity to the scene. As Spier (1920) notes, "In every sun dance a forked tree is set up as the center pole" (465).

19. The red section "symbolizes the sun rising in the east and with it the beginning of new life," while the yellow area "stands for the warmth from the south that makes all things grow that are good to eat." The black quadrant "points to the thunder beings coming from the west who bring life-giving rain along with the danger of storm and flood," and the white sector "represents the cold wind from the north that cleanses and purifies all of earth's inhabitants" (Wallace 2005, 42).

Conclusion

The Call to Infinite Responsibility

One of the central tenets of Levinasian ethics is the notion of infinite responsibility, which Emmanuel Levinas (1994) frames as follows: "I can be responsible for that which I did not do and take upon myself a distress which is not mine" (85). Here, Levinas expresses the idea that the rights and needs of the other—and the suffering of the other—are our ethical obligations. It is via the face-to-face relation that we are able to recognize our call to responsibility, or the ethical demand, of the other. Levinas (1998) offers another way of thinking about this obligation vis-à-vis a statement made by a Dostoyevsky character: "We are all guilty for everything and everyone, and I more than all the others" (90). Levinas (1999) expands on this idea elsewhere by reflecting that "it is precisely in that recalling of me to my responsibility by the face that summons me, that demands me, that requires me—it is that calling into question—that the other is my neighbor" (25). Hent de Vries (2001) explains that "the immediacy of the one for the other, *l'un pur l'autre,* to the point of substitution . . . for Levinas constitutes the heart of responsibility" (185). Monica Osborne (2018) has usefully connected this ethical obligation to the act of reading:

> If human beings are called, according to the language of Levinasian thought, to infinite responsibility, is it not also true that the texts they create must reflect this same responsibility? Further, if literature is a medium that is meant to reveal to us the face of humanity—that is, the complex and often deeply contradictory human emotions—should that "face" not also bear the mark of responsibility? (49)

The conviction that literature carries the power to translate the ethical obligation of the face-to-face encounter to the reading experience undergirds the heart of my argument about what I view as the ethical project of the phantasmic trauma narrative: to issue an ethical summons to readers to not only acknowledge the suffering of others in the past, but also recognize the ways in which we are implicated in and responsible for that suffering in the present. As I have illustrated in the previous chapters, these narratives do so by offering powerful examples of the acceptance of ethical responsibility.

Paule Marshall's *Praisesong for the Widow* (1983) offers another example of how the phantasmic trauma narrative models the assumption of personal responsibility, and by extension, social responsibility, for the traumatic past. The novel, which uses Yoruba and Vodun traditions as vehicles for the protagonist's recognition of the painful truths about her familial legacy, tells the story of an African American widow, Avey, who has been so eager to assimilate into mainstream, middle-class American culture that she has closed herself off from ancestral knowledge. However, this ancestral knowledge pursues her in dreams in the form of her great-aunt Cuney. These dreams prompt Avey to recall that upon learning from her great-aunt about their family history and the story of Ibo Landing, she felt that "the old woman had entrusted her with a mission . . . she felt duty-bound to fulfill" (42). Her sense of responsibility to both acknowledge and *feel* in response to her family's historical suffering further manifests in a later dream about the Middle Passage, helping to put into perspective her own contemporary struggles: "Their suffering—the depth of it, the weight of it in the cramped space—made hers of no consequence" (209). The mission with which she is entrusted, as interlocutor to her great-aunt's stories, is to bear witness to her family's story and to live an ethical, socially responsible life that includes empathy for the suffering of others. In this way, *Praisesong for the Widow,* like the other novels and films that I examined in the previous chapters, demonstrates that the act of learning about historical injustices carries with it an ethical responsibility, both to remember one's own history and to acknowledge the historical suffering of others in the past and to resist the repetition of such injustices in the present.

Phantasmic trauma narratives operate on the principle that literature can inspire change by awakening readers' consciousness and influencing public discourse. Inevitably, however, a reader/interlocutor must assume the mantle of responsibility, a decision that determines "whether the act of witnessing will become transformative or not" (Fernandes 2003, 92). Similarly, in *Activism and the American Novel*, Channette Romero (2012) contends that when "readers choose to empathize with the characters and situations portrayed, they become implicated in the story of social injustice and obligated to think about their connection to the society that tolerates such injustices" (42). They must choose, she explains, between "the dominant ideology that led to the injustice or the more marginalized worldviews" represented (42). Louise Erdrich's *The Round House* (2012) provides an example of this challenge. Permeated with spectral presences and phantasmic irruptions, the novel tells the story of Joe, an adolescent who is determined to uncover the nefarious secrets that cloud both the identity of his mother's rapist as well as the deeper historical traumas that continue to affect his tribe. *The Round House* positions the reader as a witness not only to these events, but also to the failures of the American justice system and the ways in which these failures continue to perpetuate a long legacy of colonial oppression. Unable to obtain justice for his mother due to the complicated tangle of tribal, state, and federal jurisdictions, Joe instead follows the dictums of traditional Ojibwe codes of justice, which identify his mother's attacker, Linden Lark, as a "wiindigoo" and endorse his killing as "fulfill[ing] the requirements of a very old law" (360). By teaching readers about the contemporary crisis of sexual violence on reservations, as well as the ways in which such crimes are the result of a historical legacy of colonial violence and tribal disenfranchisement, *The Round House* encourages them to identify with Joe's—and, more broadly, the Ojibwe—perspective. Readers are asked to choose between the American legal codes, based on centuries of the systematic disenfranchisement of Native tribes, that permit Lark's crime to go unpunished, or alternative codes of justice that are rooted in a distinctly Ojibwe worldview. In this way, phantasmic trauma narratives like *The Round House* position their cultural worldviews in conflict with mainstream, Western epistemologies. By empathizing with the former, readers become active witnesses to historical traumas and are entreated to think critically about how mainstream worldviews not only exclude ethnic minorities, but also reinscribe historical legacies of discrimination and violence.

By bridging the distances of time and space through phantasmic means, the texts and films that I examine in this study reflect a change in both what counts as historical knowledge and the means by which we acquire such knowledge. Most important, perhaps, is the way that these phantasmic narratives extend this knowledge across ethnic boundaries. Indeed, the intercultural emphasis of phantasmic trauma narratives acts as a powerful rejoinder to the problem of multiculturalism, which fails because it inevitably reinscribes the dialectical relationship of center and margin by encouraging an essentialist, totalizing approach to racial and cultural identity and therefore depoliticizes difference while purporting to celebrate it. However, while phantasmic trauma narratives invite audiences to respond empathically to cultural histories that may not be their own, these narratives also work to emphasize the readers/viewers' awareness of their place in the present and their ethical responsibility for the plight of the other. As a result, the form of empathic identification encouraged by the phantasmic trauma narrative resolves the essentialist tendency of identity politics and the colonizing potential of multiculturalism.

The pedagogical use-value of the phantasmic trauma narrative lies in the way that it asks readers and viewers to recognize its historical trauma claim and discourages them from appropriating the history that it recounts. In so doing, the phantasmic trauma narrative instead promotes what Marianne Hirsch and Nancy K. Miller (2011) term "a contemporary politics of acknowledgment" (14), which recognizes historical traumas and which can be used to foster productive interethnic exchanges in the future. The phantasmic trauma narrative provides readers and viewers a unique opportunity to experience, as individuals, cultural memories to which they might not otherwise have proximity; in some narratives, they are given access not to the historical traumas themselves, but rather to the lingering emotional consequences of those events, while in others they are asked to witness those events through the protagonist, who serves as proxy. By emphasizing the importance of maintaining and reviving culturally specific spiritual and storytelling traditions, the phantasmic trauma narrative prompts us to consider how we can be more mindful of others' suffering while still respecting the alterity that characterizes the self-other relation. If it is possible for readers and audiences to respond with empathy to a cultural narrative to which they may not lay a cultural claim, it is also possible that their responses may condition how those individuals understand the relationship between historical trauma and the sociopolitical circumstances of the present, in turn prompting ethical thinking and perhaps even ethical action.

In its most progressive incarnations, the phantasmic trauma narrative makes it possible for readers and viewers to feel for the other while at the same time recognizing their own difference from the other; it is in this relation that opportunities for ethical engagement arise. Thinking ethically requires one to think beyond one's own wants and desires, to *regard* the other. Unlike sympathy—which risks becoming a form of emotional colonization whereby the sympathizer appropriates the other's feelings—empathy necessitates cognitive engagement, requiring the empathizer not only to feel for the other, but also to acknowledge her own difference from the other. As Alison Landsberg (2004) argues, the "connection one feels when one empathizes with another is more than a feeling of emotional connection; it is a feeling of cognitive, intellectual connection, an intellectual coming-to-terms with another person's circumstances" (149). By helping the reader develop a felt connection to cultural histories to which they may not necessarily lay a personal claim, phantasmic trauma narratives encourage this sort of "intellectual coming-to-terms."

Of course, there will always be readers who are unconvinced by the notion that literature does—or can—pose an ethical summons to the reader. The driving logic here seems to be as follows: if the reader fails to recognize or refuses to acknowledge the ethical summons in the text, how can we say that it even exists? For Levinas (2008), the response is that we cannot choose to *not* be responsible. We are always already responsible for the other regardless of choice. Indeed, it is the call to responsibility for the other that makes up the self. In *Otherwise Than Being*, Levinas (2008) argues that "this extreme accusation [of the other] excludes the declinability of the self" (113); that is, no one can assume the place of the self in the call to responsibility. Alphonso Lingis (2008) explains that for Levinas, "responsibility is . . . set forth as the determinative structure of subjectivity" (xvii). Infinite responsibility is what makes up individuality and forms the basis of our freedom. Further, as Levinas (1969) writes in *Totality and Infinity*, "the will is free to assume [its] responsibility in whatever sense it likes; it is *not* free to refuse this responsibility itself; it is *not* free to ignore this meaningful world into which the face of the Other has introduced it" (218–19, emphasis added). The phantasmic trauma narrative presents readers with a face that issues a call to responsibility, one that exists regardless of reader recognition. Indeed, the same might be true of any work that seeks to share stories of human suffering. What sets these narratives apart is the phantasmic strategies that they deploy to facilitate reader connection and the models of empathy they offer.

The degree to which readers will accept the call to responsibility and what form such a response might take are difficult, perhaps even impossible, to determine. There are, however, promising strides being made in the fields of social and cognitive psychology with regard to the question of reader empathy, most notably studies such as the one published by David Kidd and Emanuele Castano in 2013, which shows that reading literary fiction has the power to increase reader empathy. Also notable is Loris Vezzali et al.'s 2015 study, which indicates that children who identify with Harry Potter might develop greater empathy and tolerance toward people from disadvantaged backgrounds. While such studies do not definitively prove that reading fiction does make people more empathic, they do suggest that it has the potential to do so. However, it would be disingenuous to pretend that there is not a dearth of evidence that the empathy that arises from a reader's engagement with a literary text will necessarily translate to prosocial action. Suzanne Keen's *Empathy and the Novel* (2007), which examines empathy from the perspectives of literary studies, cognitive science, psychology, and neuroscience, demonstrates that there are to date no significant studies that support the claim that private reading engenders altruistic behavior. When left to their own devices, Keen explains, readers gravitate toward subject matter to which they already feel a connection and do not regularly select reading material that cuts across social and cultural boundaries (60–61). Further, when reading for pleasure, one is released from social obligations and therefore does not always feel compelled to negotiate social or ethical obligations

(88). However, she does note that best seller lists and book clubs—such as the highly successful Oprah's Book Club, and more recently Reese Witherspoon's "Reese's Book Club"—have been influential in inspiring readers to explore subjects outside of their comfort zones.[1]

The success of reading communities suggests that people may be more likely to engage a greater variety of texts—and via those texts, different perspectives—if they are guided toward it. And what is a literature course if not a reading community? Thus, we can see that what might at the outset appear a limitation in fact offers an interesting opportunity for pedagogical intervention; that is, the question becomes not simply how phantasmic trauma narrative may impact readers, but rather how can we teach these narratives in a way that best instrumentalizes the ethical potential of these narratives? In posing this question, we must also think about how we encourage readers and viewers to shift beyond the point of identification into critically assessing what their feelings of empathy for the subaltern other means in the context of their real-world coexistence and engagement with that other. Opportunities for future research and critical inquiry along these lines should consider productive strategies for introducing and teaching these texts as motivators for encouraging a greater sense of historical and ethical responsibility. I argue that a course syllabus, curated with Levinasian ethics in mind and attentive to the importance of historical and cultural contexts, can provide a powerful lens through which to view phantasmic texts. For example, when I teach Morrison's *Beloved,* I ask my students to spend a great deal of time unpacking Morrison's 2004 foreword to the text, in which she explains not only the historical roots of the novel, but also articulates the way in which the issues we encounter in the text resonate in the lives of contemporary African Americans, particularly African American women. We also discuss what it means that her narrative structure "kidnaps" readers in a gesture toward the powerlessness of the novel's characters, and we address Levinasian ideas about ethical responsibility in relation to the ethical challenges by the text. These conversations establish a foundation for later conversations about the African inflections of the novel—most notably in the appearance of Beloved, whose return can be explained as an adaptation of Kongo cosmology—but also in the text's references to the Middle Passage. Such conversations attune students to the historical and cultural reclamation projects in which the text is engaged and encourage them to think about how the experiential nature of the text invites certain lines of ethical questioning and empathic response.

Thus, future directions for this kind of study would include suggestions for improved pedagogical approaches to improving students' knowledge of important cultural contexts and cultivating reader empathy as well as the development of assessment tools designed to gauge empathy scales in the literature classroom. To this end, we may seek to use (or adapt for use) competency-based assessments from the fields of social psychology and medical education: the "Reading the Mind in the Eyes Test" (Baron-Cohen et al. 1997), the "Empathic Concern Scale" (M. Davis 1983), and the "Balanced Emotional Empathy Scale" (Mehrabian and Epstein 1972) may provide such starting points. Integrating these kinds of empathy scales in the literature classroom could, in turn, shed light on how we might develop more effective pedagogical tools for leveraging the ethical potential of phantasmic trauma narratives, which not only bear witness to the historical wounds of specific ethnic groups, but also affirm that we are all responsible for and implicated in those events. The films and novels addressed in this study raise important questions about the nature of traumatic events and the way that those traumas, when not addressed, insidiously reassert themselves into the fabric of our political and social institutions.

NOTE

1. Economist Craig Garthwaite, who published a study in 2012 analyzing the effect of Oprah's original book club on the book industry, demonstrates that while Oprah's book club did not necessarily encourage self-described nonreaders to start reading, it was successful in encouraging readers to select books outside of their comfort zone (both in terms of books with challenging narrative structures and in terms of those that focused on a demographic different from that with which the reader self-identified). Reese Witherspoon's "Reese's Book Club," which was launched in 2017, "has become an industry phenomenon with the power to catapult titles to the top of the bestseller lists" (Grady 2019). According to Sarah Harden, CEO of Witherspoon's media company Hello Sunshine, all book club selections are focused on women, and the book club also strives to spotlight "works by women of color and international writers" who are not well known in the United States (qtd. in Grady 2019).

Works Cited

Aarons, Victoria. 1996. *A Measure of Memory: Storytelling and Identity in American Jewish Fiction*. Athens: University of Georgia Press. Print.
———. 2014. "A Genre of Rupture: The Literary Language of the Holocaust." *The Bloomsbury Companion to Holocaust Literature*. Ed. Jenni Adams. New York: Bloomsbury. Print.
Achebe, Chinua. 1998. *Things Fall Apart*. New York: Fawcett. Print.
Achebe, Christie. 1980. "Literary Insights into the Ogbanje Phenomenon." *Journal of African Studies* 7: 31–38. Print.
———. 1986. *The World of the Ogbanje*. Enugu: Fourth Dimension. Print.
Acholonu, Catherine. 1988. "Ogbanje: A Motif and a Theme in the Poetry of Christopher Okigbo." *Oral and Written Poetry in African Literature Today* 16: 103–11. JSTOR. Web.
Adams, Jenni. 2011. *Magic Realism in Holocaust Literature: Troping the Traumatic Real*. London: Palgrave. Print.
Adorno, Theodor. 1992. *Notes to Literature,* Vol. 2. Ed. Rolf Tiedemann. Trans. Shierry Weber Nicholsen. New York: Columbia University Press. Print.
———. 1983. *Prisms*. Trans. Samuel Weber and Shierry Weber. 1967. Cambridge: MIT University Press. Print.
Afigbo, A. E. 1981. *Ropes of Sand: Studies in Igbo History and Culture*. Ibadan: UP Limited. Print.
Ahrenhoerster, Greg. 2004. "White S(ox) vs. Indians: Sports and Unresolved Cultural Conflict in Native American Fiction." *Upon Further Review: Sports in American Literature*. Ed. Michael Cocchiarale. Westport: Greenwood. 53–62. Print.
Akers, Donna L. 2008. "Removing the Heart of the Choctaw People: Indian Removal from a Native Perspective." *The American Indian: Past and Present*. Ed. Roger L. Nichols. Norman: University of Oklahoma Press. 127–40. Print.
Alexander, Jacqui. 2005. *Pedagogies of Crossing: Meditations on Feminism, Sexual Politics, Memory, and the Sacred*. Durham: Duke University Press. Print.
Alexander, Jeffrey C., ed. 2004. "Toward a Theory of Cultural Trauma." *Cultural Trauma and Collective Identity*. Berkeley: University of California Press. 1–30. Print.
Alexie, Sherman. 1997. "Crossroads: A Conversation with Sherman Alexie." Interview with John Purdy. *SAIL* 9.4: 1–15. Project Muse. Web.
Alkana, Joseph. 1997. "'Do We Not Know the Meaning of Aesthetic Gratification?': Cynthia Ozick's *The Shawl*, the Akedah, and the Ethics of Holocaust Literary Aesthetics." *Modern Fiction Studies* 43.4: 963–90. Print.
Appelfeld, Aharon. 2004. *The Story of a Life*. Trans. Aloma Halter. New York: Shocken. Print.
Applebome, Peter. March 28, 1999. "'The Devil's Arithmetic': Memories Count." *The New York Times*. Web.

Avrech, Robert J. April 19, 2012. "The Devil's Arithmetic." Seraphicpress.com. Web.
———. April 24, 2011. "The Devil's Arithmetic: A Passover Story." Seraphicpress.com. Web.
Barrieses, Azalea, and Susan Gingell. 2011. "Listening to Bones That Sing: Orality, Spirituality, and Female Kinship in Louise Halfe's *Blue Marrow*." *Studies in American Indian Literatures* 23.3: 69–93. Print.
Bar-On, Dan. 1998. "Transgenerational Aftereffects of the Holocaust in Israel: Three Generations." *Breaking Crystal: Writing and Memory after Auschwitz*. Ed. Efraim Sicher. Urbana: University of Illinois Press. 91–118. Print.
Baron, Lawrence. 2005. *Projecting the Holocaust into the Present: The Changing Focus of Contemporary Holocaust Cinema*. Lanham: Rowman & Littlefield. Print.
Baron-Cohen, Simon, Therese Joliffe, Catharine Mortimore, and Mary Robertson. 1997. "Another Advanced Test of Theory of Mind: Evidence from Very High Functioning Adults with Autism or Asperger Syndrome." *The Journal of Child Psychology and Psychiatry* 38.7: 735–872. Print.
Bastian, Misty. 2002. "Irregular Visitors: Narratives about Ogbaanje (Spirit Children) in Southern Nigerian Popular Writing." *Readings in African Popular Fiction*. Ed. Stephanie Newell. Bloomington: Indiana University Press. 59–67. Print.
Bayer, Gerd. 2010. "After Postmemory: Holocaust Cinema and the Third Generation." *Shofar* 28.4: 116–32. Print.
Beaulieu, Elizabeth Ann. 1999. *Black Women Writers and the American Neo-Slave Narrative*. Westport: Greenwood. Print.
Bellamy, Maria Rice. 2016. *Bridges to Memory: Postmemory in Contemporary Ethnic American Women's Fiction*. Charlottesville: University of Virginia Press. Print.
Benito, Jesús, Ana Ma Manzanaz, and Begoña Simal, eds. 2009. *Uncertain Mirrors: Magical Realisms in U.S. Ethnic Literatures*. Amsterdam: Rodopi. Print.
Berger, Alan. 1997. *Children of Job: American Second-Generation Witnesses to the Holocaust*. Albany: SUNY Press. Print.
Berger, Alan, and Victoria Aarons. 2017. *Third Generation Holocaust Representation: Trauma, History, and Memory*. Evanston: Northwestern University Press. Print.
Bergland, Renée L. 2000. *The National Uncanny: Indian Ghosts and American Subjects*. Lebanon: Univeristy Press of New England. Print.
Berlant, Lauren. August 14, 2008. "Institutionists: History and the Affective Event." *American Literary History*. Oxford: Oxford University Press. Accessed October 9, 2018. https://lucian.uchicago.edu/blogs/politicalfeeling/files/2009/01/berlant-intuitionists.pdf.
Berman, Jessica. 2011. *Modernist Commitments: Ethics, Politics, and Transnational Modernism*. New York: Columbia University Press. Print.
Bernard-Donals, Michael, and Richard Glejzer. 2001. *Between Witness and Testimony: The Holocaust and the Limits of Representation*. Albany: State University of New York Press. Print.
Bernstein, Susan David. 2003. "The Problem of Identification and Anne Frank's Diary." *Witnessing the Disaster: Essays on Representation and the Holocaust*. Ed. Michael Bernard-Donals and Richard Glejzer. Madison: University of Wisconsin Press. 141–61. Print.
Bettanin, Guiliano. 2008. "Memory Work in Octavia Butler's *Kindred* and Women's Neo-Slave Narratives." *Cultural Memory and Multiple Identities*. Eds. Rüdiger Kunow and Wilfried Raussert. Berlin: Lit Verlag. 91–107. Print.
Blades, John. April 21, 1993. "Along with Scalps, Bows and Arrows, and Other Clichés, American Indian Writers Are . . ." *Chicago Tribune*. Accessed December 12, 2018. https://www.chicagotribune.com/news/ct-xpm-1993-04-21-9304210026-story.html.
Blum, Lawrence. 1980. *Friendship, Altruism, and Morality*. New York: Routledge. Print.
Boskin, Joseph, and Joseph Dorinson. 1987. "Ethnic Humor: Subversion and Survival." *American Humor*. Ed. Arthur Power Dudden. New York: Oxford University Press. 97–117. Print.
Brogan, Kathleen. 1998. *Cultural Haunting: Ghosts and Ethnicity in Recent American Literature*. Charlottesville: University Press of Virginia. Print.
Brooks, Kinitra. 2012. "Maternal Inheritances: Trinity Formations and Constructing Self-Identities in *Stigmata* and *Louisiana*." *FEMSPEC* 12.2: 17–46. Print.

Brown, Laura S. 1995. "Not Outside the Range: One Feminist Perspective on Psychic Trauma." *Trauma: Explorations in Memory*. Ed. Cathy Caruth. Baltimore: Johns Hopkins Univeristy Press. 100–12. Print.

Browne, Nick. 1976. "The Spectator in the Text." *Film Quarterly* 29.2: 26–38. Project Muse. Web.

Bruns, Gerald L. 1987. "Midrash and Allegory: The Beginnings of Scriptural Interpretation." *The Literary Guide to the Bible*. Ed. Robert Alter and Frank Kermode, 625–46. Cambridge: Harvard University Press. Print.

Boyarin, Daniel. 1994. *Intertextuality and the Reading of Midrash*. Bloomington: Indiana University Press. Print.

Boyd, Colleen E., and Coll Thrush. 2011. "Introduction: Bringing Ghosts to Ground." *Phantom Past, Indigenous Present: Native Ghosts in North American Culture and History*. Lincoln: University of Nebraska Press. vii-xl. Print.

Buse, Peter, and Andrew Stott. 1999. "Introduction: A Future for Haunting." *Ghosts: Deconstruction, Psychoanalysis, History*. London: Palgrave. 1–20. Print.

Butler, Octavia. 1977. *Mind of My Mind*. New York: Doubleday. Print.

———. 1979. *Kindred*. Boston: Beacon. 2003. Print.

———. 1980. *Wild Seed*. New York: Doubleday. Print.

———. 1986. "Black Women and the Science Fiction Genre: Interview with Octavia Butler." Interview by Frances M. Beal. *Black Scholar* 17.2: 14–18. Web.

———. 2003. "A Conversation with Octavia Butler." *If All of Rochester Read the Same Book*. Rochester, NY. Web.

———. 2004. "Interview with Octavia Butler." *In Motion Magazine*. By Joshunda Saunders. Web.

Carabí, Angels. 2004. "Interview with Gloria Naylor." *Conversations with Gloria Naylor*. Jackson: University Press of Mississippi. 111–22. Print.

Cariou, Warren. 2006. "Haunted Prairie: Aboriginal 'Ghosts' and the Spectres of Settlement." *University of Toronto Quarterly* 75.2: 727–34. Print.

Caruana-Loisel, Valerie. 2010. "Flying African Stories." *Encyclopedia of African American History*, Vol. 1. Ed. Leslie Alexander. Santa Barbara: ABC-CLIO. 198–99. Print.

Caruth, Cathy. 1990. *Unclaimed Experience*. Baltimore: Johns Hopkins University Press. Print.

———. 1995. *Trauma: Explorations in Memory*. Baltimore: Johns Hopkins University Press. Print.

———, ed. 2013. *Literature in the Ashes of History*. Baltimore: Johns Hopkins University Press. Print.

Chabon, Michael. 2000. *The Amazing Adventures of Kavalier and Clay*. New York: Random House. Print.

Cham, Mbye. 2004. "Film and History in Africa: A Critical Survey of Current Trends and Tendencies." *Focus on African Films*. Ed. Françoise Pfaff. Bloomington: Indiana University Press. 48–68. Print.

Chanady, Amaryll Beatrice. 1985.*Magical Realism and the Fantastic: Resolved Versus Unresolved Antimony*. New York: Garland. Print.

Chavkin, Allan, and Nancy Feyl Chavkin. 1994. "An Interview with Louise Erdrich." *Conversations with Louise Erdrich and Michael Dorris*. Jackson: University Press of Mississippi. 220–54. Print.

Chou, Isoje. 2011. "I Have Always Meant to Fail: From Abiku to Abikuisms (Speaking of Nigeria and Road Desire)." *African Cities Reader* 2.1: 174–82. Print.

Codde, Philippe. 2011. "Keeping History at Baby: Absent Presences in Three Recent Jewish American Novels." *MFS* 57.4: 675–96. Print.

———. 2009. "Transmitted Holocaust Trauma: A Matter of Myth and Fairy Tales?" *European Judaism* 42.1: 62–75. Print.

Coleman, Monica A. 2008. *Making a Way Out of No Way: A Womanist Theology*. Minneapolis: Fortress. Print.

Collado-Rodriguez, Francisco. 2008. "Ethics in the Second Degree: Trauma and Dual Narratives in Jonathan Safran Foer's *Everything Is Illuminated*." *Journal of Modern Literature* 32.1: 54–68. Print.

Cooper, J. California. 1991. *Family*. New York: Anchor Books. Print.
Coulombe, Joseph L. 2011. *Reading Native American Literature.* New York: Routledge. Print.
Cox, Karen Castalucci. 1998. "Magic and Memory in the Contemporary Short Story Cycle: Gloria Naylor and Louise Erdrich." *College English* 60.2: 150–72. Print.
Craps, Stef. 2016. "On Not Closing the Loop: Empathy, Ethics, and Transcultural Witnessing." *The Postcolonial World.* Ed. Jyotsna G. Singh and David D. Kim. New York: Routledge. 53–67. Print.
———. 2013. *Postcolonial Witnessing: Trauma Out of Bounds.* New York: Palgrave. Print.
Craven, Avery, and Walter Johnson. 1952. *The United States, Experiment in Democracy.* New York: Ginn. Print.
Crossley, Robert. 2003. "Reader's Guide." *Kindred.* Boston: Beacon. 265–84. Print.
Dash, Julie. 1999. *Daughters of the Dust: A Novel*. New York: Plume. Print.
Davis, Cristina. 1994. "An Interview with Toni Morrison." 1986. Reprinted in *Conversations with Toni Morrison.* Ed. Danille Taylor-Guthrie. Jackson: University Press of Mississippi. 223–33. Print.
Davis, Mark H. 1983. "Measuring Individual Differences in Empathy Evidence for a Multidimensional Approach." *Journal of Personality and Social Psychology* 44.1: 113–26. Print.
de Vries, Hent. 2001. "Derrida and Ethics: Hospitable Thought." *Jacques Derrida and the Humanities: A Critical Reader.* Ed. Tom Cohen. Cambridge: Cambridge University Press. 172–92. Print.
Deloria, Vine, Jr. 2003. *God Is Red: A Native View of Religion.* 1973. Golden: Fulcrum. Print.
den Dulk, Allard. 2015. *Existential Engagement in Wallace, Eggers, and Foer: A Philosophical Analysis of Contemporary American Literature.* London: Bloomsbury. Print.
Dennis, Geoffrey. 2007. *The Encyclopedia of Jewish Myth, Magic, and Mysticism.* Woodbury: Llewellyn. Print.
Derrida, Jacques. 1997. *Specters of Marx: The State of the Debt, the Work of Mourning and the New.* Trans. Peggy Kamuf. New York: Routledge. 1994. Hopkins University Press. Print.
The Devil's Arithmetic. 1999. Dir. Donna Deitch. Showtime Films. Film.
De Weever, Jacqueline. 1991. *Mythmaking and Metaphor in Black Women's Fiction.* New York: St. Martin's. Print.
Dubey, Madhu, and Elizabeth Goldberg. 2011. New Frontiers, Cross-Currents and Convergences: Emerging Cultural Paradigms." *The Cambridge History of African American Literature.* Ed. Maryemma Graham and Jerry W. Ward, Jr. Cambridge: Cambridge University Press. 566–617. Print.
Dusenberry, Verne. 1998. *The Montana Cree: A Study in Religious Persistence.* 1968. Norman: University of Oklahoma Press. Print.
Due, Tananarive. 1996. *The Between*. New York: HarperCollins. Print.
Eaglestone, Robert. 1997. *Ethical Criticism: Reading after Levinas.* Edinburgh: Edinburgh University Press. Print.
———. 2004. "One and the Same? Ethics, Aesthetics and Truth." *Poetics Today: Literature and Ethics* 25.4: 595–608. Print.
Echema, Austin. 2010. *Igbo Funeral Rites Today: Anthropological and Theological Perspectives.* Berlin: Lit Verlag. Print.
Eisen, George. 1995. "Early European Attitudes toward Native American Sports and Pastimes." *Ethnicity and Sport in North American History and Culture.* Ed. George Eisen. Westport: Greenwood. 1–19. Print.
Ekwunife, Anthony Nwoye Okechukwu. 1999. *Meaning and Function of the "Ino Uwa" (Reincarnation) in Igbo Traditional Religious Culture.* Onitsha: Spiritan. Print.
El Hafi, Fethia. 2010. "Punished Bodies in Soyinka's *The Bacchae of Euripides* and Morrison's *Beloved.*" *Journal of Black Studies* 41.1: 89–107. doi:10.1177/0021934709331917.
"Empathy," Def. 1. *Oxford English Dictionary Online.* Web.
Englander, Nathan. 1999. "The Tumblers." For the Relief of Unbearable Urges. New York: Knopf. 25–55. Print.
Enns, Peter. 2010. *Exodus.* Grand Rapids: Zondervan. 2000. Print.
Epstein, Helen. 1981. *Children of the Holocaust: Conversations with Sons and Daughters of Survivors*. New York: Bantam. Print.

Erdrich, Louise. July 28, 1985. "Where I Ought to Be: A Writer's Sense of Place." *The New York Times Book Review* 91: 1, 23–24. Print.
———. 1989. *Tracks*. New York: Harper Collins. Print.
———. April 2002. "The Progressive Interview." *The Progressive*. By Mark Anthony Rolo.
———. 2005. *The Painted Drum: A Novel*. New York: Harper Collins. Print.
———. 2012. *The Round House: A Novel*. New York: Harper Collins. Print.
Eyerman, Ron. 2001. *Cultural Trauma: Slavery and the Formation of African American Identity*. Cambridge: Cambridge University Press. Print.
Faris, Kade M. 2004. "Ojibwa Shamanism." *Shamanism: An Encyclopedia of World Beliefs, Practices, and Culture*, Vol. 1. Ed. Mariko Namba Walter and Eva Jane Neumann Fridman. Santa Barbara: ABC-CLIO. 334–36. Print.
Faris, Wendy B. 1995. "Scheherazade's Children: Magical Realism and Postmodern Fiction." *Magical Realism*. Ed. Lois Parkinson Zamora and Wendy B. Faris. Durham: Duke University Press. 163–89. Print.
Farrell, Kirby. 1998. *Post-Traumatic Culture: Injury and Interpretation in the Nineties*. Baltimore: Johns Hopkins University Press. Print.
Fernandes, Leela. 2003. *Transforming Feminist Practice: Non-Violence, Social Justice and the Possibilities of a Spiritualized Feminism*. San Francisco: Aunt Lute Books. Print.
Feuer, Menachem. 2007. "Almost Friends: Post-Holocaust Comedy, Tragedy, and Friendship in Jonathan Safran Foer's *Everything Is Illuminated*." *Shofar: An Interdisciplinary Journal of Jewish Studies* 25.2: 25–48. Print.
Fink, Ida. 1987. "A Scrap of Time." *A Scrap of Time and Other Stories*. Trans. Madeline Levine and Francine Prose. New York: Pantheon. Print.
Fisher, Mary Pat. 1997. *Living Religions: An Encyclopedia of the World's Faiths*. London: Tauris. Print.
Fishman, Boris. 2014. *A Replacement Life*. New York: Harper Collins. Print.
Fixico, Donald L. 2004. "History of the Western Southeast since Removal." *Handbook of North American Indians, Volume 14: Southeast*. Washington, DC: Government Print Office. 162–73. Print.
Flanzbaum, Hilene. 2012. "The Trace of Trauma: Third Generation Holocaust Survivors." *Phi Beta Kappa Forum*: 13–15. Print.
Floreani, Tracy. 2001. "Metafictional Witnessing in *Everything Is Illuminated*." *Unfinalized Moments: Essays in the Development of Contemporary Jewish American Narrative*. Ed. Derek Parker Royal. West Lafayette: Purdue University Press. 139–49. Print.
Foer, Jonathan Safran. 2002. *Everything Is Illuminated*. New York: Harper. Print.
———. 2011. *The Heavens are Empty: Discovering the Lost Town of Trochenbrod, by Avrom Bendavid-Val*. New York: Pegasus. Print.
———. September 12, 2012. "Interview with Jonathan Safran Foer." HarperCollins.com. n.d. Web.
Forbes. Jack D. 2006. "The Name Is Half the Game: The Theft of 'America' and Indigenous Claims of Sovereignty." *Eating Fire, Tasting Blood: An Anthology of the American Indian Holocaust*. Ed. Marijo Moore. New York: Thunder's Mouth. 32–51. Print.
Foreman, P. Gabrielle. 1995. "Past-On Stories: History and the Magically Real, Morrison and Allende on Call." *Magical Realism: Theory, History, Community*. Ed. Lois Parkinson Zamora and Wendy B. Faris. Durham: Duke University Press. 285–304. Print.
Foster, John Burt. 1995. "Magical Realism, Compensatory Vision, and Felt History: Classical Realism Transformed in *The White Hotel*." *Magical Realism*. Ed. Lois Parkinson Zamora and Wendy B. Faris. Durham: Duke University Press. 267–83. Print.
Francis, Lee. 2003. "We, the People: Young American Indians Reclaiming Their Identity." *Genocide of the Mind: New Native American Writings*. Ed. Marijo Moore. New York: Thunder's Mouth. 77–84. Print.
Franco, Dean J. 2006. *Ethnic American Literature: Comparing Chicano, Jewish, and African American Writing*. Charlottesville, VA: University of Virginia Press. Print.
Friend, Beverly. 1982. "Time Travel as a Feminist Didactic in Works by Phyllis Eisenstein, Marlys Millhiser, and Octavia Butler." *Extrapolation* 23.1: 50–55. Print.

Gagnon, Gregory O. 2007. "North America: Ojibwe Culture." *The Wiley-Blackwell Companion to Religion and Social Justice.* Oxford: Wiley-Blackwell. 425–37. Print.

Garrett, Michael T. 2004. "Sound of the Drum: Group Counseling with Native Americans." *Handbook of Group Counseling and Therapy.* Ed. Janice L. DeLucia-Waack. Thousand Oaks: Sage. 169–82. Print.

Garthwaite, Craig L. 2012. "You Get a Book!: Demand Spillovers, Combative Advertising, and Celebrity Endorsements." *National Bureau of Economic Research.* NBER Working Paper 17915. https://www.nber.org/papers/w17915.pdf.

Gates, Jr., Henry Louis. 2014. *The Signifying Monkey: A Theory of African American Literary Criticism.* 1988. New York: Oxford University Press. Print.

Genette, Gérard. 1980. *Narrative Discourse: An Essay in Method.* Trans. Jane E. Lewin. Ithaca: Cornell University Press. Print.

Gerima, Haile. 1994. "Filming Slavery: A Conversation with Haile Gerima." Interview with Pamela Woolford. *Transition* 64: 90–104. JSTOR. Web.

Glass, Michael. 2009. "Assimilation and Resistance." *Encyclopedia of American Religious History.* 3rd ed. Ed. Edward L. Queen II, Stephen R. Prothero, and Gardiner H. Shattuck, Jr. Boston: Facts on File. 163–65. Print.

Glissant, Édouard. 1999. *Caribbean Discourse: Selected Essays.* 1989. Charlottesville: University of Virginia Press. Print.

Gomez, Michael A. 1998. *Exchanging Our Country Marks: The Transformation of African Identities in the Colonial and Antebellum South.* Chapel Hill: University of North Carolina Press. Print.

Goodhart, Sandor. 2008. "'A Land That Devours Its Inhabitants': Midrashic Reading, Emmanuel Levinas, and Prophetic Exegesis." *Shofar* 26.6: 13–35. Print.

———. 2017. *Mbian Nights: Literary Reading in a Time of Crisis.* New York: Bloomsbury. Print.

Gordon, Avery. 1997. *Ghostly Matters: Haunting and the Sociological Imagination.* Minneapolis: University of Minnesota Press. Print.

Gourdine, Angeletta. 2003. *The Difference Place Makes: Gender, Sexuality, and Diaspora Identity.* Columbus: Ohio State University Press. Print.

Govan, Sandra Y. 1986. "Homage to Tradition: Octavia Butler Renovates the Historical Novel." *MELUS* 13: 79–96. Project Muse. Web.

Grady, Constance. September 20, 2019. "How Reese Witherspoon Became the New High Priestess of Book Clubs." *Vox.* Accessed October 31, 2019. https://www.vox.com/the-highlight/2019/9/13/20802579/reese-witherspoon-reeses-book-club-oprah.

Grayson, Sandra M. 2000. *Symbolizing the Past: Reading* Sankofa, Daughters of the Dust, *and* Eve's Bayou *as Histories.* Lanham: University Press of America. Print.

Gubkin, Liora. 2007. *You Shall Tell Your Children: Holocaust Memory in American Passover Ritual.* New Brunswick: Rutgers University Press. Print.

Halfe, Louise Berniece. 1998. *Blue Marrow.* Regina, SK, Canada: Coteau Books. Print.

Hampton, Gregory James. 2010. *Changing Bodies in the Fiction of Octavia Butler: Slaves, Aliens, and Vampires.* Lanham: Lexington Books. Print.

Hartman, Geoffrey. 1994a. *Holocaust Remembrance: The Shapes of Memory.* Cambridge: Blackwell. Print.

———. 1994b. "Reading, Trauma, Pedagogy." *The Geoffrey Hartman Reader.* Ed. Daniel T. O'Hara. New York: Fordham. 291–302. Print.

Hartman, Geoffrey, and Sanford Budick, eds. 1986. *Midrash and Literature.* New Haven: Yale University Press. Print.

Hausman, Blake. 2011. *Riding the Trail of Tears.* Lincoln: University of Nebraska Press. Print.

Hearne, Joanna, and Lindsey Foat. 2014. "Thoughts on Filming *Older Than America*: An Interview with Georgina Lightning." *Post Script: Essays in Film and the Humanities* 33.2: 70–80. Print.

Herman, Judith. 1994. *Trauma and Recovery: From Domestic Abuse to Political Terror.* London: Pandora. Print.

Hicks, John D. 1949. *A Short History of American Democracy.* Boston: Houghton. Print.

Hirsch, Marianne. 1997. *Family Frames: Photography, Narrative, and Postmemory.* Cambridge: Harvard University Press. Print.

———. 2001. "Surviving Images: Holocaust Photographs and the Work of Postmemory." *Yale Journal of Criticism* 14.1: 5–37. Print.

———. 2012. *The Generation of Postmemory: Writing and Visual Culture after the Holocaust.* New York: Columbia University Press. Print.

Hirsch, Marianne, and Nancy K. Miller, eds. 2011. "Introduction." *Rites of Return: Diaspora Poetics and the Politics of Memory.* New York: Columbia University Press. 1–20. Print.

Horn, Dara. 2002. *In the Image.* New York: Norton. Print.

Horowitz, Sara R. 1998. "Auto/biography and Fiction after Auschwitz: Probing the Boundaries of Second-Generation Aesthetics." *Breaking Crystal: Writing and Memory after Auschwitz.* Ed. Efraim Sicher. Urbana: University of Illinois Press. 276–94. Print.

Howe, LeAnne. 2002. "Tribalography: The Story of America." *Clearing a Path: Theorizing the Past in Native American Studies.* Ed. Nancy Shoemaker. New York: Routledge. 29–50. Print.

———. 2005. "The Unknown Women." *Evidence of Red: Poems and Prose.* Cambridge, UK: Salt Publishing. 9–19. Print.

———. 2006. Interview. *Indian Country Diaries: Spiral of Fire.* Dir. Carol Cornsilk. Native American Public Telecommunications. Film.

———. 2007. *Miko Kings: An Indian Baseball Story.* San Francisco: Aunt Lute. Print.

———. 2008a. "Blind Bread and the Business of Theory Making, by Embarrassed Grief." *Reasoning Together: The Native Critics Collective.* Ed. Craig S. Womack. Norman: University of Oklahoma Press. 325–39. Print.

———. 2008b. "Ohoyo Chishba Osh: The Woman Who Stretches Way Back." *Pre-Removal Choctaw History: Exploring New Paths.* Ed. Greg O'Brien. Lincoln: University of Oklahoma Press. 26–46. Print.

———. 2010. "Choctawan Aesthetics, Spirituality, and Gender Relations: An Interview with LeAnne Howe." Interview with Kirsten Squint. *MELUS* 35.3: 211–24. Print.

Hua, Linh U. 2011. "Reproducing Time, Reproducing History: Love and Black Feminist Sentimentality in Octavia Butler's *Kindred.*" *African American Review* 44.3: 391–407. Print.

Iser, Wolfgang. 1980. *The Act of Reading: A Theory of Aesthetic Response.* Baltimore: Johns Hopkins University Press. Print.

Jaffe, Daniel M. 2001. *With Signs and Wonders: An International Anthology of Jewish Fabulist Fiction.* Ed. Daniel M. Jaffe. Montpelier: Invisible Cities Press. Print.

Jarrett, Gene Andrew. 2014. "Octavia Butler." *The Wiley-Blackwell Anthology of African American Literature, Volume 2: 1920-Present.* Ed. Gene Andrew Jarret. Malden: Wiley-Blackwell. Print. 778–79. Print.

Johnson, Wendy. December 6, 2006. "Movie Cast Members Visit Ojibwe School." *The Pine Journal.* Web.

Jones, Gayl. 1975. *Corregidora.* Boston: Beacon. Print.

Keen, Suzanne. 2006. "A Theory of Narrative Empathy." *Narrative* 14.1: 207–36. Print.

———. 2007. *Empathy and the Novel.* New York: Oxford University Press. Print.

Keizer, Arelene P. 2004. *Black Subjects: Identity Formation in the Contemporary Narrative of Slavery.* Ithaca: Cornell University Press. Print.

Kellerman, Natan. 2013. "Epigenetic transmission of Holocaust trauma: Can nightmares be inherited?" *The Israel Journal of Psychiatry and Related Sciences* 50.1: 33–37. Print.

Kent, Alicia A. 2007. *African, Native, and Jewish American Literature and the Reshaping of Modernism.* New York: Palgrave. Print.

Kidd, David Comer, and Emanuele Castano. October 18, 2013. "Reading Literary Fiction Improves Theory of Mind." *Science.* Web.

Kim, Daniel Y. 2005. *Writing Manhood in Black and White: Ralph Ellison, Frank Chin, and the Literary Politics of Identity.* Stanford: Stanford University Press. Print.

Krauss, Nicole. 2005. *The History of Love.* New York: Norton. Print.

Kreyling, Michael. 2010. *The South That Wasn't There: Postsouthern Memory and History.* Baton Rouge: Louisiana University Press. Print.

Krijnen, Joost. 2016. *Holocaust Impiety in Jewish American Literature: Memory, Identity, (Post-)Postmodernism*. Leiden: Brill Rodopi. Print.

LaCapra, Dominick. 2001. *Writing History, Writing Trauma*. Baltimore: Johns Hopkins University Press. Print.

Lacey, Lauren J. 2014. *The Past That Might Have Been, the Future That May Come: Women Writing Fantastic Fiction, 1960s to the Present*. Jefferson: McFarland. Print.

Lambert, Valerie Long. 2007. *Choctaw Nation: A Story of American Indian Resurgence*. Lincoln: University of Nebraska Press. Print.

Landsberg, Alison. 2004. *Prosthetic Memory: The Transformation of American Remembrance in the Age of Mass Culture*. New York: Columbia. Print.

Lang, Berel. 2000. *Holocaust Representation: Art within the Limits of History and Ethics*. Baltimore: Johns Hopkins University Press.

Lang, Jessica. 2009. "*The History of Love*, the Contemporary Reader, and the Transmission of Holocaust Memory." *Journal of Modern Literature* 33.1: 43–56. Print.

Langer, Lawrence. 1991. *Holocaust Testimonies: The Ruins of Memory*. New Haven: Yale University Press. Print.

Laub, Dori. 1992. "Bearing Witness, or the Vicissitudes of Listening." *Testimony: Crises of Witnessing in Literature, Psychoanalysis, and History*. Ed. Shoshana Felman and Dori Laub. New York: Routledge. 57–74. Print.

Lawrence, Tonja. 2010. *An Africentric Reading Protocol: The Speculative Fiction of Octavia Butler and Tananarive Due*. Diss. Wayne State University.

Lemberg, Jennifer M. 2011. "'Unfinished Business': Journeys to Eastern Europe in Thane Rosenbaum's *Second Hand Smoke* and Jonathan Safran Foer's *Everything Is Illuminated*." *Unfinalized Moments: Essays in the Development of Contemporary Jewish American Narrative*. Ed. Derek Parker Royal. West Lafayette: Purdue University Press. 81–96. Print.

Levecq, Christine. 2000. "Power and Repetition: Philosophies of (Literary) History in Octavia E. Butler's *Kindred*." *Contemporary Literature* 41.3: 525–53. Print.

Levinas, Emmanuel. 1969. *Totality and Infinity: An Essay on Exteriority*. Trans. Alphonso Lingus. Pittsburgh: Duquesne University Press. Print.

———. 1986. "The Trace of the Other." *Deconstruction in Context*. Ed. Mark C. Taylor. Trans. Alphonso Lingus. Chicago: University of Chicago Press. 345–59. Print.

———. 1987. "Diachrony and Representation." *Time and the Other*. Trans. Richard A. Cohen. Pittsburgh: Duquesne University Press. 97–120. Print.

———. 1989. "Ethics as First Philosophy." *The Levinas Reader*. Ed. Séan Hand. Trans. Séan Hand and Michael Temple. Cambridge: Basil Blackwell. 75–86. Print.

———. 1989. "Reality and Its Shadow." Trans. Alphonso Lingis. *The Levinas Reader*. Ed. Séan Hand. Malden, MA: Blackwell Publishing. Print.

———. 1994. *Nine Talmudic Readings*. Trans. Annette Aronowicz. Bloomington: Indiana University Press. Print.

———. 1996. "God and Philosophy." *Emanuel Levinas: Basic Philosophical Writings*. Ed. Adriaan T. Peperzak, Simon Critchley, and Robert Bernasconi. Bloomington: Indiana University Press. 129–48. Print.

———. 1998. *Entre Nous: Thinking-of-the-Other*. Trans. Michael B. Smith and Barbara Harshav. New York: Columbia University Press. Print.

———. 1999. *Alterity and Transcendence*. Trans. Michael B. Smith. London: Althone. Print.

———. 2000. *God, Death, and Time*. Trans. Bettina Bergo. Stanford: Stanford University Press. Print.

———. 2008. *Otherwise Than Being or Beyond Essence*. Trans. Alphonso Lingus. Pittsburgh: Duquesne University Press. Print.

Levine, Rabbi Yosie. 2011. "Chronos, Kairos and Chaos: The Collapse of Time on Seder Night." *Shabbat Hagadol*. Web.

Lightning, Georgina. n.d. "Interview with Fox 21 News." Fox News Online. Web.

Lindbeck, Kristen H. 2010. *Elijah and the Rabbis: Story and Theology*. New York: Columbia University Press. Print.

Lingus, Alphonso. 2008. Translator's Introduction. *Otherwise Than Being or Beyond Essence*. Emmanuel Levinas. Pittsburgh: Duquesne University Press. Print.

Long, Lisa A. 2009. "A Relative Pain: The Rape of History in Octavia Butler's *Kindred* and Phyllis Alesia Perry's *Stigmata.*" *College English.* 64.4: 459–83. Print.
López, Alfred J. 2001. *Posts and Pasts: A Theory of Postcolonialism.* Albany: SUNY Press. Print.
Lucci-Cooper, Kathryn. 2003. "To Carry the Fire Home." *Genocide of the Mind: New Native American Writing.* Ed. Marijo Moore. New York: Thunder's Mouth. 3–12. Print.
Mann, Barbara A. 1998. "The Four Mothers." *The Encyclopedia of Native American Legal Tradition.* Ed. Bruce Elliott Johansen. Westport: Greenwood. 99–101. Print.
Marable, Manning. February 25, 2000. "We Need New and Critical Study of Race and Ethnicity." *Chronicle of Higher Education.*
Marshall, Paule. 1983. *Praisesong for the Widow.* New York: Penguin. Print.
Martin, Gerald. 1995. "On 'Magical' and Social Realism in García Márquez." *García Márquez.* Ed. Robin Fiddian. London: Longman. 100–20. Print.
Mayer, Ruth. 2002. *Artificial Africas: Colonial Images in the Times of Globalization.* Hanover: University Press of New England. Print.
McHale, Brian. 1987. *Postmodernist Fiction.* New York: Methuen. Print.
Mehrabian, A., and N. Epstein. 1972. "A Measure of Emotional Empathy." *Journal of Personality* 40: 525–43. Print.
Meland, Carter, Joseph Bauerkempter, LeAnne Howe, and Heidi Stark. 2005. "The Bases Are Loaded: American Indians and American Studies." *American Studies* 46.3–4: 391–416. Print.
Meland, Carter. 2007. "Baseball Is Past Time: A Review of *Miko Kings: An Indian Baseball Story.*" *Yellow Medicine Review: A Journal of Indigenous Literature, Art and Thoughts*: 226–29. Print.
———. 2014. "Talking Tribalographies: LeAnne Howe Models Emerging Worldliness in 'The Story of America' and *Miko Kings.*" *Studies in American Indian Literatures* 26.2: 26–39. Print.
Messent, Peter. 2007. "Liminality, Reptition, and Trauma in Hemingway's 'Big Two-Hearted River' and Other Nick Adams Stories." *Mapping Liminalities: Thresholds in Cultural and Literary Texts.* Ed. Lucy Kay and Zoe Kinsley. Bern: Peter Lang. 137–66. Print.
Miller, Nancy K., and Jason Tougaw. 2002. "Introduction: Extremities." *Extremities: Trauma, Testimony, and Community.* Ed. Nancy K. Miller and Jason Tougaw. Chicago: University of Illinois Press. 1–24. Print.
Milton, Sybil. 2001. "Memorials." *The Holocaust Encyclopedia.* Ed. Walter Laqueur and Judith Tydor Baumet. New Haven: Yale University Press. 415–19. Print.
Mitchell, Angelyn. 2001. "Not Enough of the Past: Feminist Revisions of Slavery in Octavia E. Butler's *Kindred.*" *MELUS* 26.3: 51–75. Print.
———. 2002. *The Freedom to Remember: Narrative, Slavery, and Gender in Contemporary Black Women's Fiction.* Piscataway: Rutgers University Press. Print.
Mitchell, John Hanson. 1999. "Ceremonial Time." At Home on the Earth: Becoming Native to Our Place: A Multicultural Anthology. Ed. David Landis Barnhill. Berkeley: University of California Press. 227–39. Print.
Momaday, N. Scott. 2010. *House Made of Dawn.* 1966. New York: HarperCollins. Print.
Moore, Marijo. 2006. "Introduction." *Eating Fire, Tasting Blood: An Anthology of the American Indian Holocaust.* New York: Thunder's Mouth. Print.
Morrison, Toni. 1973. *Sula.* New York: Knopf. Print.
———. 1977. *Song of Solomon.* New York: Vintage Books. Print.
———. 1994a. "The Pain of Being Black: An Interview with Toni Morrison." Interview with Bonnie Angelo. *Conversations with Toni Morrison.* Ed. Danille Taylor-Guthrie. Jackson: University Press of Mississippi. 255–61. Print.
———. 1994b. "Toni Morrison." Interview with Charles Ruas. *Conversations with Toni Morrison.* Ed. Danille Taylor-Guthrie. Jackson: University of Mississippi Press. 93–118. Print.
———. 1995. "The Site of Memory." *Inventing the Truth: The Art and Craft of Memoir.* 2nd ed. Ed. William Zinsser. Boston: Houghton Mifflin. 83–102. Print.
———. 2004. *Beloved.* 1987. New York: Vintage. Print.
Mould, Tom. 2004. *Choctaw Tales.* Jackson: University of Mississippi Press. Print.

Mulvey, Laura. 1975. "Visual Pleasure and Narrative Cinema." *Screen* 16.3: 6–18. Project Muse. Web.
Najita, Susan Y. 2006. *Decolonizing Cultures in the Pacific: Reading History and Trauma in Contemporary Fiction.* New York: Routledge. Print.
Naylor, Gloria. 1988. *Mama Day.* New York: Random House. Print.
Newton, Adam Zachary. 1995. *Narrative Ethics.* Cambridge: Harvard University Press. Print.
Nora, Pierre. 1989. "Between Memory and History: Les Lieux de Mémoire." *Representations* 26: 7–24. Project Muse. Web.
Novick, Peter. 2000. *The Holocaust in American Life.* New York: Houghton Mifflin. Print.
Nzewi, Esther. 2001. "Malevolent Ogbanje: Recurrent Reincarnation or Sickle Cell Disease?" *Social Science & Medicine* 52: 1403–16. Print.
Obama, Barack Hussein. July 11, 2009. "Remarks By the President at Cape Coast Castle." Cape Coast Castle, Cape Coast, Ghana.
O'Brien, Greg. 2002. *Choctaws in a Revolutionary Age, 1750–1830.* Lincoln: University of Nebraska Press. Print.
Ogunyemi, Chikwenye Okonjo. 1996. *Africa Wo/Man Palava: The Nigerian Novel by Women.* Chicago: The University of Chicago Press. Print.
———. 2002. "An Abiku-Ogbanje Atlas: A Pre-Text for Rereading Soyinka's *Aké* and Morrison's *Beloved.*" *African American Review* 36: 663–78. Print.
Okonkwo, Christopher N. 2008. *A Spirit of Dialogue: Incarnations of Ogbanje, the Born-to-Die, in African American Literature.* Knoxville: University of Tennessee Press. Print.
Older Than America. 2008. Dir. Georgina Lightning. Tribal Alliance Productions. Film.
"Older Than America." October 18, 2006. *The Pine Journal.* Web.
Olitzky, Kerry M. 2002. *Preparing Your Heart for Passover: A Guide for Spiritual Readiness.* Philadelpia: Jewish Publication Society. Print.
Orringer, Julie. 2010. *The Invisible Bridge.* New York: Knopf. Print.
Ortiz, Simon. 2004. "Empowerment." *American Indian Quarterly* 28.1–2: 112–14. Print.
Osborne, Monica. 2018. *The Midrashic Impulse and the Contemporary Literary Response to Trauma*. Lanham: Lexington Books. Print.
Osundare, Niyi. 1988. "The Poem as a Mytho-linguistic Event: A Study of Soyinka's 'Abiku.'" *Oral and Written Poetry in African Literature Today* 16: 91–102. JSTOR. Web.
Owens, Louis. 1990. "Afterword." *Bearheart: The Heirship Chronicles.* By Gerald Vizenor. Minneapolis: University of Minnesota Press. 247–54. Print.
Ozick, Cynthia. 1989. *The Shawl.* New York: Knopf. Print.
Parham, Marisa. 2009. "Saying 'Yes': Textual Traumas in Octavia Butler's *Kindred.*" *Callaloo* 32.4: 1315–31. Print.
Passalacqua, Camille. 2010. "Witnessing to Heal the Self in Gayl Jones's *Corregidora* and Phyllis Alesia Perry's *Stigmata.*" *MELUS* 35.4: 139–63. Project Muse. Web.
Patton, Venetria. 2013. *The Grasp That Reaches beyond the Grave: The Ancestral Call in Black Women's Texts.* Albany: SUNY Press. Print.
Perry, Phyllis Alesia. 1998. *Stigmata.* New York: Anchor. Print.
———. 2005. *A Sunday in June.* Westport: Hyperion. Print.
Peterson, Nancy. 2001. *Against Amnesia: Contemporary Women Writers and the Crises of Historical Memory.* Philadelphia: University of Pennsylvania Press. Print.
Petty, Sheila. 2008. *Contact Zones: Memory, Origin, and Discourse in Black Diasporic Cinema.* Detroit: Wayne State University Press. Print.
Pflug, Melissa. 1996. "'Pimadaziwin': Contemporary Rituals in Odawa Community." *American Indian Quarterly* 20:3/4: 489. Print.
Pietri, Arturo Uslar. 1996. "Realismo mágico." *Godos, insurgents, y visionarios.* Barcelona: Seix Barral. Print.
Pratt, Richard Henry. 2012. "Kill the Indian . . . and Save the Man." 1892. *Reading the American Past: Selected Historical Documents.* Ed. Michael P. Johnson. New York: Bedford/St. Martins. 36–39. Print.
Pozorski, Aimee. 2013. "'A Charming Picture': Photographic Images of Holocaust Perpetrators." *Picturing the Language of Images.* Ed. Nancy Pedro and Laurence Pedri. Newcastle-upon-Tyne: Cambridge Scholars. 345–54.

Quayson, Ato. 1997. *Strategic Transformations in Nigerian Writing: Orality and History in the Work of Samuel Johnson, Amos Tutuola, Wole Soyinka and Ben Okri.* Bloomington: Indiana University Press. Print.
Rabaté, Jean-Michel. 1996. *The Ghosts of Modernity.* Gainesville: Univeristy Press of Florida. Print.
Raczymow, Henri. 1994. "Memory Shot Through With Holes." Translated by Alan Astro. *Yale French Studies* 85: 98–105. Print.
Rader, Dean. 2011. *Engaged Resistance: American Indian Art, Literature, and Film from Alcatraz to the Nmai.* Austin: University of Texas Press. Print.
Radstone, Susannah. 2007. "Trauma Theory: Contexts, Politics, Ethics." *Paragraph: A Journal of Modern Critical Theory* 30.1: 9–29. Print.
Rainwater, Catherine. 1999. *Dreams of Fiery Stars: The Transformations of Native American Fiction.* Philadelphia: University of Pennsylvania Press. Print.
Ramadanovic, Petar. 2008. "'You Your Best Thing, Sethe': Trauma's Narcissism." *Studies in the Novel* 40.1: 178–88. Print.
Ranger, T. O., and Kimambo, Isaria. 1972. *The Historical Study of African Religion.* Berkeley: University of California Press. Print.
Rapaport, Herman. 2011. *The Literary Theory Toolkit: A Compendium of Concepts and Methods.* Malden: Wiley-Blackwell. Print.
Ratti, Manav. 2013. *The Postsecular Imagination: Postcolonialism, Religion, and Literature.* New York: Routledge. Print.
Reid, Mark A. 2005. *Black Lenses, Black Voices: African American Film Now.* Lanham: Rowman & Littlefield. Print.
Reilly, John M. 1986. "History-Making Literature." *Studies in Black American Literature, Volume II: Belief vs. Theory in Black American Literary Criticism.* Ed. Joe Weixlmann and Chester J. Fontenot. Greenwood: Penkevill. 85–120. Print.
Reisner, Rosalind. 2004. *Jewish American Literature: A Guide to Reading Interests.* Westport: Libraries Unlimited. Print.
Rhines, Jesse Algeron. 1996. *Black Film/White Money.* New Brunswick: Rutgers University Press. Print.
Robbins, Jill. 1999. *Altered Reading: Levinas and Literature.* Chicago: University of Chicago Press. Print.
Rody, Caroline. 2009. *The Interethnic Imagination: Roots and Passages in Contemporary Asian American Fiction.* Oxford: Oxford University Press. Print.
———. 2013. "Jewish Post-Holocaust Fiction and the Magical Realist Turn." *Moments of Magical Realism in US Ethnic Literatures.* Ed. Lyn Di Iorio Sandín and Richard Perez. New York: Palgrave. Print.
Romero, Channette. 2012. *Activism and the American Novel: Religion and Resistance in Fiction by Women of Color.* Charlottesville: University of Virginia Press. Print.
———. 2014. "Expanding Tribal Identities and Sovereignty through LeAnne Howe's 'Tribalography.'" *Studies in American Indian Literature* 26.2: 13–25. Print.
Rosen, Norma. 1992. *Accidents of Influence: Writing as a Woman and a Jew in America.* Albany: State University of New York Press. Print.
Rosenberg, Meisha. 1999. "Cynthia Ozick's Post-Holocaust Fiction: Narration and Morality in the Midrashic Mode." *Journal of the Short Story in English* 32: 1–11. Print.
Rosenbaum, Thane. 1999. "An Act of Defiance." *Elijah Visible.* New York: St. Martin's. 57–86. Print.
———. 2002. *The Golems of Gotham.* New York: Perennial. Print.
Rosenfeld, Alvin. 1995. "The Americanization of the Holocaust." *David W. Belin Lecture in American Jewish Affairs.* Ann Arbor: University of Michigan Press. 1–42. Print.
———. 2011. *The End of the Holocaust.* Bloomington: Indiana University Press. Print.
Rothberg, Michael. 2000. *Traumatic Realism: The Demands of Holocaust Representation.* Minneapolis: University of Minneapolis Press. Print.
Rushdy, Ashraf. 1999. *Neo-Slave Narratives: Studies in the Social Logic of a Literary Form.* New York: Oxford University Press. Print.
Salanskis, Jean-Michel. 2006. *Levinas Vivant.* Paris: Les belles lettres. Print.

Sandín, Lyn Di Iorio, and Richard Perez, eds. 2013. *Moments of Magical Realism in US Ethnic Literatures*. New York: Palgrave. 1–15. Print.

Sankofa. 1993. Dir. Haile Gerima. Channel Four Films. Film.

Saper, Bernard. 1993. "Since When Is Jewish Humor Not Anti-Semitic?" *Semites and Stereotypes: Characteristics of Jewish Humor*. Ed. Avner Ziv and Anat Zajdman. Westport: Greenwood. 71–86. Print.

Schwab, Gabriele. 2010. *Haunting Legacies: Violent Histories and Transgenerational Trauma*. New York: Columbia University Press. Print.

Schwartz, Howard. 1983. *Elijah's Violin and Other Jewish Fairy Tales*. New York: Oxford University Press. Print.

Schwenger, Peter. 1999. *Fantasm and Fiction: On Textual Envisioning*. Stanford: Stanford University Press. Print.

Sellman, Tamara Kaye. December 16, 2005. "Jewish Magical Realism: Writing to Tell the Tale." *Margin*. http://www.angelfire.com/wa2/margin/nonficSellmanJewishMR.html.

Sender, Yitzchak. 1991. *The Commentators' Haggadah: An Anthology of Inspiring Halachic Insights of Torah Luminaries*. Nanuet: Feldheim. Print.

Setka, Stella. 2015. "Bastardized History: How *Inglourious Basterds* Breaks through American Screen Memory." *Jewish Film & New Media: An International Journal* 3.2: 141–69. Print.

———. 2014. "Haunted by the Past: Traumatic Rememory and Black Feminism in Gayl Jones's *Corregidora*." *Mosaic* 47.1: 129–44. Print.

Sidhu, Jatinder. December 7, 1999. "Africa's Cinema: Setting the Record Straight." *BBC News*. Web.

Sicher, Efraim. 2009. "The Future of the Past: Countermemory and Postmemory in Contemporary American Post-Holocaust Narratives." *History & Memory* 12: 56–91. Project Muse. Web.

Sigal, J. J., D. Silver, et al. 1973. "Some Second-Generation Effects of Survival of Nazi Persecution." *American Journal of Orthopsychiatry* 43.3: 320–27. Print.

Silko, Leslie Marmon. 1977. *Ceremony*. New York: Penguin. Print.

Silverman, Kaja. 1986. "Suture." *Narrative, Apparatus, Ideology*. Ed. Philip Rosen. New York: Columbia University Press. 219–35. Print.

———. 1990. "Historical Trauma and Male Subjectivity." *Psychoanalysis and Cinema*. Ed. E. Ann Kaplan. New York: Routledge. 110–27. Print.

Singer, Isaac Bashevis. 1966. *Zlateh the Goat and Other Stories*. New York: Harper. Print.

Sivan, Miriam. 2009. *Belonging Too Well: Portraits of Identity in Cynthia Ozick's Fiction*. Albany: SUNY Press. Print.

Skibell, Joseph. 1997. *A Blessing on the Moon: A Novel*. Chapel Hill, NC: Algonquin Books. Print.

Skibell, Joseph. 2011. *A Curable Romantic*. Chapel Hill, NC: Algonquin Books. Print.

Smith, Andrea. March 26, 2007. "Soul Wound: The Legacy of Native American Schools." *Amnesty International Magazine*. Web.

Soyinka, Wole. 1976. *Myth, Literature, and the African World*. London: Cambridge University Press. Print.

Spargo, R. Clifton. 2004. *The Ethics of Mourning: Grief and Responsibility in Elegiac Literature*. Baltimore: Johns Hopkins University Press. Print.

Spaulding, Timothy A. 2005. *Re-Forming the Past: History, the Fantastic, and the Postmodern Slave Narrative*. Columbus: The Ohio State University Press. Print.

Spiegelman, Art. 1980. *Maus*. New York: Pantheon Books. Print.

Spier, Leslie. 1920. *The Sun Dance of the Plains Indians: Its Development and Diffusion*. Google Books. Web.

Steele, Meili. 2012. "The Social Imaginary as a Problematic for Human Rights." *Theoretical Perspectives on Human Rights and Literature*. Ed. Elizabeth Swanson Goldberg and Alexandra Schultheis Moore. New York: Routledge. 87–102. Print.

Steinberg, Marc. 2004. "Inverting History in Octavia Butler's Postmodern Slave Narrative." *African American Review* 38.3: 467–77. Print.

Stelzriede, Danelle Dyckhoff. 2017. "Representing Spectral Subjects in Historical Crime Fiction." *Arizona Quarterly: A Journal of American Literature, Culture, and Theory* 73.3: 77–100. *Project MUSE*, doi:10.1353/arq.2017.0016. Web.
Stephenson, Maanna. 2008. *The Sage Age: Blending Science with Intuitive Wisdom*. Letchworth, UK: Nightengale. Print.
Stern, David. 1998. *Midrash and Theory: Ancient Jewish Exegesis and Contemporary Literary Studies*. Evanston: Northwestern Univeristy Press. Print.
Strhan, Anna. 2012. *Levinas, Subjectivity, Education: Towards an Ethics of Radical Responsibility*. Oxford: Wiley-Blackwell. Print.
Stout, Mary A. 2012. *Native American Boarding Schools*. Santa Barbara: ABC-CLIO. Print.
Suleiman, Susan Rubin. 1994. "War Memories: On Autobiographical Reading." *Auschwitz and After: Race, Culture, and "the Jewish Question" in France*. Ed. Lawrence D. Kritzman. New York: Routledge. 47–62. Print.
———. 2002. "The 1.5 Generation: Thinking about Child Survivors and the Holocaust." *American Imago* 59.3: 277–95. Print.
———. 2006. *Crises of Memory and the Second World War*. Cambridge: Harvard University Press. Print.
"Sympathy," Def. 1a. *Oxford English Dictionary Online*. Web.
Tillet, Salamishah. 2012. *Sites of Slavery: Citizenship and Democracy in the Post-Civil Rights Imagination*. Durham: Duke University Press. Print.
Tillman, Aaron. 2017. *Magical American Jew: The Enigma of Difference in Contemporary Jewish American Short Fiction and Film*. Lanham: Lexington Books. Print.
Tribunella, Eric L. 2010. *Melancholia and Maturation: The Use of Trauma in American Children's Literature*. Knoxville: University of Tennessee Press. Print.
Tudor, Rachel. 2010. "Latin American Magical Realism and the Native American Novel." *Teaching American Literature: A Journal of Theory and Practice* 3:3/4: 1–14. Print.
Turner, Stephanie S. 2004. "'What Actually Is': The Insistence of Genre in Octavia Butler's *Kindred*." *Femspec* 4.2: 259–80. Print.
Varsam, Maria. 2003. "Concrete Dystopia: Slavery and Its Others." *Dark Horizons: Science Fiction and the Dystopian Imagination*. Ed. Raffaella Baccolini and Tom Moylan. New York: Routledge. 203–24. Print.
Vezzali, Loris, Sofia Stathi, Dion Giovanni, Dora Capozza, and Elena Trifiletti. July 23, 2014. "The Greatest Magic of Harry Potter: Reducing Prejudice." *Journal of Applied Social Psychology* 45.2: 55–121. https://doi.org/10.1111/jasp.12279.
Vickroy, Laurie. 2002. *Trauma and Survival in Contemporary Fiction*. Charlottesville: University of Virginia Press. Print.
Visser, Irene. 2015. "Decolonizing Trauma Theory: Retrospect and Prospects." *Humanities* 4: 250–65.
Wagers, Kelley. 2009. "Seeing 'from the Far Side of the Hill': Narrative, History, and Understanding in *Kindred* and *The Chaneysville Incident*." *MELUS* 34.1: 23–45. Print.
Wallace, Mark I. 2005. *Finding God in the Singing River: Christianity, Spirit, Nature*. Minneapolis: Fortress. Print.
Walters, Anna Lee. 1988. *Ghost Singer*. Albuquerque: University of New Mexico Press. Print.
Warnes, Christopher. 2005. "Naturalizing the Supernatural: Faith, Irreverence, and Magical Realism." *Literature Compass* 2: 1–16. Print.
———. 2009. *Magical Realism and the Postcolonial Novel: Between Faith and Irreverence*. London: Palgrave. Print.
Weinstock, Jeffrey Andrew. 2004. *Spectral America: Phantoms and the National Imagination*. Madison: University of Wisconsin Press. 3–17. Print.
Weissman, Gary. 2004. *Fantasies of Witnessing: Postwar Efforts to Experience the Holocaust*. Ithaca: Cornell University Press. Print.
Whitehead, Anne. 2004. *Trauma Fiction*. Edinburgh: Edinburgh University Press. Print.
Wideman, John Edgar. 1997. *The Cattle Killing*. Boston: Mariner Books. Print.
Wiesel, Elie. 1977. "The Holocaust as Literary Inspiration." *Dimensions of the Holocaust*. Ed. Elliot Lefowirtz. Evanston: Northwestern University Press. 4–19. Print.

Wilson, Ivy. 2011. *Specters of Democracy: Blackness and the Aesthetics of Politics in the Antebellum US*. Oxford: Oxford Univeristy Press. Print.
Wittmann, Rebecca. January 26, 2019. "As a Country, Germany Has Confronted Its Past. But for Families, Angst about the War Persists." *University of Toronto Magazine*. Accessed January 30, 2019. https://magazine.utoronto.ca/research-ideas/culture-society/as-a-country-germany-has-confronted-its-past-but-for-german-families-angst-about-the-war-persists/
Woolfork, Lisa. 2009. *Embodying American Slavery in Contemporary Culture*. Urbana: University of Illinois Press. Print.
Yogev, Michael P. 1993. "The Fantastic in Holocaust Literature: Writing and Unwriting the Unbearable." *Journal of the Fantastic in the Arts* 5.2: 32–49. Print.

Index

Aarons, Victoria, 52, 57
abiku. See ogbanje
Achebe, Christie, 30
Acholonu, Catherine, 39
Adams, Jenni, 13, 52
Adorno, Theodor, 54
Akers, Roger L., 90
Alexander, Jeffrey C., 87
Alexie, Sherman, 86
alterity, 5, 8, 97, 104, 111, 140
Amazing Adventures of Kavalier and Clay, The, 16, 59
Amistad, 109
Antopol, Molly, 52
Appelfeld, Aharon, 54
Avrech, Robert J., 116

Baron, Lawrence, 120
baseball, 100–101
Bastian, Misty, 30
Beaulieu, Elizabeth, 38, 40
Bellamy, Maria Rice, 3, 11
Beloved, 16, 35, 133, 142
Berger, Alan, 52
Bergland, René, 11
Berman, Jessica, 104
Bernstein, Susan David, 41, 44
Between, The, 31, 47
Beulens, Gert, 6
Big Drum ceremony, 126, 132
Bingo Palace, The, 84

Birth of a Nation, The, 109
Blessing on the Moon, A, 59
Blue Marrow, 85
Booth, Wayne, 5
Brogan, Kathleen, 3, 11, 52, 95, 108
Brown, Laura, 6
Butler, Octavia, 3, 30, 31, 32

Cattle Killing, The, 31
Carpentier, Alejo, 13
Caruth, Cathy, 4, 6, 46, 82
Ceremony, 83
Chabon, Michael, 52, 55
Cham, Mbye, 111
Chanady, Amaryll, 15
Choctaw: history and culture, 81, 90, 91–92, 93, 95; language, 81, 89, 91, 95, 96, 97, 98–99, 100, 104; time, 93–95
Coulombe, Joseph L., 86
Cooper, J. California, 25
Corregidora, 47
Cox, Karen Castalucci, 14
cra, 110, 111
Craps, Stef, 4, 6
cross-cultural empathy. *See* empathy
cross-cultural engagement, 4, 12, 17, 19, 20, 52, 62, 68, 81, 82, 87, 89, 92, 100–102, 103, 110, 116, 124, 124–125, 127, 130–131, 132, 132–133, 140
Crossley, Robert, 41
Curable Romantic, A, 59

Dash, Julie, 25
Daughters of the Dust, 25, 47
Dawes Act, 92, 101, 105n3
Deloria, Vine Jr., 33
Dennis, Geoffrey, 68
Derrida, Jacques, 9
Devil's Arithmetic, The, 1, 19, 51, 82, 107–108, 116–124
Due, Tananarive, 31

Eaglestone, Robert, 5, 8
empathy, 2–3, 5–6, 7, 8, 10, 12, 20, 34, 121; cross-cultural empathy, 23–24, 34, 44–45, 47, 53, 68, 116, 124, 130; reader empathy and engagement, 24, 26–28, 32, 33, 34, 41, 53, 59, 62, 65, 68, 86, 86–88, 89, 91, 94, 95, 97, 98, 102, 104, 110, 114, 139–142
Englander, Nathan, 59
enslavement. *See* slavery
epistemology, 13, 15, 18, 31, 33
Erdrich, Louise, 14, 84
ethics, 3, 5–6, 8–10, 11, 20, 34, 41, 43, 52, 53, 59, 61, 96, 97, 99, 104, 108, 123, 140; ethical engagement, 64, 88, 89, 107; ethical reading, 63, 97, 104; as responsibility, 20, 27, 35, 41, 68, 86, 88, 97, 104, 108, 121, 130, 137–138, 140–142
Everything Is Illuminated, 15, 18, 51, 53, 57, 59, 62–76, 82, 117, 124

Family, 25, 47
fantastic, the, 58–59, 88
Farrell, Kirby, 4
Felman, Shoshanna, 4
felt connection, 2, 7, 10, 12, 15, 16–17, 18–19, 20, 23–24, 26–27, 28, 41, 44, 47, 52, 53, 58, 62, 63–64, 64, 68, 72, 81, 104, 107, 108, 110–111, 116, 117–118, 126, 131, 133, 138, 140
Fernandes, Leela, 10, 138
Fishman, Boris, 52, 55
Fixico, Donald L., 101
Flanzbaum, Hilene, 56
Franco, Dean J., 17, 52
Freedman, Jonathan, 52
Foer, Jonathan Safran, 3, 51, 52, 55, 63–64
Foreman, P. Gabrielle, 88

Foster, John, 12
Four Mothers Society, 101–102

Gates, Henry Louis Jr., 25
Genet, Gérard, 66
genocide, 2, 15, 17, 82
Gerima, Haile, 109
ghosts. *See* haunting
Ghost Singer, 85
Glissant, Édouard, 12
Golems of Gotham, The, 59
Gone With the Wind, 109
Goodhart, Sandor, 60–61
Gourdine, Angeletta, 112
Grass Dancer, The, 85

Halfe, Louise, 85
Hampton, Gregory Jerome, 41
Hampton Normal School, 92, 100
Hartman, Geoffrey, 4, 9, 55
haunting, 2, 11–12, 84–85
Hausman, Blake, 84
Herman, Judith, 82
Hirsch, Marianne, 2, 7, 55
History of Love, The, 59
Holocaust, 1, 7, 17, 18, 45, 52–53, 56, 58, 60, 61–62, 67, 122–124; survivor literature, 53, 54; second-generation literature, 53, 55, 56; third-generation literature, 52, 53, 55–57, 60
Horn, Dara, 59
Horowitz, Sara R., 60–61
House Made of Dawn, 83
Howe, LeAnne, 3, 88, 90
Hua, Linh, 23, 27

In the Image, 59
Indian boarding schools, 124–126, 129, 132
Invisible Bridge, The, 56–57
Iser, Wolfgang, 8

Jaffe, Daniel M., 58
Jewish history and culture, 2, 18, 52, 57, 57–60, 65, 67, 76, 117, 120, 122
Judaism, 52, 58–59, 64, 65, 68, 118–119

Kaplan, Amy, 6
Keen, Suzanne, 27, 34, 141

Kindred, 18, 23–24, 26, 27, 29–47, 51, 53, 82, 110–111, 117
Krauss, Nicole, 52, 55
Kreyling, Michael, 43
Krijnen, Joost, 55

LaCapra, Dominick, 4, 6, 53
Lacey, Lauren J., 3, 41
Landsberg, Alison, 6, 12
Lang, Berel, 54
Lang, Jessica, 55, 57
Langer, Lawrence, 120
LaRose, 84
Laub, Dori, 4, 10
Levinas, Emmanuel, 5, 8–9, 27, 123, 137, 140
Lieux de mémoire, 17–18, 108, 109, 116, 117–118, 123–124, 131, 132
Lightning, Georgina, 124
Lingus, Alphonso, 140
Long, Lisa, 23, 26, 27, 41
López, Alfred J., 14
Love Medicine, 84

Magical realism, 13–15, 32, 52, 57, 59
Mama Day, 25, 47
Marable, Manning, 17
Márquez, Gabriel García, 13
Marshall, Paule, 25
McHale, Brian, 67
Meland, Carter, 96
memory: historical and cultural, 2, 3, 12, 20, 23, 25, 31, 46, 56, 108; text as site of memory, 1, 4, 17, 19, 42, 56; tradition, 84; and trauma, 4–5, 7, 16, 18, 26, 45, 47, 52, 54, 55, 108
midrash, 18, 51, 52–53, 57, 59–62, 64; as a practice of reading, 52, 53, 60–61, 62, 64, 66, 67
Miko Kings: An Indian Baseball Story, 15, 19, 51, 81–82, 87, 91–104, 126–127
Mitchell, Angelyn, 38
Momaday, N. Scott, 83
Moore, Marijo, 81
Morrison, Toni, 14, 30, 35, 40

Najita, Susan Y., 93
Naylor, Gloria, 14, 25
neoslave narratives, 23, 26, 28

Nora, Pierre, 17
Nussbaum, Martha, 5

Obama, Barack, 116
ogbanje, 23, 24, 27, 28, 28–29, 30, 35, 37, 45, 46; as border-shifting agent, 16, 18, 23, 29, 31, 33, 34, 39, 43
Ogunyemi, Chikwenye Okonjo, 16, 37, 39
Okonkwo, Christopher, 16, 28, 31, 33, 37
Older Than America, 19, 51, 82, 107–108, 119, 124–133
ontology, 12–13, 18, 23, 26, 29, 32–33
Orringer, Julie, 56
Ortiz, Simon, 87
Osborne, Monica, 8, 60–61, 61–62
Owens, Louis, 14

Painted Drum, The, 84
Passover, 1, 19, 117–121, 123
Patton, Venetria A., 30
Perez, Richard, 12
Perry, Phyllis Alesia, 25
Petty, Sheila, 114
Pflug, Melissa, 131
phantasmic trauma narratives, 2, 6, 7, 8–10, 11, 12–14, 15, 15–18, 19–20, 23–24, 25, 26–28, 44–45, 47, 59, 67, 68, 84, 88, 97, 104, 107–108, 110, 111, 116, 137–140, 142
phantasmic elements or irruptions, 2, 4, 6, 8, 11, 12–13, 18, 20, 25, 28, 47, 52, 57, 59–60, 62, 64, 65, 67, 69, 74, 76, 82, 84–86, 88, 89, 92, 94–95, 97, 103, 110, 111, 112, 113, 116, 117, 119, 123, 124, 126, 127, 128, 129–130, 131, 132, 138, 140
Pianist, The, 122
Piano Lesson, The, 25
Praisesong for the Widow, 25, 47, 138
postmemory, 2, 7, 55
Power, Susan, 85
Pozorski, Aimee, 9

Raczymow, Henri, 56
Radstone, Susannah, 6
Raeff, Anne, 55
Rainwater, Catherine, 86
Reilly, John M., 31
reincarnation, 2, 18, 25, 28, 30, 47, 110

Replacement Life, A, 59
responsibility. *See* ethics
Riding the Trail of Tears, 84, 87
Robbins, Jill, 9, 97
Rody, Caroline, 3, 57, 59
Romero, Chanette, 3, 13, 33, 102, 138
Rosenbaum, Thane, 53, 55
Rothberg, Michael, 6
Round House, The, 84, 87, 138

Sacred Wheel, 129
Sandín, Lyn Di Iorio, 12
Sankofa, 19, 51, 82, 107–108, 109–116, 119
Schindler's List, 122
Schwartz, Howard, 57
Sellman, Tamara Kaye, 57, 59
Silko, Leslie Marmon, 12
Simon, Andrea, 52
Skibell, Joseph, 52, 59
slavery, 2, 7, 15, 16, 18, 23, 29, 31, 32, 34, 35, 39, 40, 43, 45, 56
Song of Solomon, 16
Spaulding, Timothy A., 23, 44
Spiegelman, Art, 55
Steinberg, Marc, 23
Stigmata, 25, 26, 47, 110–111
storytelling, 47, 60, 64, 66–67, 81, 82, 88, 90, 93, 96, 99, 103, 140
Strhan, Anne, 123
Suleiman, Susan Rubin, 27, 46
Sun Dance, 126, 127–129, 132
Sunday in June, A, 25

Tillman, Aaron, 52, 58
time travel, 1–2, 4, 19, 26, 28–29, 32, 33, 34, 35, 40, 44, 46, 49n22, 82, 89, 91, 92, 95, 96, 97, 111, 113, 118–119, 120, 127
Tracks, 16, 84
tribalography, 19, 88, 89–92, 95, 100, 103, 104
trauma: fiction, 27, 52; historical and cultural, 2, 8, 10, 12, 15, 17, 23, 46, 47, 56, 59, 61, 82, 84, 108, 138; theory, 4, 5, 6, 8, 10, 82
Tribunella, Eric, 122
Tudor, Rachel, 13

Vickroy, Laurie, 27
viewer identification, 108, 111, 113–114, 117, 119, 121–122, 129, 133
Visser, Irene, 6, 82

Wagers, Kelley, 23, 31, 40
Walters, Anna Lee, 85
Warnes, Christopher, 59
Weinstock, Jeffrey, 11
Weissman, Gary, 56
Wideman, John Edgar, 31
Wiesel, Elie, 54
Wilson, August, 25
Wilson, Ivy, 11
Woolfork, Lisa, 27, 43, 110–111

Yogev, Michael, 58

About the Author

Stella Setka is an associate professor of English at West Los Angeles College, where she teaches courses on American literature and film. She holds a Ph.D. in English from Purdue University, and her scholarship on ethnic American literature and women's studies has been published in *MELUS, Mosaic, American Periodicals,* and *Jewish Film & New Media.* She serves as vice president and program chair of MELUS: The Society for the Study of Multi-Ethnic Literature of the United States. She lives in Los Angeles with her husband, Ethan Alexander, and their daughter, Zelda.

www.ingramcontent.com/pod-product-compliance
Lightning Source LLC
Chambersburg PA
CBHW050908300426
44111CB00010B/1434